# Animal
# Bone
# Archeology

# ANIMAL BONE ARCHEOLOGY

## FROM OBJECTIVES TO ANALYSIS

**BRIAN HESSE** and **PAULA WAPNISH**

UNIVERSITY OF ALABAMA-BIRMINGHAM AND SMITHSONIAN INSTITUTION

TARAXACUM WASHINGTON

**THE MANUALS ON ARCHEOLOGY**

*are guides to the excavation, preservation, classification, analysis, description, and interpretation of special categories of archeological remains. The authors have drawn upon their experience and the contributions of other experts to formulate instructions for dealing with delicate, complicated or unobtrusive kinds of phenomena. Their intent is to enable those who are not specialists in the particular subject matter to classify and describe finds in a useful manner and to observe details easily overlooked during excavation or analysis. The manuals will be revised periodically to incorporate new information. Suggestions for improving the clarity or completeness of the instructions, illustrations, and data are welcome, as well as recommendations of topics appropriate to the series.*

To the memory of
PATRICIA DALY PERKINS
CLIFFORD EVANS
DEXTER PERKINS, JR.
ROBERT L. STIGLER

*First published 1985 by*
*Taraxacum Inc., 1227 30th Street, Washington, D.C. 20007*
*ISBN 0-9602822-3-8*

*Library of Congress Catalog Card Number: 83-51521*

*Designed by John B. Goetz*
*Cover motif by George Robert Lewis*
*Printed in the United States of America*

# Preface

This book was written out of the conviction that animal bone studies are too often relegated to appendices in archeological reports. We think of ourselves as social scientists first and as natural scientists second. Thus, we view bones as artifacts, and our primary interest is to make them inform on the activities of past cultures. Doing that is a cooperative venture. Modern archeological techniques make it possible to recover thousands of osseous specimens. Deciding what to study, what to observe, and how to summarize the data are jobs often left entirely to the specialist, when in fact the decisions involved require constant interaction between the project director and the animal bone archeologist. The suggestions we offer here are intended to pave the way for better collaboration by clarifying the problems and potential of animal bone studies in archeology.

A difficult task in writing the book was transforming words into pictures. Thus, we are extremely grateful to Nancy Carney and Les Barnhart for their creative input and long hours of careful artistry that produced most of the drawings. Helen Barbara Gibbs drew the goat-horn cores from Tepe Ganj Dareh. Wilma Nappier was a patient and painstaking typist through numerous revisions of the manuscript.

The whole project is the inspiration of the series editor, Betty Meggers. With infinite patience, she has shaped the text, trying to insure that it speaks to its proper audience, archeologists. We thank her for having given us the opportunity to write this book.

# Contents

# Figures

x **FIGURES**

60. Preliminary sorting and numbering fragments in a field laboratory.
61. Boxes containing fragments sorted into provisional categories prior to packing for shipment.
62. A paper label used by the Tel Miqne project.
63. Sand box for supporting glued fragments during drying.
64. Donkey skull encased in plaster.
65. Flow chart of the process of sorting in animal bone research.
66. Y-shaped spinous processes of bovid thoracic vertebrae.
67. Stencils used to record preserved portions of bones and locations of cut marks.
68. Annual growth in deer antlers.
69. Developmental sequence in horn cores of male and female sheep.
70. Stages of tooth wear in cattle, sheep/goat, and pig.
71. Dial calipers in use.
72. Measuring box in use.
73. Relationship between age and size in cattle molars.
74. Relationship between age and size in equid teeth.
75. Three goat horn cores from Tepe Ganj Dareh.
76. Varieties of facial morphology differentiating three races of pigs.
77. Malformations in sheep/goat teeth from Tell Jemmeh.
78. Arthritic modifications on the articular surfaces of cattle phalanges.
79. Pathological alterations of the diaphysis portions of herbivore bones.
80. Bones from Tell Jemmeh modified by disease.
81. Root marks on a cattle phalanx from Tell Jemmeh.
82. Cut marks on phalanges of cattle from Tell Jemmeh.

83. Cut marks produced using metal tools.
84. Closely spaced, parallel grooves diagnostic of gnawing by rodents.
85. Defining units of dispersion of fragments.
86. Axes of variability in three factors relevant for identifying spaces within an archeological site.
87. The use of skeletal outlines to illustrate an archeological animal.
88. Aerial view of the Iranian site of Tepe Ganj Dareh and its environs.
89. Closeup of the stratigraphy at Tepe Ganj Dareh.
90. Histograms of measurements on foot bones of camelids.
91. Histograms of three measurements on goat bones.
92. Bivariate plot of two distal widths of the distal metapodials of goats.
93. Ages at death for sheep/goat samples from Tepe Ganj Dareh.
94. "Fat" harvest profile constructed using the ranges of estimates for fusion.
95. Comparison of the sheep/goat harvest profiles obtained for five late Pleistocene and four early Holocene sites in the Near East.
96. Harvest profiles for male and female goats during the basal and architectural periods at Tepe Ganj Dareh.
97. The proportion of fused epiphyses in samples of camelid bone from two Chilean sites.
98. Reducing error for comparing MNI's.
99. The manner in which the relationship between MNI and TNF is controlled by ENI.
100. Attritional samples with equal proportions of fetal, immature, and mature individuals.

# Tables

# 1    Introduction

## PHILOSOPHY

The analysis of animal bones is a rapidly expanding subdiscipline within archeology. One measure of growth is the list published annually by the International Council of Archaeozoology (ICAZ). From an initial group of several dozen, the roll has expanded to hundreds of practitioners in dozens of countries. Simultaneously, the interests of archeozoologists have spread to all corners of prehistory and history. Specialization has begun, with individual scientists concentrating on subjects defined taxonomically, temporally, geographically or culturally.

A second measure of expanded interest is the appearance of specialist publications. The quadrennial meetings of the International Council of Archaeozoology have generated a number of important proceedings (Clutton-Brock and Grigson 1983). For nearly a decade, the Swedish journal, *Ossa*, has devoted a significant portion of its pages to archeozoological research. During 1983, an archeozoological newsletter was initiated in Canada. A third measure of growth is the publication of archeozoological bibliographies. Among recent efforts are the review focused on eastern North America by Bogan and Robison (1978) and a serial compiled by Müller (1982).

Recognition of animal bone archeology as a legitimate subdiscipline has been a good thing. Previously, project director/archeologists often thought in terms of a Renaissance figure called a "bioarcheologist," capable of collecting, preserving, identifying, and interpreting plant, animal, and human remains. Few, if any, such individuals exist. It is the theme of this book that the biological specialist is an integral component

of an archeological research design in which the categories of excavated material are the template for positions on the research team. A primary segregation isolates those concerned with "artifacts" from those concerned with "ecofacts." Both the artifact and the ecofact teams may be subdivided depending on the size and complexity of the excavated sample. Information flows back from each component in the analytic structure to the central figure (the project director/archeologist), who is responsible for integrating the disparate data sources and for interpreting them in cultural historical terms (Fig. 1).

All of us who "do bones" have had the experience of analyzing a collection in a vacuum, in the sense that we learned of significant results of other specialists only after our own work was completed. In these circumstances, the project director/archeologist must appreciate the analytical nuances in each of the particular studies commissioned in order to integrate the results. In practice, this seldom happens. Archeological reports consequently become collections of appendices from which summary conclusions can be drawn, but the potential for interdisciplinary cross-fertilization is lost.

A different philosophy motivates this book. For us, the primary structure of the research design of an archeological project is defined by the historical and cultural questions that stimulate it (Fig. 2). The project director/archeologist still heads the research, but the subdivision of work is based on descriptive (culture history) and explanatory (culture process) objectives. For example, teams of researchers might focus

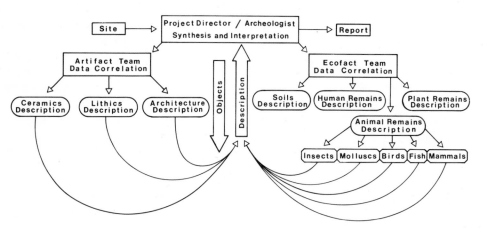

**Fig. 1.** Traditional research design in animal bone archeology, in which the work is divided according to the category of artefact or ecofact to be studied.

on techno-environmental relationships, social organization, and ideology. The members of each team would be concerned with linking categories of remains (bone, stone, etc.) to their area of special interest. The same objects might be relevant to all three realms of culture. Thus, the animal bone archeologist might provide data on different attributes of a faunal collection to each team.

The emergence of the discipline of animal bone archeology allows the precise juxtaposition of skills with questions, so that synthetic results can be generated. For example, our primary objective in analyzing a collection of sheep and goat bones from the Roman villa of San Giovanni was understanding the degree to which the villa's husbandry economy was integrated into regional systems of animal and animal-product exchange (Steele 1981). A measure of this variable was developed by applying the culling strategy prescribed by ancient Roman agricultural manuals

to the proportions of the different age classes represented in the San Giovanni bone sample. The absence of expected categories may imply export. A similar study compared bone refuse from a colonial North American site to the contemporary probate record (Bowen 1975). In analyzing remains from a Bronze Age tomb in Jordan, by contrast, our focus was on ideological content, the nature of a burial association, and its relationship to a ritual meal (Hesse and Wapnish 1981). In the first case, the collaborative team included historians; in the second, physical anthropologists.

This insistence on the primacy of questions over data explains the subtitle of this book, "From Objectives to Analysis." The time to do research and the funds to support and publish it are limited. Efficiency, if nothing else, demands that analysis be done for some other reason than that it is possible. This position is not shared by all our colleagues. Some insist

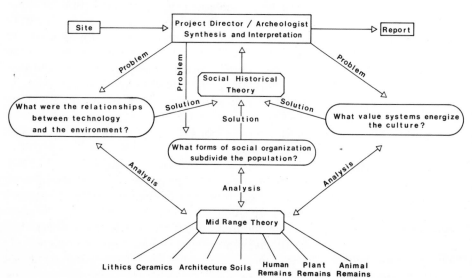

**Fig. 2.** Integrated research design in animal bone archeology, in which the work is divided according to the questions to be asked.

that animal bone reports contain certain standardized data, perhaps as a consequence of all-too-frequently discovering that the data presented in a paper are inadequate for evaluating the conclusions. In our opinion, this problem should be resolved by improving pre-publication reviews rather than by establishing a rigid set of descriptive requirements. Better reviews depend on understanding the relationship between theory and data, and this will be the focus of our attention. This manual does not provide a simple set of procedures for generating the "right" data. Animal bone archeology is collaborative; the suggestions made here are intended to illustrate the problems likely to be encountered rather than prescribe solutions.

The title of this volume reflects our experience and philosophy. By "animal," we mean primarily mammals and birds, rather than fish, reptiles, amphibians, and invertebrates, and we devote most of our attention to these remains. We avoid the terms "archeozoology" and "zooarcheology" because we do not believe we are doing zoology with archeological materials or archeology with zoological principles. We are doing archeology with one kind of residue—bone—in a way analogous to what is done using potsherds and stone tools. As the principles of pyrotechnology may condition the study of pottery and those of lithology the interpretations of stone-tool assemblages, so zoology is a component of animal bone archeology. The emphasis, however, is on human activity and how it may be inferred. Thus, the structure of analysis is cultural rather than biological.

## FOR WHOM THIS BOOK IS WRITTEN

If you are a practitioner of animal bone archeology, this book is not directed primarily at you. All specialists have their own patterns of work, some of which may differ from those we propose based on our experience. Many of the examples are drawn from our work and have been published in greater detail elsewhere. Those portions devoted to research design and to interaction with project director/archeologists may be of interest.

### Project Directors and Archeologists

Project director/archeologists may find themselves in two kinds of situations where the comments

here will prove useful. First, an archeologist may have acquired a sample of animal bones and wonder what, if anything, can be done with it. Modern archeological sampling strategies include the use of screens, water sieves, and flotation equipment, which enhance recovery of bones. After excavation has finished, an archeologist may become attracted to one of the ecological-environmental modes of explanation (such as optimal foraging theory, environmental possibilism, population pressure) and wonder if the sample provides potentially relevant data.

Other archeologists put off establishing collaboration until several seasons of excavation have passed, despite the fact that a slot for an animal bone archeologist is included in their research team. At this point, surrounded by crates of unwashed, unsorted material and facing a reporting deadline, the archeologist makes frantic calls searching for a specialist and discovers that although we are increasing in number, there are still not enough of us to go around. Archeologists confronted with this problem may find help from the International Council for Archaeozoology, which publishes a list of animal bone experts and their current research projects. The Association for Field Archaeology also maintains a file, which identifies taxonomic specialities.

Secondly, project directors and archeologists may find this book useful if animals are a significant element in their research design. Extracting the maximum information is facilitated if they plan the research so as to provide answers to the following three basic questions: (1) What is an animal bone archeology research design? (2) What demands will collaboration make? and (3) How is animal bone research integrated into traditional objectives of archeological excavation? Answering the first question involves exploring variables such as the nature of accumulation and preservation of animal bone refuse, the effects of different collecting techniques on bone samples, the patterns of cross-cultural regularity in perception of animals by prehistoric human groups, and the linkages between animal-related behavior and animal bone remains. The answer to the second question embraces procedures of recovery and stabilization of bones, availability of comparative osteological material, requirements of storage, computer facilities, and training of the excavation crew. Responding to the third question is complicated by conflicts in sampling strategies. A usual archeological goal is the elucidation of a statistically reliable portrait of the interaction between an extinct population and its material culture. Hypothetical models of how humans used and discarded pottery differ from similar constructs for bones. Each model demands that different parts of a site be excavated and different collecting techniques be employed. These conflicts can be resolved by establishing the relative priorities of various kinds of data and the kinds of correlations between categories of finds that are relevant to the problems to be solved.

### Excavators

The second group that should find this book useful is the excavators, whether supervisors or team members, whose astuteness plays an important role in determining whether bone finds have a chance to be reported. This assertion can be supported by an example. Some years ago, we studied some large collections from preceramic sites in northern Chile. The matrix had been screened, allowing retrieval of abundant bones of birds and small rodents. Examination of large flotation samples from the same sites suggested, however, that one kind of camelid bones was underrepresented in the screened samples. This was the sesamoid, a small olive-pit-shaped bone from the foot. Sesamoids are considerably larger than most of the rodent bones that were saved, but were unrecognized and discarded because they were confused with the small stones occurring naturally in the soil (cf. Fig. 51).

Another important category of field observation is the presence of articulations. Because bones remaining in correct anatomical relationship can be assigned to a single individual, their recognition enhances the accuracy of estimates of the relative abundances of the animal categories in a sample. Finally, excavators need to know how to preserve fragile bones, which often include the most taxonomically significant features of a species.

### Novice Animal Bone Archeologists

The third group of potential consumers are novice animal bone archeologists. A former bone specialist once confided that he had turned to this area of archeology in graduate school because the other students in his cohort had preempted ''better'' categories of artifacts. However you got to this point, you will need to learn a number of things. These include: (1) how to prepare a reference collection of skeletons as a basis for identifications, (2) how to label and sort a collection in the field, (3) how to stabilize fragile

specimens, and (4) how to formulate research designs compatible with archeological fieldwork and analysis. This manual will not provide universal or standardized solutions, but it may help you avert disaster.

## ORGANIZATION

In accord with our conviction that the structure of animal bone archeology rests on a cultural base, we begin by discussing the manner in which animals and cultures are integrated. The compilation of folk taxonomies has revealed a number of regularities in the way animals are conceptualized by societies at similar levels of political, social, and technological complexity. These regularities underscore the point that the precise biological distinctions we make do not necessarily correspond to those made by the people whose remains we study. This potential disconformity can be resolved only for samples with historical documentation, but ethnographic analogies may prove useful in interpreting prehistoric samples. Folk categories do not simply partition nature; they reflect social, ideological, and economic spheres of human thought and activitiy, as well as subsistence concerns.

The variables affecting the surviving remains are reviewed in Chapter 3. Archeologists have devoted considerable attention in recent years to processes of site formation (e.g., Cowgill 1970, Schiffer 1976, 1983; Sullivan 1978). We draw on these syntheses to identify various processes that deposit bone and destroy it.

Chapters 4 and 5 address the practical aspects of finding and saving bones. Chapter 4 discusses the nature and terminology of the vertebrate skeleton; Chapter 5, the categories of finds, collecting procedures, field conservation, and record keeping. We offer guidelines to bone identification, including keys to help recognizing skeletal parts, articulations, and general taxonomic categories. Finally, we provide some suggestions for shipping specimens.

Chapters 6, 7, and 8 correspond to the three levels of analysis that characterize animal bone archeology: (1) the analysis of single bones or single animals, (2) the analysis of taxonomic categories, and (3) the analysis of collections from habitation sites. Each chapter includes case studies from our own research, not because they are necessarily the best examples but because they are familiar to us. They reaffirm our central point, namely, that animal bone archeology is not a mere scientific appendix, but is a cultural-historical discipline in its own right.

# 2    Identifying Animal Categories

## OBJECTIVES OF ANIMAL BONE ARCHEOLOGY

Two objectives guide animal bone archeology: (1) to portray the interactions between animals and people in a cultural setting and (2) to understand the processes motivating the zoocultural system. The materialist perspective of most animal bone archeologists leads them to be concerned primariily with questions of diet and environment. This channels the interpretive focus towards the animals as the unit of study and emphasizes information about how the animals appear, where they may be found, how they should be raised, and what their useful products may be. Any faunal study overlooking these aspects would be remiss, but it is equally important in a fully anthropological approach to consider how animals were conceptualized by the people who interacted with them. Zoological categories may correspond completely, partly or not at all to those employed in the cultures archeologists study. The scope of a research design must attempt to include culturally valid categories and part of our job is to try to find out what those categories were.

## SOURCES FOR UNDERSTANDING ZOOCULTURAL SYSTEMS

Animal species provide clues to the boundaries within which human adaptation takes place and animal bone archeologists must decipher them using the literature of zoology, ethology, and game management.

Zoology establishes the biological and morphological parameters of adaptation; ethology, the behavioral patterns. Game-management studies are the least familiar, yet potentially one of the richest sources of archeological modelling. The experimental domestication of novel species, the movement of animals to new environments, and the application of alternative hunting and herding techniques enhance understanding of the possibilities of systems for exploiting animals.

### Bibliographic Resources

Important bibliographic resources in these fields include the *Zoological Record*, which annually publishes an indexed bibliography. This listing can be used to search for publications on a species or a region. The *Journal of Mammalogy, American Midland Naturalist, Journal of Animal Ecology, Saugetierkundliche Mitteilungen*, and *Zeitschrift für Tierpsychologie* are a few of the potential sources in animal ethology. A useful introduction to modern experiments in animal management is the *World Animal Review*, published quarterly by the Food and Agriculture Organization of the United Nations, which also issues numerous monographs on the management of animal resources in Third World countries. Additional relevant articles appear in the literature on zoo management (e.g., *Zoologisches Garten*) and livestock management (e.g., *The Journal of Animal Science* and *Dairy Goat Journal*).

### Zoological and Folk Taxonomy

A cultural-ethological portrait includes environmental information and a rough guide to the strategies of human exploitation. The sources mentioned above deal with animals in the context of the taxonomic hierarchy devised by the Swedish botanist Carolus Linnaeus in the mid-18th century. Since the categories employed in western science may not be relevant to different cultures, and folk taxa shape and express human-animal interactions, we need a method by which to recognize native categories of animals.

Historical documents and ethnographic accounts concerning either the culture being studied or groups temporally and spatially related to it or at a similar level of technological development may allude to or describe animals that were favored, tabooed, used in rituals, viewed as totems, etc.; in other words, identify culturally valid categories. Recognizing native categories is only a beginning, however. These need to be evaluated against a larger framework of zoocultural systems for their information potential to be realized. We believe such a framework is provided by the branch of ethnoscience known as folk biology or the ethnography of concepts and behavior concerning animals.

### Folk Biology

Folk biologists have developed techniques to delimit and describe native categories of plants and animals and the structure of folk classifications. The native's universe is thought to be embodied in his lexicon and consequently the appropriate cognitive models and their related behavior are sought in lexical domains. These studies have revealed a typology that appears to have wide applicability. Further, the technological levels of societies appear to correlate with classificatory and lexical depth. Levels of abstraction for category salience in cultures of varying complexity can also be predicted. These last observations have special utility for animal bone archeologists working with preliterate societies, since the absence of written data requires them to employ broader concepts when looking for native categories.

Bones are initially sorted according to their anatomical part and Linnaean identification. Meaningful cultural and historical interpretation requires that the resulting groups be rearranged into ethnographically relevant units. Folk biology provides tools for making this transformation.

## DEFINING TAXONOMIC CATEGORIES

Folk biology is concerned with the similarities and differences between folk and scientific classifications. While contrasts and overlaps occur at a number of levels, both systems recognize objective discontinuities in nature. Rosch (1978) shows that general categories closely describe real-world structures, meaning that folk classifications are more than in the heads of the natives. Hunn (1975, 1978) predicts that most categories in a folk classification will correspond to scientific taxa, but many scientific taxa will have no native counterparts. Zoological classifications therefore act as an etic grid rather than as a set of equivalents for understanding native taxonomies.

This imbalance stems from the fundamental difference in motivation between scientific and folk systems. The aim of evolutionary classification is to be consistent with regard to phylogeny (Simpson 1961). While folk classifications are concerned with reducing the chaos of a particular domain in its cultural setting, reduction is not consciously carried to the highest possible degree. Freed of the limitations imposed by the goal of general explanation, folk classification uses elements for partitioning that are irrelevant to science. Criteria such as age, sex, manageability, and disease resistance are often the hallmarks of native categories because they represent a highly practical human response to objective reality.

Biological taxonomists arrange plants and animals into related groupings on the basis of criteria judged important to the evolutionary context, be they morphology, embryology, biochemistry, etc. Elements of physical appearance must be analyzed if they are to be used as discriminants. Their reason for being is as important as their existence. Folk classifications have no theory to guide the selection of criteria for defining and arranging categories. Elements of physical appearance are taken at face value; that is, they are descriptive and little else. When scientific and folk biological taxa overlap at the descriptive level, it is because the bundle of physical characters defining the group of organisms is cognized in the folk system and reflects phylogenetic relationships in the scientific system.

### The Perspective of the Zoologist

Most biologists are concerned with creating classifications that express natural relationships consistent with evolutionary theory. Taxonomy—the theory and practice of classifying animals—involves three processes: (1) distinguishing natural groups (or category delineation), (2) ordering those groups on the basis of their relationships, and (3) assigning type names.

Traditional taxonomists classify populations, "defined in the broadest sense as any group of organisms systematically related to each other" (Simpson 1961:11), using a combination of deductive and inductive reasoning. Deductive reasoning takes the form of determining a priori what attributes will be significant to express natural relationships. Inductive reasoning involves intensive empirical consideration of the attributes. Those showing strong statistical patterning in line with known objectives are weighted a posteriori.

The hallmark of population systematics is the uniqueness of individuals. No two are identical genetically, even those belonging to the same "category." Mayr (1982:47) makes this explicit:

The differences between biological individuals are real, while the mean values which we may calculate in the comparison of groups of individuals (species, for example) are man-made inferences. This fundamental difference between the classes of the physical scientists and the populations of the biologists has various consequences. For instance, he who does not understand the uniqueness of individuals is unable to understand the working of natural selection.

The systematic framework of zoological classification is an elaborate hierarchy. The basic form is a sequence of seven ranks decreasing in inclusiveness from top to bottom:

> Kingdom
> > Phylum
> > > Class
> > > > Order
> > > > > Family
> > > > > > Genus
> > > > > > > Species

Seven levels are insufficient to classify all the organisms known today and new levels have been created by adding the prefixes super-, sub-, and infra- to the basic category names. Convention requires that any animal classified be placed in one of the seven basic levels, but use of other levels is optional. Each rank contains varying numbers of named entities, known as *taxa*. According to Simpson (1961:19), a taxon is "a group of real organisms recognized as a formal unit at any level of a hierarchic classification." Mayr (1982:207) defines a taxon as "a group of organisms of any taxonomic rank that is sufficiently distinct to be worthy of being named and assigned to a definite category." Simpson's definition underscores the fact that taxa are real, concrete objects whereas Mayr stresses the subjectivity inherent in delimiting taxa of equal rank. Taxa at all ranks are real organisms; that

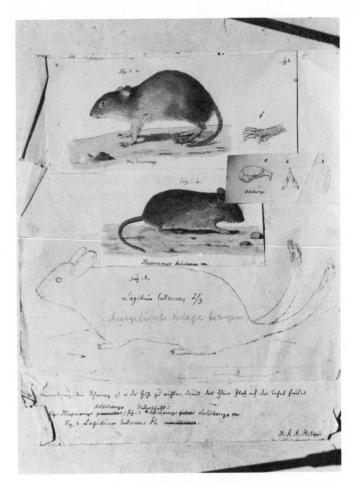

**Fig. 3.** Illustrations prepared by the Chilean scientist, R.A. Phillippi, for his review of South American fauna. Note the particular attention paid to pelage and dentition.

is, they are sufficiently distinct natural entities to be delimited. Categories, however, are artificial constructs that designate levels in a hierarchic classification.

The core of modern systematics is the species. As defined by Mayr (1969:4), "species are groups of interbreeding natural populations, that are reproductively isolated from other such groups." Boundaries can be drawn objectively between species, but not between taxa at higher levels. One taxonomist's family may be another's genus or super-family, and so on. The absence of clear, objective criteria for defining categories above the species level makes it necessary to emphasize the distinction between taxa and categories.

The range of criteria used to define taxa has increased dramatically over the past twenty years. Biological data, such as gross and micromorphology, cytogenetic and serological composition, geographic and ecological distribution, are evaluated for objectivity, kinds and degrees of affinity, antiquity of the taxon, etc. A taxonomist working with mammals might pay attention to skin color, dentition, skull configuration, and tail length, among other characters (Fig. 3).

The complexity of zoological classification is exemplified by sheep (Schaller 1977). The criteria for subdividing the genus *Ovis* have included horn shape and size, coloration, body build and size, chromosome number, geographic range, and habitat preference. Since 1873, the number of species recognized in the Old World has varied between 1 and 17 and the number of subspecies from 8 to 38 (Valdez 1982). This is largely a result of changes in the kinds of information employed for making distinctions as the species concept developed and population systematics were incorporated into evolutionary taxonomy. In the most recent classification by Valdez (1982), overall body size, chromosome number, and habitat preference were used to divide the genus into three major groups, while horn shape and coloration were emphasized for species and subspecies distinctions.

One of the striking innovations in the Valdez classification concerns wild sheep in the Middle East. While recognizing that they "are the most diverse group of wild sheep," he places them (including populations on Cyprus, Corsica, and Sardinia) into one species, *Ovis orientalis* (Valdez 1982:70). This taxon includes the mouflon and the urial, which are assigned to separate taxa in classifications that rely on phenotypic characters. Valdez has demonstrated, however, that these two forms interbreed in the wild and produce fertile offspring. Since reproductive isolation is a cornerstone of the modern zoological concept of species, this discovery indicates the diverse group has to be treated taxonomically as a single species.

Why is this example important for animal bone archeologists? First, it demonstrates the need for understanding the basis of distinctions among zoological categories. Second, it shows that, although zoologists strive for consistent classification, wide differences in perception may lead to disparate results. Third, it reveals that the criteria important in zoological classification (reproductive behavior often being the most important) may have limited bearing on the questions of animal bone archeology, which focus on human-animal interactions and the environments in which they took place. Finally, it should be noted that zoologists consistently avoid dealing with the complexities of domestic stock. Domestic sheep are at least as variable as their wild counterparts, yet until recently zoologists treated them as a single species, *Ovis aries*. The expanding literature on domestic breeds (e.g., Epstein 1971 and Mason 1980) has begun to address this situation and is especially valuable to animal bone archeologists.

## The Perspective of the Folk Biologist

In animal bone reports, a vernacular term is usually provided for each scientific taxon. While this practice has the salutory effect of communicating more effectively with non-zoologist readers, it masks considerable and important complexities in the ways non-scientists think about their animal world. The following guidelines for discovering useful categories for animal bone analysis emerge largely from observations made by scholars in one branch of cognitive anthropology: the formalists of folk biology.

We would be remiss to omit mention of another large school concerned with folk biological studies, whose theories and methodologies stand in contrast to those of the formalists. This symbolic school emphasizes the priority of the specific social context in attaching meaning to labels, focuses on the multiplicity of uses to which single labels may be put, views cultural and real-world factors as equivalent stimuli in cognitive processes, and is little concerned with eliciting classificatory structures relevant to groups of people. Formalists, by contrast, emphasize the priority of real-world structures in cognition, the existence of discrete domains, and the classificatory arrangement by which they may be defined. Since archeologists collect real-world specimens and use them to infer patterns of behavior for social units over time, the formalist approach offers them greater opportunities for practical application.

***Kinds of Classifications.*** Classifications fall into two broad categories. General-purpose classifications employ a wide variety of data and therefore have a high information content, which may make their manipulation in specific contexts difficult. Special-purpose classifications, by contrast, employ few attributes to define and arrange categories.

Most cultures classify animals in several ways. The categories of the various schemes and their arrangements may vary greatly, little, or not at all. They may relate to a small part of the activities of a wide variety of people, as for example, in the United States, where animal parts are classified into cuts of meat in a consumer lexicon that crosscuts a wide swath of social groups. Or they may relate to a major portion of the activities of a segment of a society, as in ancient Mesopotamia, where domestic sheep were conceptualized differently by the priestly class, which shared a specialized vocabulary.

In short, we can assume that societies will have classifications of their animals related to economic,

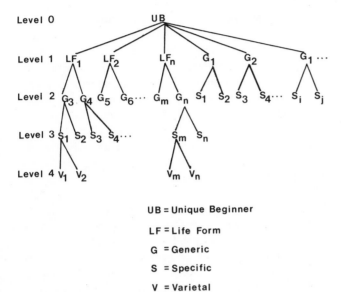

UB = Unique Beginner

LF = Life Form

G = Generic

S = Specific

V = Varietal

**Fig. 4.** The relationships between categories in folk classification systems. The five categories commonly recognized and assigned hierarchical significance range from unique beginner (the most general) to varietal (the most specific).

social, and ideological variables, together with classifications relevant to specific activities and groups within the society. For animal bone archeology, this implies that selecting the proper categories for analysis may depend on establishing what segment of a society was responsible for the remains.

***General Principles of Folk Classification.*** The folk taxonomic model widely used today is a typology of folk taxa based on psychological criteria that link patterns of nomenclature with principles of classification. Nine principles of folk biological classification have been proposed for the structural similarities in otherwise diverse arrangements of organisms (adapted from Berlin, Breedlove and Raven 1973):

1. All languages recognize groups of organisms or taxa.
2. Taxa are allocated to five categories identified by name. Those usually recognized are: unique beginner, life form, generic, specific, and varietal.
3. The five categories are arranged hierarchically and the taxa at each rank are mutually exclusive.
4. Taxa of the same ethnobiological category usually belong to the same taxonomic level (Fig. 4). The unique-beginner taxa occur at

level zero: life-form taxa at level one. Generic taxa usually occur at level two, but sometimes at level one. Specific taxa occur at level three, but occasionally at level two. Varietal taxa occur at level four or level three.
5. Unique beginners (e.g., plant, animal, living thing) may not be distinguished linguistically or labels may not be consistent.
6. Life-form taxa are few (5 to 10), polytypic, and labelled by primary lexemes (e.g., tree, vine, bird, grass).
7. Generic taxa are the most numerous (up to 500) and are the basic units of folk classification.
8. Specific and varietal taxa are less numerous.
9. Intermediate taxa are covert categories, included in life-form taxa and superordinate to generic taxa. These taxa are rare and not distinguished linguistically.

***Relevance to Animal Bone Archeology.*** Several details of folk classifications are relevant to animal bone archeology. Generic taxa constitute the smallest natural groupings of organisms distinguished by gross morphology and thus may be considered natural, logical, general-purpose categories. As such, they correspond most closely with species in the scientific system. Hunn (1975) points out, however, that some folk generics equate with higher scientific taxa (e.g., the generic "bat" in folk English corresponds to the scientific order *Chiroptera*). In other instances, folk specifics correlate with scientific species (e.g., the specifics "striped skunk" and "hooded skunk" in folk English correspond to the scientific species *Mephitis mephitis* and *Mephitis macroura*).

Folk taxonomic studies contribute two important warnings to animal bone archeologists: (1) scientific zoological categories are not necessarily the most appropriate units of analysis for making cultural inferences and (2) the relevant zoological category may be higher or lower than the species level. A category of considerable significance in many cultures is labelled in folk English "vermin," defined in Webster's Dictionary as "noxious, mischievous, or disgusting animals of small size, of common occurrence, and difficult to control including various insects . . . , various mammals . . . , and sometimes birds." This category has no scientific equivalent, since it contains organisms from distinct phyla. For cultural analysis, however, these disparate forms must be grouped for comparison with non-vermin.

If the core of a folk biological classification need

CASH HERD
(sold for cash)

**Toklu**- Male Yearling

PRODUCTIVE HERD

**Koyun sürüsü**- Herd used for
continuing production

**Koyun**- Ewe

**Kart Koyun**- Ewe, 6 yrs. +
(candidates for sale even if still
lambing)

**Dörter**- A ewe who has lambed 4
times

**Kĭsĭr**- A barren ewe

**Şişek**- Yearling ewe

**Toklu**- Yearling ram

**Koç**- Ram, 2 yrs. +

**Kuzu**- Lamb

**Fig. 5.** The Yörük folk classification of sheep. Two general groups
are recognized: (1) a cash herd containing one category and (2) a
productive herd containing nine categories.

not be limited to taxa of generic rank, how may taxa of
other ranks acquire "basic" status? That is, how do
such categories become well differentiated and reduce
internal diversity? Studies of urban Americans, whose
contact with plants and animals is limited, show that
significant categories are more inclusive than among
human groups whose interaction and dependence on
the local biota are stronger. Urban dwellers are un-
aware of distinctions between species. For them, the
basic level may be the life-form, the most inclusive
rank at which category members share significant
numbers of characteristics (Rosch et al 1976). In
hunter-gatherer societies, by contrast, folk taxonomies incorporate few or no higher-level categories.
Fine distinctions are used for grouping organisms and
a high percentage of the genera and species distinguished by zoologists is recognized and labelled.

Most folk biologists agree that the existence of
many finely discriminated categories of animals reflects their use, often as food. Other researchers

maintain that the existence of lower-level categories
for organisms that serve no utilitarian purpose implies
a general interest in the environment. There is no way
at present to prove either view. We have seen, however, that salience levels in general-purpose classifications are determined by utilitarian concerns. When
utilitarian factors reach a critical level, they spawn
special-purpose classifications. When a special-purpose classification encompasses "the animals we eat,
hunt, and raise," it acquires paramount importance to
the animal bone archeologist. Bates (1973) study of the
Yörük, a pastoral people of southeast Turkey, provides an excellent example of such a classification,
giving the relevant folk terms for components of a
sheep herd as a unit of production (Fig. 5).

Assigning a bone to the Linnaean category *Ovis* is
not sufficient. For answering cultural questions, the
zoological unit must be subdivided by age and sex.
Because the experimental methods used to establish
age baselines result in finely graded categories, there
are generally not enough archeological specimens of
any given species in each category to permit statistical
comparison. If, however, folk categories such as
those provided by Bates are used to produce culturally meaningful groupings by age and sex, these
analytic units may contain enough specimens to permit statistical manipulation.

When confronted by physically similar organisms, peoples of diverse cultures frequently make fine
distinctions on the basis of size. The Rofaifo of the
Papua New Guinea highlands recognize three taxa
differentiated by size rather than two species of ma-
cropods (marsupials including kangaroos and walla-
bees), cross-cutting the boundaries drawn by biologists (Fig. 6; Dwyer 1977:431).

Size may also serve for grouping animals of het-
erogeneous nature. In a series of studies concerning
the definition and linguistic encoding of life-form taxa
in 112 languages, Brown (1979, 1981) identified five
categories that consistently conformed to Berlin's
(1976) conceptual criteria for taxa of this rank. The
categories FISH, SNAKE, and BIRD were encoded

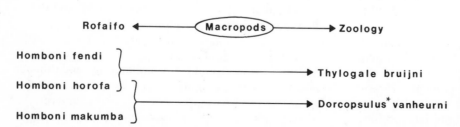

**Fig. 6.** Folk classification of large
mammals by the Rofaifo of Papua
New Guinea. Three taxa
differentiated by size equate with two
taxa recognized by biologists.

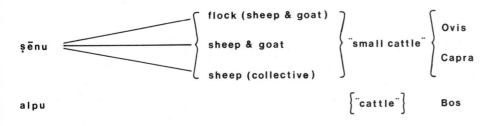

**Fig. 7.** The classification of domestic stock in ancient Mesopotamia. Goats and sheep are given the same term because size is the primary criterion by which they are differentiated from cattle.

first; WUG and MAMMAL were added last to accommodate animals not classified in the first three categories. WUG signifies "small residual animal" and always includes insects and spiders; it sometimes is expanded to incorporate worms, snails, crabs, lizards, small frogs, and tortoises. MAMMAL signifies "large residual animal" and is usually restricted to mammals of western science, but may include crocodiles, tortoises, and frogs of sufficient size. In sum, size appears to be an important criterion in the formation of higher and lower animal categories of a folk system, often overshadowing other phenotypic characters as an organizing principle.

If written records or relevant ethnographic studies exist, they may reveal life-form categories comparable to WUG or MAMMAL that justify lumping seemingly diverse fauna into a single analytic unit. WUG, in particular, offers such a possibility for more complex societies, since it is likely to include animals not routinely exploited for food. The occasional occurrence of the bones of complete or partly articulated small lizards, snakes, frogs, and snails (even insect cases) might warrant this treatment. In this case, the animal bone archeologist may decide that fine taxonomic identification is unnecessary, providing that environmental information is not sacrificed.

Size can also be the deciding factor in grouping animals ordinarily considered separately because of morphological distinctiveness, practical use, etc. The Akkadian term *senu* means (1) a flock of sheep and goats, (2) sheep and goats, or (3) a collective term for sheep. In many Mesopotamian texts, *senu* is contrasted with "cattle," in which case it is often translated as "small cattle" rather than as "sheep and goats" (Fig. 7).

The textual evidence may provide insights into animal-management procedures. Two passages from the cuneiform corpus illustrate what we mean. One is an invocation of good fortune: "May your cattle pen be wide, your fold for sheep and goats large"; the other, part of a law from the Code of Hammurapi: "a shepherd to whom have been handed over cattle or sheep and goats to pasture" (Oppenheim 1962). Both passages reveal features of a stocking or herding strategy that may justify using "small cattle" as the analytic unit for certain interpretations.

The final point we wish to make about ethnobiological categories and classifications concerns their utility in the absence of historical sources and ethnographic accounts. If we look again at the Mesopotamian category "small cattle," we see that the label and concept are comprehensible because such a category exists in folk English. In instances where non-phenotypic characters are emphasized in scientific classification, it may be more productive for the purpose of defining significant analytic units to examine a modern (but not necessarily related) folk classification of the same animals. Field manuals and identification guides give descriptions of how animals may be recognized. While these guides are organized according to the scientific system, they often include popular names as well; in essence, a modern folk classification. Zoogeographic reports also frequently supplement scientific names with modern folk labels. Such materials are useful provided they are employed with care. Zoologists can make mistakes in applying popular names, just as lexicographers can confuse scientific labels. The dangers posed by working with several sets of terms for the same animals can be overcome and even turned to advantage when the categories involved are understood.

## ART HISTORICAL SOURCES

Depictions in sculpture, relief, painting, and other media reveal something about how the artist viewed the animal and in what contexts. More productively, they may highlight features useful as analytic criteria.

But art historical literature must be used with caution since problems may arise when animal identifications are made without understanding the zoological categories involved (Reed and Osborn 1978). The perspective of the art historian is essential, however, for understanding the stylization and context of potentially useful features.

We do not recommend that an animal bone archeologist become immersed in the relevant art historical literature, any more than the discussion on ethnobiology was meant to suggest a similar plunge into cognitive studies. If the problems are complex, the response should be to consult a specialist rather than abandon the approach. We have been gratified by the cooperation we have received over the years from art historians, linguists, and zoologists.

Art historical sources may identify questions posed incompletely or not at all by other lines of evidence. The pictorial record of the ancient Near East suggested that the two-humped Bactrian camel as well as the one-humped dromedary camel may have been used on the international trade routes that passed Tell Jemmeh in Israel. Since the dromedary would be expected because of location and context, and the presence of the Bactrian would indicate important commercial lines to the east, it was necessary to establish whether both forms were present. The morphological criteria usually used for identification (mostly length-breadth ratios of whole bones) were not applicable to the fragmentary archeological remains, however, and new criteria had to be developed (Wapnish 1981, 1984). Animal bone archeologists often initiate such studies, but they can become lengthy digressions. When time and publication deadlines are pressing, the decision to go ahead will be determined by the importance of answering the question involved.

## THE INTEGRATION OF ANIMALS AND SOCIETY

Creating categories for analysis requires a look at the different ways humans integrate animals into society. An analogy may be drawn with ceramic studies. Archeologists examine features such as surface treatment, decoration, temper, vessel shape, and firing because they reveal techniques and procedures of manufacture and use. Whether the categories of analysis were appreciated or recognized by the potters is an issue disconnected from whether the characteristics are useful for analysis. If variations in some of the characteristics correlate with variations in another set of archeological attributes, they are useful.

Animal bone archeologists are just beginning a similar exploration of the variability manifested by osseous debris. We have leaned too long and too hard on zoological categories as the sole structure for investigation. Zoological units may or may not be useful for cultural inferences. How can we develop more informative measures of variability? Precisely the same way that other archeological specialists have created theirs: by examining how animals are integrated into techno-environmental systems, sociopolitical relationships, and ideological behavior, both secular and sacred.

## Animals as Technofacts

A rich source for the discovery of analytic categories is an understanding of how each biotic resource can be exploited successfully. This requires identifying the tasks that ancient societies had to accomplish and the kinds of categories associated with them. For example, the methods, timing, and success of hunting depend on several variables in the game population, especially (1) availability, associated with density, seasonality, and daily activity cycle; (2) vulnerability, related to coloration, habitat preference, ferocity, and social organization; (3) productivity, linked to size, carcass yield, and possible use as a multiple resource, and (4) cost, determined by the effort needed for transport to the home site and the complexities of preparation and use. In considering the variable "availability" as it relates to a daily activity cycle, animals may be classified as diurnal, nocturnal, and crepuscular. Patterning in the frequency of animal remains grouped in this way permits reconstructing the daily activities of the hunters. Likewise, vulnerability as it relates to habitat preference produces plains-dwelling, forest-loving, and mountain-climbing categories of animals. These distinctions may provide insights into catchment utilization. Each variable, as well as others not listed above, can contribute useful qualitative and quantitative information.

Herders are concerned with a different set of variables. These include (1) pasture quality, controlled by stocking rate, seasonal movement, and nutritional value of the forage; (2) herd management, related to temperament of the flock, protection from predators, and number of herdsmen; and (3) profitability, dependent on scheduling of extractive activities, timing of slaughter, access to markets, resistance to disease, and relative value of the products (hide, meat, milk). In considering seasonal movements, a distinction can be made between the herds of sedentary communities, which are rotated across local pastures and returned to the fold each evening, and the flocks of nomads, which are moved along a seasonal round and available to the home community only during brief periods each year. Examining the scheduling of extractive activities brings out the contrast between animals that are milked (a daily activity) and animals that are sheared (an annual activity).

Hunters and herdsmen are the providers of animal resources. The second part of the techno-environmental equation is the consumers. Once dead, an animal becomes a collection of parts: hide, bone, cuts of meat, tendon, sinew, teeth, and hair. This "classification" reflects a number of activities aimed at utilizing one or more of these parts: skinning, butchering, cooking, tool and textile manufacturing. When species or anatomical parts are grouped according to parts, the variations may reveal activity areas or different functions (domestic versus ritual).

Defining techno-environmental categories is a natural procedure in research designs emphasizing diet, environmental reconstruction, and the organization of production and consumption. A popular and productive strategy draws on optimal foraging theory to interpret animal bone collections "as the joint product of environmental and behavioral 'givens' (constraints) and the goals and choices exhibited by foragers attempting to maximize the benefits obtained per unit foraging time" (Smith 1983:640). A theoretical model of this type places a tremendous premium on using techno-environmental variables in analysis.

## Animals as Sociofacts

In many societies, animals symbolize social distinctions. Possession of or access to some species may be restricted to a kin group or social stratum. In medieval Europe, for example, certain species of birds of prey were the exclusive property of the nobility. Access to game animals, such as stags, was denied members of the lower classes by prohibiting trespass on large tracts of land. The Egyptians and Assyrians both used cheetahs as hunting aids, and the Egyptians domesticated the hyena as an exotic food (Clutton-Brock 1981; Zeuner 1963). Unusual pets conferred status in antiquity, as they do today. The Assyrian kings instructed their representatives in the far reaches of the empire to send exotic animals to the court. To evaluate such possibilities, rare and novel species should be dealt with analytically as a category separate from the more usual debris.

Animals may also reflect economic differences within a society. The age and sex classes of slaughtered stock or game are often ranked in terms of palatability. Old camel is known as the meat of the urban poor in parts of Arabia because of its toughness and gamy quality (Cole, D.P. 1975). The occupants of the Anatolian site of Korucutepe are described as having discriminating tastes because of their apparent preference for young pig (Boessneck and Von den Driesch 1975).

Differences in representation of parts of animals can also provide economic and cultural information. Schulz and Gust (1983) grouped animal bone fragments from four 19th century archeological contexts in Sacramento, California according to the cuts of meat to which they belonged. When they ranked the cuts using the retail prices obtained from contemporary sources, the relative frequencies of the categories of bones correlated with the differences in status attributed to the archeological contexts by the historical documents (Fig. 8). The cut of meat, rather than the species, may in fact be the appropriate unit of comparison in many situations. In the modern United States, differential representation of two categories, one composed of chicken wings, chuck steaks, and lamb breasts, and the other of chicken breasts, T-bone steaks, and lamb chops, provides clearer evidence of differing economic status than can be derived using the whole animals represented.

Animals also figure in the establishment and maintenance of social ties. Herd animals are frequently exchanged as part of marriage contracts. In mixed pastoral economies, each species has a distinct value based on its utility for such exchanges. The gift of an animal may accompany rituals associated with achieving adulthood. Among the Nuer, the animal's name is assumed by the young man in the course of these rites, so that the names of cattle are guides to kinship relationships within the society. Among hunting groups, complex rules of redistribution guarantee community-wide access to animal resources. In these cases, the units of exchange may be either parts or whole animals. Some small animals may be classed as gathered rather than hunted resources and so fall under different rules of redistribution.

Animal names are often used to label kin or other social groups. The selection of labels for totemic designations is tied to social complexity. In hunting and

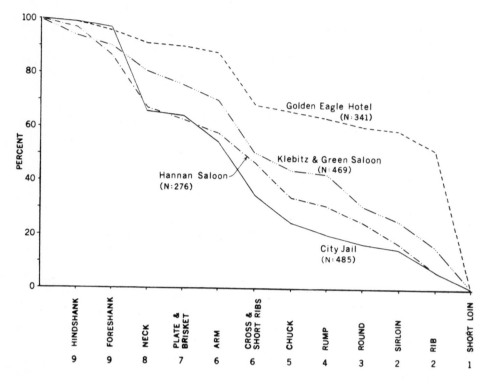

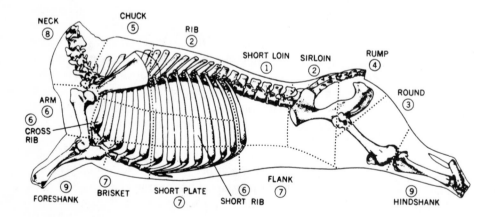

**Fig. 8.** Economic information obtained from bones grouped according to cuts of meat. The fragments collected from four late 19th-century sites in Sacramento, California with different functions were assigned to the cuts of beef they represented. When these were ranked according to contemporary retail prices and their frequencies at each site were plotted by ascending value as cumulative curves, a high correlation emerged between the more expensive cuts and the hotel. The least costly cuts predominated at the city jail; the two saloons were intermediate (reprinted from Schulz and Gust 1983, Figs. 1 and 2 by permission of the Society for Historical Archaeology).

gathering societies, animals important in everyday use tend to be chosen; in more complex societies, distance from daily interaction with animals renders the choices more arbitrary and mythical animals, such as griffins and dragons, may be used (Bulmer 1979).

In sum, it is often desirable to regroup zoological categories and anatomical parts according to criteria of social distinction. The utility and advisability of such regroupings are subject to the same rules of ar-

gument by analogy that govern other kinds of archeological reasoning (Gould and Watson 1982; Wylie 1982).

## Animals as Ideofacts

People have different degrees of attachment to the animals around them. The affection of owners toward pets is often expressed by burial of animal companions with ceremonies comparable to those employed for humans. This relationship contrasts with that between ranchers and cattle. As described by Bennett (1964:37, 42), "when animals are herded in fairly large numbers . . . utilitarian attitudes toward the animals tend to become dominant . . . [and] attitudes toward cattle contain almost no element of sympathy or compassion, and very little tendency toward the establishment of relationships between single men and single animals." This attitude contrasts sharply with the links between ranchers and their horses and dogs, or those between milkers and their dairy cows. Such relationships are also reflected in the propriety of killing and eating species or individuals.

Much animal bone archeology "begins with an implicit nul hypothesis: that human beings will eat anything that contributes to their biological well being. Instantly, we know this is false—and not only because the total range of possible foods is rarely if ever known by its possible consumers. The fact is, even within the realm of what is admittedly edible, people exercise amazing discrimination in their choice of foods. The question is, how come?" (Tuzin 1981:187). Tuzin's comments, made in the context of an appraisal of food taboos and their genesis in lowland South America, are supported by Beckerman and Sussenbach, who observed a weak correlation between the availability of various protein resources and their exploitation by South American forest peoples. Their interpretation, which animal bone archeologists may be able to test, is:

It is the normal case for the people of a particular culture to focus on a single species or, at most a genus. As game depletion occurs . . . , this focal species tends to be depleted at a faster rate than others. Hunters supplement their dwindling bag of the focal species with other species *of the same general size*. It is likely that it will be only after all the animals of that size class are depleted that a shift to another, almost certainly smaller, size class will occur (Beckerman and Sussenbach 1983:346).

This observation that size is a determinant in prey selection seems likely to account for the importance of size as a category organizer in many folk systems of classification. Taking this point further, Bulmer (1979) notes that the Kalam of the New Guinea highlands use size as a criterion for assigning mystical significance to species of birds. This is an example of the general proposition that "birds and other animals are not selected randomly as totems and for other forms of ritual and mystical marking" (Bulmer 1979:71). He further

suggests that animals singled out for special recognition will be those important in everyday uses.

An alternative formulation argues that animals singled out for ritual significance are "anomalous" taxa that do not fit comfortably into the overall structure of the classification system (Douglas 1966; Tambiah 1969). As ambiguous categories, they threaten the cultural order. Therefore, they are given special treatment to neutralize their potential danger. The most famous example of this behavior is the dietary rules of the Hebrews in the Old Testament (Deuteronomy and Leviticus). Mammals that may be eaten must have cloven hooves and chew the cud. The camel and the pig, among others, are explicitly proscribed, the camel because it ruminates but does not have split hooves and the pig because it has split hooves but does not ruminate. This ideology is expressed in an elaborate system of ritual avoidance and prescribed consumption, purification and defilement. Once an ideological system of this kind develops, it tends to acquire added functions, such as maintenance of social solidarity and marking of social boundaries. Behavior motivated by such ideological concerns may be reflected in the kinds and distributions of animal remains.

In many societies, animals are killed in a ritual context. Hunters often have elaborate mythologies that mediate their relationship with game. Herdsmen frequently slaughter their animals for ceremonial occasions, and the suitability of a particular species is determined by the context of the sacrifice.

Ideologies are difficult to infer from archeological evidence. Our objective is (1) to call attention to the fact that animal-related behaviors are affected by these phenomena and (2) to suggest some general guidelines for sorting animal bones into categories appropriate for their recognition. In these matters, it is particularly important for the animal bone archeologist to collaborate with the project director and specialists on the culture involved, who can suggest behaviors potentially reflected in the samples.

## RESEARCH DESIGN IN ANIMAL BONE ARCHEOLOGY: AN EXAMPLE

An animal bone research design should address two questions: (1) What animal categories are important and (2) how should they be contrasted? The procedures can be illustrated by a research design we developed for studying the animal bones from Tel Miqne on the western border of Israel's central hill country. This walled city, occupied during the late second and early first millennium B.C., covers some 50 acres. It has been identified as Ekron, one of the five major cities of the Philistines mentioned in the Old Testament. Ekron was at the political boundary between Israelite and Philistine lands. Biblical accounts leave open the question whether Ekron was a wholly Philistine city or Israelites were a significant part of the population during some periods. Excavations directed by Trude Dothan and Seymour Gitlin, aimed at establishing the site's chronology, yielded a collection of about 11,000 bone fragments. Our task was to extract information from this sample relevant to understanding the function of the site and the behavior of the inhabitants.

## Indices of Military Function

Since Ekron seems to have figured in numerous military adventures during its occupation, it was reasonable to ask if specialized military functions might be reflected in the bone deposit. Several indices were selected to measure the military character of the settlement.

*Index 1.* The ratio of transport animals to barnyard stock. Literary and artistic evidence attests that donkeys, horses, and camels were used for military transport and chariotry. This group of taxa contrasts with the sheep-goat-cattle-(pig) complex that was the domestic mainstay of the ancient Middle East. Transport animals should be more frequent with respect to the domestic category during periods of heightened military activity.

*Index 2.* Ages at death of the transport animals. Transport animals used by the military were likely to be purchased, commandeered from local sources, or raised in protected locations for the government. Therefore, prime adults should far outnumber young, juvenile, and aged animals at military encampments. We would also expect higher than normal frequencies of trauma.

*Index 3.* Ages at death of the barnyard stock. Military installations are often supplied externally, a practice that would provide a frequency of market-age animals above the average mortality normally associated with pastoral flocks.

*Index 4.* Higher than normal frequency of wild game. Soldiers may have leisure between official duties and hunting would be a natural form of diver-

sion. Therefore, we may expect gazelles, other antelopes, deer, and large carnivores to be more abundant in military than non-military contexts.

## Indices of Sociocultural Behavior

Another goal was to characterize the range of production, consumption, and discard activities during each historic period as a basis for observing differences of possible cultural and chronological significance. Three indices are relevant:

*Index 1.* Distributions of animal parts. Butchering reduces a carcass to packets for consumption. Therefore, the skeletal recovery pattern must be examined for each species. The fragments must be grouped into categories (head, back and chest, shoulder and hip girdles, fore and hind limbs, feet, fragments of shaft and articular ends) that can be mapped across contexts defined archeologically. These distributions should reveal areas devoted to specialized activities, such as skinning, tool manufacturing, and refuse disposal. They might also shed light on social differences.

*Index 2.* Composition of the diet. Diet can be examined either by species or by animal part. Dietary estimations at complex sites must be treated with caution because it is not always clear how segments of the human population correlate with animal remains.

*Index 3.* Patterns of mortality. The age categories of domestic stock can provide an index of the degree of involvement in pastoral activities. Generally, pastoralist flocks are divided into two categories: (1) animals intended for sale and (2) animals needed to maintain and increase the herd (e.g. Fig. 5). Three kinds of patterns of animal bone remains are expectable, each reflecting a different pattern of use. A self-sufficient pastoral community should be associated with a mortality pattern closely comparable to the normal mortality of each herded species. A consuming community should be associated with an abundance of animals of marketable age. A group of producers involved in a market economy should be represented by abnormal frequencies of sub-adults and females.

## Indices of Ideological Differences

Biblical accounts are equivocal about the presence or absence of Israelites in Ekron. Were such a group to have lived there and practiced the dietary rules described in the Old Testament, their presence might be detected through the animal bone record. Investigation should focus on the prohibited and prescribed species since they are most clearly defined. Edible animals are those with cloven hooves that also chew their cud. Israelites were also enjoined from eating the back end of the animal unless the ischiatic nerve was first removed. Since this is a difficult and costly procedure, the effect of the injunction was to render the hindquarters unfit to eat. The Hebrew ritual code was not static. Of significance here were the reforms of Hezekiah during the late 8th to early 7th century B.C., which made game animals a ritually acceptable category of food. Three indices are relevant to this problem:

*Index 1.* The presence of profane animals. This criterion is insufficient alone because equids and camels served non-dietary functions among Israelites. The question to be answered is whether they were used for food. If Ekron had a mixed population, we would expect the prohibited species to be segregated spatially. Pig remains should also exhibit this separation.

*Index 2.* Uses of equids and camels. These animals were commonly used for transport by the Israelites, but we would not expect to find evidence of dismemberment and butchering in an Israelite context. Whole or partly articulated skeletons would be more likely.

*Index 3.* Ratio of fore and hind parts of permitted species. In a mixed community, we would anticipate a higher proportion of back quarters in some areas than in others.

## Indices of Environmental History

Finally, we want to employ animal remains to tell something about the environmental history of the site: facts that can be coordinated with paleobotanical and sedimentological data. The ratio between wet-adapted and dry-adapted species is one index. The best evidence is provided by owl-pellet deposits, since their context identifies the precise reason for the presence of the bone fragments. A contrast between the frequencies of water fowl and ground birds is another indicator of local conditions.

## Conclusion

The indices listed above exemplify three kinds of variables that can be used to examine a variety of questions about ancient animal exploitation. The point to keep in mind is that the bone fragments must be grouped and regrouped in numerous ways to make full use of their archeological potential. The criteria for these combinations are zoological, technological, social, and ideological. The kinds of categories range from groups of species to selected bones of particular animals of a given age and sex. Many of the categories employed for one index have obvious utility for others. Before we can evaluate these measures, however, we must consider how information about animal use is transmitted by the archeological record.

# 3

# The Nature of a Sample of Bones

The factors that can potentially influence the condition and location of organic remains in archeological sites are so numerous and so daunting that some investigators doubt the quantitative attributes of animal bone samples can ever be linked with certainty to cultural and environmental variables (Grayson 1979). This gloom is darkened by the demonstration that numerous "natural" processes can produce assemblages similar to those predicted to result from human behavior. For example, killing more animals when young than when old would produce a sample with a large relative proportion of immature bones. Since immature bones are usually less dense than mature ones, they are less resistent to attritional factors. A contrast in the relative proportions of immature and mature specimens between two samples might thus reflect differential preservation rather than cultural preferences. In other situations, natural factors can distort the cultural patterns sufficiently that legitimate distinctions are masked.

Nevertheless, animal bones are wonderful records of human activity. Most of the fragments collected and subjected to analysis derive from refuse. While refuse is a socially determined concept, subject to considerable cross-cultural variability, it has proved in ethnoarcheological research to be a relatively robust measure of the behavior, if not directly the values, of groups of people. Some animal bone specialists have been impressed with the rough fit between the expectations developed from cultural/historical/environmental models and the observed frequencies and locations of bone fragments in ancient middens. In some historical sites in the United States, for example, the relative socio-economic status of certain social strata, inferred from architectural evi-

dence, is reflected both in the species represented and the quality of the cuts of meat indicated by the bones in the refuse, the lower classes discarding more remains of hunted and trapped wild game and the cheaper cuts of butchered domestic livestock (cf. Fig. 8).

## LEVELS OF ANALYSIS

As with all other kinds of archeological data, there are several ways of extracting information from samples of animal bones. The simplest method is tabulating the presence or absence of taxons, bones or features of bones. When taxa are index markers for environmental conditions, comparing their distributions in Late Wisconsin times and today permits reconstructing Pleistocene environments (Graham 1976, Graham and Semken 1976). When specific morphologies are evidence for the domestic status of a species, their presence or absence can distinguish hunters from herders.

Other kinds of questions require knowing the relative frequencies of taxa, the age and sex categories within taxa or the types of bones represented. Quantitative information may be expressed at ordinal, interval or ratio scales of measurement. The ordinal was employed in analyzing remains of sheep and goats at the early Neolithic site of Ganj Dareh in western Iran. Comparing lists of sheep and goat bones, ranging from the most frequent to least frequent skeletal element, made it possible to discern if the butchered carcasses were being discarded in different manners during different periods of occupation at the site (Hesse 1978).

The interval and ratio scales can provide other

information. In the southeastern United States, for instance, the most common animal recovered is usually the white-tailed deer. Other species, such as raccoon, squirrel, and opposum, served as alternative resources or were exploited for their unique charactertistics (Larson 1980). A change in the relative relationship of these two categories, dominant and less frequent, may indicate subsistence stress, during which the latter served as a buffer resource (Wilkinson 1975).

In the cases described above, the relative abundances of bones and taxa were estimated. It may be inferred that eight deer were killed for each squirrel, but whether nine, nine hundred, or nine thousand animals were harvested is left moot. Sometimes, however, animal bone samples are used to estimate the actual number of animals killed. This is commonly done with catastrophic assemblages, such as bison kills, where the accumulation is presumed to have resulted from a short-term event (Voorhies 1969). Less commonly, it is attempted with attritional assemblages, such as middens, where accumulation is presumed to have been a long-term process and the goal is to estimate the total amount of food used as a basis for deducing the size of the group and the length of occupation of the site.

As one moves from nominal-level statistics to a ratio scale, the risk of distortion from biasing factors increases. If the historical or cultural questions asked demand higher order statistics, the research design must include procedures to identify and estimate the strength of such distortions. The first step in that direction is to construct a rough model of the potential effects that must be considered.

## PROCESSES AFFECTING SAMPLES

The objects recovered by archeologists bear traces impressed not only by their experiences as active elements in past cultural systems, but during their long period of burial (Sullivan 1978). Probably only one thing is certain about the histories of all archeological samples: the total amount of information declines over time, obeying the law of entropy.

The process is diagrammed in Figure 9 (for other versions, see Gilbert, A.S. 1979 and Meadow 1980). The vertical axis represents time, travelling from past to present as one goes from top to bottom. The sizes of the boxes arranged along this axis reflect the quality of

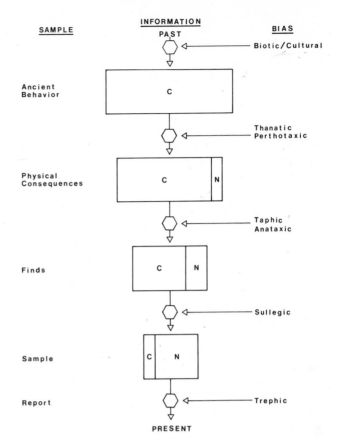

**Fig. 9.** The process of distortion of the information potentially encoded in animal bone remains. Information about cultural events (C) gradually decreases through time as the bones are subjected to a succession of natural influences (N). This diagram divides the process into five categories separated by five kinds of biasing agents. The animal bone archeologist must attempt to allocate the data extracted from a collection among these variables.

information available at various points in time. That this is a mixture of effects of cultural and natural processes is indicated by subdividing each box into two parts, labelled "C" and "N". The positions of the boxes reflect the existence of several distinct "populations" of information (Cowgill 1970).

The "primary target population" is the system of values, beliefs, behaviors, and activities of the society being studied, as they actually occurred in the past. Unfortunately, not all values, beliefs, behaviors, and activities involve material objects. Hence, some measure of the richness and texture is inevitably lost.

A secondary population of information, the "physical consequences population," consists of facts about morphology and location that result from past cultural activities (Schiffer 1976). Three transformational processes can be distinguished, depending on whether the object is entering, leaving or persisting in the web of ongoing cultural activities. Entering processes may be typified by mining (the extraction of raw materials from the buried state) and looting abandoned sites (the extraction of finished objects from the buried state). Leaving processes are exemplified by loss (the inadvertent burial of objects) and discard (the deliberate burial of objects). Persisting processes include the social custom of inheritance and the institution of museums, both of which accomplish the orderly transfer of objects from one historical context to another.

The tertiary population is the "physical finds population," composed of all those objects actually buried, together with the spatial relationships between them. Unfortunately, the slim sliver of surviving information is not a static time capsule (Johnson 1960). The buried state is an active environment, full of physical, chemical, and biological processes capable of transforming the information originally encoded into the physical remains. The study of these processes is known as "taphonomy" (Efremov 1940). The seven principal processes affecting the information content of samples of animal bones have been designated as biotic, thanatic, perthotaxic, taphic, anataxic, sullegic, and trephic (Clark and Kietzke 1967).

## Biotic Processes

The nature of the environment when the site was formed is the primary determinant of the species likely to be encountered. Biotic factors establish both the species and their seasonality.

All animals are limited to a range of habitats and employ two basic approaches to solving the problems of survival. One is the sedentary option: the acquisition of a suite of physiological and behavioral traits that enable the successful exploitation of a range of conditions experienced in a single locale. The more variable these conditions, the greater the flexibility needed. The sedentary option does not necessarily require year-round activity; estivation and hibernation are alternative strategies. The other main approach is the nomadic option. Numerous birds and mammals are able to specialize on a limited range of foods by moving to exploit seasonal differences in availability. These movements may be dramatic, such as undertaken by storks and reindeer, which encompass tremendous horizontal distances. Other species adapt through short vertical movements correlated with seasonal changes at different elevations in rugged terrain.

Cultural factors act in conjunction with biotic factors. As environment is to biotic factors, so perception is to cultural factors. Both are enabling conditions that permit rather than insure the representation

of a locally available species at a site. Although it is difficult to incorporate economic, social and ideological factors into the analysis, it is critical to keep them in mind lest our interpretations of animal bone debris become reduced to reporting biological regularities rather than attempting to reconstruct the perceptions of the human inhabitants. Perception is reflected not only in what animals were exploited, but how far away from the site the interactions occurred. Attempts to deal with these questions have led to a body of theory known as "catchment analysis" (Higgs 1975).

In sum, biotic factors establish: (1) the character and magnitude of the environment exploited, (2) the species available and their abundances, seasonal and otherwise, and (3) the species perceived as useful by the prehistoric inhabitants.

## Thanatic Processes

Thanatic processes remove members from living populations and deposit them in archeological contexts. While it is usual to think of animal bones as evidence of killing by humans, numerous variables affect the composition of the record encountered by the archeologist. The most important are contributions by non-human predators, selective predation by humans, other selective processes, and conditions of accumulation.

***Non-human Predators.*** Non-human predators may contribute bones during or after occupation of a site. Predatory birds accumulate remains of small animals beneath their roosts. At the Roman site of Stobi in Macedonia, James Wiseman discovered that an entrance to an abandoned theater had been occupied by owls, probably for centuries. The density of the remains and the partial articulation of many skeletons made the origin of this deposit readily identifiable, but other accumulations by predatory birds may be less distinctive (Fig. 10).

Other non-human predators may also contribute to archeological sites. Differentiating the debris of human killers from that of other large carnivores has been a subject of intense controversy (e.g. Binford 1981, 1983; Freeman 1983). The distinction is crucial for early-man studies because of the importance of hunting and meat-eating in many of the scenarios constructed to explain human origins. Brain's work (1980, 1981) exemplifies the kinds of experiments that must be conducted before the debris of leopards, hyaenas, and other carnivores can be segregated with confi-

**Fig. 10.** An accumulation of bird and rodent bones created by predatory birds, found while excavating a cistern of Byzantine construction in southern Israel.

dence from those of humans in early Paleolithic sites.

A further complication derives from the fact that domestic or commensal carnivorous species have shared human habitations for at least 10,000 years. In studying animal remains recovered during National Park Service excavations at historic sites in the eastern United States, we have encountered samples from basements that could be described as "pussycat accumulations." These consist of songbirds, chipmunks, field mice, and occasional chicken bones and sheep-rib fragments. Domestic dogs may kill animals and accumulate their remains. Wild or commensal predators often inhabit ruins of abandoned houses and the risk of wrongly interpreting the resulting small-animal remains as of human origin is real.

The opposite kind of error is also possible. Small

species may not be classified as human game because of their inadequate size and unpalatability to modern Euro-American tastes. "Rodent husbandry" among the ancient Romans (dormice), the ancient and contemporary inhabitants of the Andes (guinea pigs), and modern West Africans (rats) provide cautionary examples (Fig. 11; Clutton-Brock 1981).

*Selective Predation.* All forms of human and animal predation are selective. A number of general factors affect the selection. One is the activity pattern of the predator relative to the prey. Many species have restricted periods of activity, being active only during daylight (diurnal) or night (nocturnal). Still others move about only during early morning and evening (crepuscular). The thanatic effect of a nocturnal predator, such as an owl, would be to cull only nocturnally active rodents, birds, and reptiles. Similar patterning may characterize human predation. Comparison of the rodent remains from a series of Archaic (3000–2000 B.C.) sites in northern Chile revealed that more recent sites contained a larger proportion of small mammal and bird remains than earlier ones. When the species were identified, they showed

**Fig. 11.** Examples of ancient and modern rodent husbandry. **a,** Dormouse. **b,** West African rat.

the increase resulted from intensified pursuit of diurnal species, the exploitation of crepuscular forms remaining relatively constant (Hesse 1983).

A second factor is the relative abundance of prey. The sizes of populations of predators and prey are linked into complex relationships that have been the subject of much field observation and mathematical modeling (Caughley 1977). The relative sizes of age and sex classes vary depending on whether a population is increasing, decreasing or stable. Consequently, even if a predator is absolutely random in chosing its victims, the representation of animals it kills over time will be affected by changes in the composition of the prey population. Applying this factor to samples of sheep and goat remains in early Holocene sites in southwest Asia has led to the hypothesis that the abundance of young animals reflects overhunting, which changed the demographics of the wild flocks, making young animals relatively more numerous than they are in stable herds (Uerpmann 1979).

A third factor is the vulnerability of the prey. Natural attributes affecting vulnerability include coloration, locomotion, defensive weapons, alertness, and size. Their importance is illustrated by the interaction between wolves (a species that has been used as an analog for humans), deer, and moose. Deer

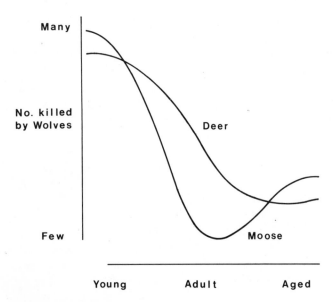

**Fig. 12.** The interaction of predator and prey. The vulnerability of a prey animal is related to its age and physical maturity and to the size and power of the predator. This diagram showing that wolves are more successful in killing adult deer than adult moose reflects the latter's superior capacity for self defense (after Mech 1970).

King Assurbanipal's Lion Hunt
From Nineveh  Ca. 650 B.C.

**Fig. 13.** Ancient depiction of a Near Eastern king killing a lion. Art historical resources of this kind supplement the faunal record.

have only one realistic defensive option: to flee. Topographic and weather conditions figure largely in determining which individuals survive. Moose have another option: to stand and fight. Those that do tend to survive. The thanatic pattern associated with these two predator-prey interactions is different. Wolves are more ''random'' in their take of deer, making the age distributions of the victims similar to the living population. By contrast, moose killed are either young and weak or old and feeble (Fig. 12). The same distinction has been reported for samples of animal bones from Paleolithic sites, suggesting that early hunters were able to kill all age classes of small game, but only the young and the old of large species (Klein 1978).

The primary cultural component of vulnerability is technology. Long before the advent of firearms, humans acquired the skills and equipment to subdue any prey. Egyptian and Near Eastern kings during the first and second millennia B.C. created hunting preserves where they dispatched game ranging from lions to elephants for ritual or for sport (Fig. 13). Andean rulers coordinated massive harvests of vicuña (Murra 1965).

Even with superior technology, decisions must be made about when and where it is applied. Some cultures seem guided by protectionist behavior, expressed in taboos that mitigate the impact on the local populations of various prey species (Kensinger and Kracke 1981). Contrary attitudes also occur, as among the Algonkian of North America, who appear to have harvested intensively without regard to long-term effects on the prey populations. The only general conclusion that can be drawn is that the variability and complexity of human thanatic effects are likely to be both large and difficult to predict.

**Other Selective Processes.** Among other thanatic processes are disease, starvation, and old age (Shipman 1981). Wild sheep and goats suffer greater decimation from late snows and epidemic diseases

**Fig. 14.** Mummified cat from ancient Egypt.

than from predation (Murie 1944). Disease, starvation, and old age also kill animals that are incorporated into archeological sites. While digging in Iran, we saw a herdsman struggling to get an obviously ill sheep back to his village for proper ritual slaughter. The animal would stagger a few feet, fall, then be rousted back up by the owner, only to fall again. After several repetitions of this sequence, the man picked the animal up and carried it off. Perhaps it was finally slaughtered, but its death was not a consequence of a managerial decision by the herdsman.

Cultural practices are another source of bias. Cattle in India are sometimes managed in "old age homes," although they often end up in the food chain anyhow (Harris 1966). Numerous species were mummified in ancient Egypt (Fig. 14). As with predation, these thanatic processes are selective.

*Conditions of Accumulation.* Thanatic processes differ with respect to their duration. Catastrophic assemblages represent one extreme. At the Jones-Miller site in Colorado, large numbers of animals were killed in a single episode (Frontispiece; Stanford 1984). Bone samples created this way are particularly rewarding because they usually represent populations; that is, "biological unit(s) at the level of ecological integration where it is meaningful to speak of a birth rate, a death rate, a sex ratio and an age structure in describing the properties of the unit(s)" (Caughley 1977:1, citing L.C. Cole 1957). In other words, they provide direct insight into a portion of the biotic environment. Another example of a catastrophic thanatic process is provided at the Jordanian site of Pella, where a roof collapsed and killed a group of camels. Here, the population culled was not a natural one, but a culturally determined one: a group of animals once part of a caravan.

Attritional assemblages are much more common. They are produced by repeated episodes of culling, often spread over long periods of time. A classic example of a natural attritional assemblage is the tarpits of La Brea, California, where thousands of animals were trapped during millennia. An attritional archeological assemblage is typified by the Neolithic village of Erbaba in west-central Anatolia (Fig. 15). Attritional assemblages seldom represent natural populations; rather, they are samples from a long sequence of such populations. Thus, they must be distinguished terminologically. Wilson (1975:9) suggests using the term "group," "when the nature of the organization (of the assembly of animals) is still unknown or there is no desire to specify it." He also recommends

adopting terms of venery. These words, codified in the 15th century, label groups of animals—a pride of lions, a school of fish, a trip of goats, a gang of elk, a husk of hares (Lipton 1968:9–11). They are appropriate for two reasons: (1) their unfamiliarity calls attention to their lack of conformity with a "normal" biological unit, and (2) they spring from the activity of hunting, a reminder of the thanatic process responsible for the assemblage.

In sum, thanatic processes cull animals from living populations and deposit their remains in archeological sites. To identify and characterize them, we need to know (1) what processes were active during accumulation at the site, (2) what selective patterns characterized the interactions between the thanatic processes and each category of animal, and (3) what pace of culling is responsible for the assemblage of animals encountered.

## Perthotaxic Processes

Perthotaxic processes move and destroy fragments of bone before they come to rest and are buried. It can be said that animals, particularly those caught in cultural webs, die twice. The first time, their lives are snuffed out by thanatic processes. Once dead, their parts enter the cultural stream where they are used, reused, and eventually discarded. Use produces two important effects: disarticulation and differential preservation of skeletal parts.

*Disarticulating Agents.* Except under special circumstances, such as the deeper parts of bison-kill sites where the hunters could not get at the carcasses (Wheat 1972), burials of animals that were not butchered (Clutton-Brock 1974), and very small sites

**Fig. 15.** An attritional deposit of animal bones. This scatter of fragments was found in a trash accumulation at the Neolithic site of Erbaba in Turkey.

where few individuals were processed, it is generally impossible to reassemble the parts of an animal. The disarticulating actions of some natural perthotaxic factors have been investigated. When dead animals fall into fluvial environments, the tissue holding the joints together disintegrates and each bone or bone fragment moves downstream in a manner predictable by its size and shape, the nature of the streambed, and the velocity of the stream (Behrensmeyer 1975, Shipman 1981, Wolff 1973). Live animals also act as perthotaxic agents, scavenging kills and selectively removing skeletal elements.

*Weathering.* Another factor that selectively destroys bone prior to burial is weathering (Behrensmeyer 1978). The contrast between exposed and unexposed bone can be dramatic. Buried fragments from 5000-year-old sites in northern Chile are frequently remarkably fresh in appearance (Fig. 16). By contrast, bones of sheep, llama, and donkey scattered on the surface near modern camps are almost invariably bleached white and in some stage of exfoliation. Clearly, rapid burial is essential for preservation in this arid, sun-drenched environment. The rate of accumulation of debris, whether by natural or cultural

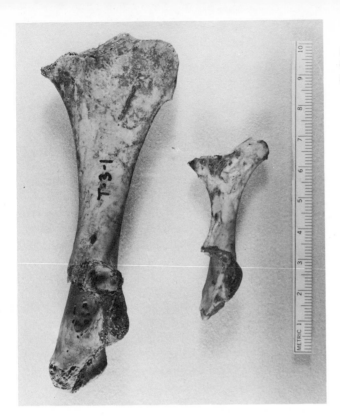

Fig. 16. Bird bones from the Archaic site of Tiliviche in northern Chile. Because of favorable conditions for preservation, they appear almost fresh after 6000 years of burial.

processes, is thus a significant variable.

**Gnawing.** Gnawing is one of the most extensively discussed perthotaxic agents. Many carnivores and herbivores gnaw selectively on various bone elements (Fig. 17). Experimental and observational research on a wide variety of predators indicates that the structure of a bone determines its likelihood of survival. Spongy areas are far more easily destroyed by chewing than solidly packed material (Binford 1981, Brain 1980,

Haynes 1980). Furthermore, the relative abundance of chewing marks on bones of different species may not accurately reflect the intensity of this perthotaxic agent (Lyon 1970). At Tell el-Hayyat in Jordan, for example, the percentage of gnawed pig bone was much higher than that of sheep and goat bone. This difference seems to reflect greater vulnerability of sheep and goat bones to complete destruction by gnawing, rather than lower incidence of attack (Metzger 1984).

**Trampling.** Trampling is another perthotaxic factor. The feet of both humans and animals selectively crush and bury bones of different shapes and compositions. In Bushman camps, a kind of microstratigraphy is created as bones of different shapes and sizes are sorted to differing depths by trampling (Yellen, pers. commun.). Also, bones may be moved to the fringes of Bushman camps, at least in part to make walking less hazardous (Yellen 1977).

The two most important perthotaxic processes of cultural origin are butchering and tool use. There are innumerable ways of butchering an animal, depending on such variables as size, parts considered valuable, cooking method, and further processing anticipated. At an aboriginal site in Pennsylvania, for example, it has been shown that the size of parts to which a car-

Fig. 17. Damage from gnawing by carnivores (probably dogs) on cattle bones from Tell Jemmeh, Israel.

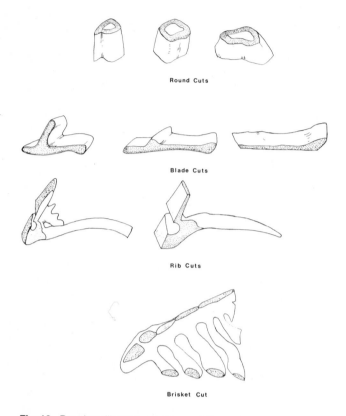

Round Cuts

Blade Cuts

Rib Cuts

Brisket Cut

**Fig. 18.** Drawings illustrating patterns of dismemberment employed by butchers in the United States for cattle, pigs, and lambs.

cass was reduced is related to the size of the pots used for cooking (Guilday, Parmalee, and Tanner 1962). In the United States today, butchers have well established patterns of dismemberment for cattle, pigs, and lambs (Fig. 18).

Tools and other cultural uses are not always easy to recognize. Bone fragments can be employed for cutting and scraping without extensive remodeling, but may be identifiable as tools by polish or microwear (Gilbert and Steinfeld 1977). Skulls of animals have been used to ornament buildings, as in the case of sheep skulls mounted on plastered pilasters at Tepe Ganj Dareh (Smith, P. 1975). Cattle bones were structural components in some buildings in medieval England. In some situations, tool manufacture may be sufficiently extensive to overwhelm other perthotaxic factors. At Tepe Godin, an early urban center in Iran, A.S. Gilbert (1979) concluded that tool use was responsible for the preservation and provenience of many of the animal bones encountered.

***Selective Deposition.*** Perthotaxic processes may be passive as well as active. An important passive factor is topography. Slopes, hollows, and gullies are natural collecting points for bones being transported by one or another active factor. Cultural equivalents are trash pits and abandoned buildings. Meadow (1975, 1978a) has shown how the architectural context of a bone accumulation is related to the kinds of fragments encountered.

As thanatic processes select bones from the faunal environment created by biotic forces, so perthotaxic factors select bones from the carcasses of dead animals and arrange for their disposition. To identify and characterize them we need to know (1) what factors were redistributing carcasses and destroying some of their parts during burial, (2) over what horizontal space these factors operated, and (3) what topographic features influenced the likelihood of preservation.

### Taphic Processes

The variety of mechanical and chemical actions affecting bones subsequent to burial are subsumed under this label. Like those previously discussed, taphic processes are selective.

Mechanical factors may be natural or cultural. Freeze-thaw cycles create movements of the soil that tend to grind up bones that are shallowly buried. Plowing may accomplish the same thing. At the Rogers-CETA site in Alabama, the ratio of bones to sherds was much lower in the plow zone than below it (Fig. 19; Hesse and Henson 1983). Although some of this variability may reflect increased rates of fragmentation of the pottery, the absolutely lower frequencies of bone in the upper samples indicate that not all the variation can be explained in this way.

Freeze-thaw cycles and plowing change the locations of bone fragments, as well as selectively destroying them. Burrowing by rodents, insects, and crustacea can also churn the deposit. Plant roots are another effective transporter of archeological materials.

The chemical environments of archeological sites can affect buried bone in three principal ways: (1) by dissolving it gradually, (2) by replacing the calcium with soil minerals, and (3) by augmenting the structure by depositing material in interbone spaces (Goffer 1980, Newesely and Herrmann 1980). Experimental work has shown that the rate at which organic material is removed is not constant. Initial resistance to dissolution is followed by a period of rapid loss, which then

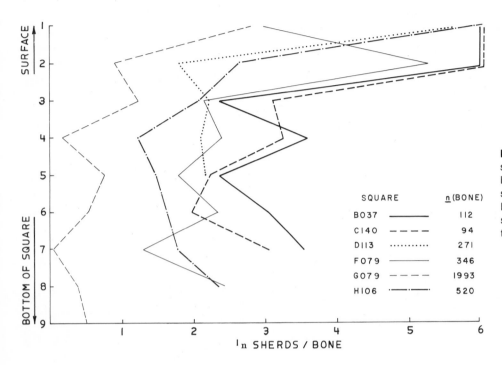

**Fig. 19.** Detecting differential survival of animal bones. Plotting the logarithmic sherd/bone ratio by square and depth at the Rogers-CETA site in Alabama shows reduced survival of bones in the plow zone (Levels 1–3).

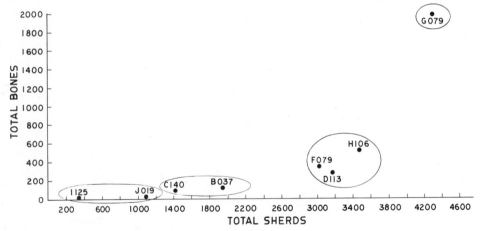

**Fig. 20.** Recognizing horizontal variability in survival of animal bone at the Rogers-CETA site. The ovals group squares with similar rates of bone recovery. Squares I125 and J019 produced only traces. Squares C160 and B037 produced small samples. Bone was abundant in Square G079.

slows as organic leaching nears completion (Hare 1980). As a consequence, two bones with quite different degrees of organic preservation may not differ significantly in age, and two parts of a single bone may show radically different degrees of amino-acid preservation.

There can be considerable intrasite variability in the degree of organic preservation. At the Rogers-CETA site, there was a greater contrast in variability in the horizontal than in the vertical dimension (Fig. 20; Hesse and Henson 1983). Low rates of recovery

reflected survival of bones with the most resistant structural compositions, whereas high rates implied survival of less resistant types. At the site of Tell Jemmeh in Israel, a wide range of animo-acid preservation has been observed in the bones (first phalanges) of cattle buried approximately contemporaneously (Von Endt, pers. commun.).

Extensive leaching of either the organic or inorganic portion of a bone destroys its internal microstructure and weakens its resistance to mechanical stress, but in the absence of grinding-crushing proc-

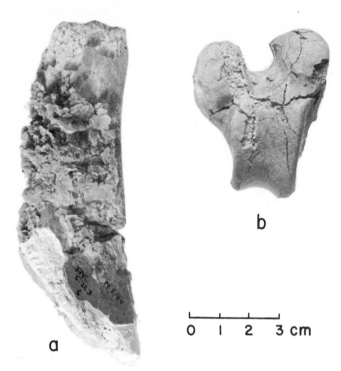

b

a

0  1  2  3 cm

**Fig. 21.** Bones affected by crystalline growth. **a,** Spinous process from a bovid thoracid vertebra showing extensive crystalline growth. **b,** Epiphysis of a sheep or goat distal femur beginning to split on the surface as a consequence of internal crystalline growth.

action as a perthotaxic process. The distinction between the two is important, however. Perthotaxic processes act on carcasses and the important variables determining what bones are affected are the characteristics of the remains. Anataxic processes act on perthotaxic spaces and the most important factor in determining what is destroyed is the location of the remains.

Among other natural anataxic processes are the activities of burrowing animals. The ejecta from their holes form small piles of exposed and redeposited material. A classic example of a cultural anataxic

**Fig. 22.** Highly magnified bone cells containing crystals.

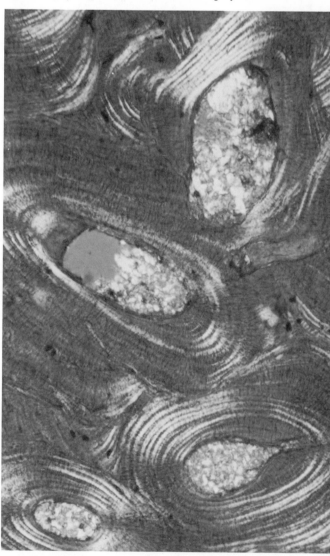

esses, the original contours remain intact (Sillen 1981). Another destructive force is the growth of crystals in intra-bone spaces (Figs. 21–22). Bone does not shrink like a bar of soap. Its deterioration is more like the disassembly of a house of cards, where elimination of the cards one by one leaves a shell and one final removal causes all to collapse.

Taphic processes can be identified by investigating (1) what mechanical processes are likely to have been active in the matrix of the site, (2) how variable and how active the chemical environment has been, (3) whether chemical changes have proceeded sufficiently to affect the mechanical resistance of bone fragments, and (4) what historical sequence of factors may have affected various loci within a site.

### Anataxic Processes

These are recycling processes, by which bones are extracted from a buried state and exposed to agents of attrition. The most importatnt, and the one often responsible for the discovery of archeological sites, is erosion. This may be dramatic, as in the steady destruction of Tell Jemmeh in Israel by the Nahal Besor (Fig. 23), or it may be unobtrusive, involving only the exposure and movement of bone fragments in a small part of a site.

Erosion as an anataxic process is similar to fluvial

**Fig. 23.** Erosion of Tell Jemmeh by the Besor River, which is gradually destroying the site.

process is the mining of bison-kill sites in the North American Plains for bones to be ground into fertilizer (Davis 1978). Archeology is another anataxic process.

Humans are active redepositors. A frustrating example comes from the Israeli site of Tell Jemmeh. The basic material used for construction during the several thousand-year occupation of the site was sun-dried mud brick. Unfortunately, during some periods, the masons obtained the dirt for their bricks from earlier middens. The effect was to reexpose and redeposit older bone samples in new construction. When the new buildings eventually eroded away, the older material became mixed with the more recent debris.

To summarize, anataxic factors (1) reexpose older material to new perthotaxic conditions, (2) act on perthotaxic spaces, and (3) are particularly important in sites representing complex societies.

## Sullegic Processes

This category covers the procedures of the archeologist that bias the sample obtained from a site or excavation. Many sites are too large to be excavated completely. Even when small, it is impossible to record all the information about the location, orientation, and association of every object. Field methods are selective; whatever the manner of digging, objects differ in the likelihood of being collected.

A basic part of a research design is deciding how rigorous the searching procedures will be. At one extreme is the excavation of a site in blocks that are separated later in a laboratory. This is often done when the matrix has been transformed into stone, as in some Paleolithic sites. Sometimes, soil columns are removed from large sites, although the matrix has not been consolidated. At the other extreme is selecting for retention only the "important" objects encountered. Between these poles are a variety of procedures, such as dry screening, water screening, and flotation, all of them selective. The finer the screen, the smaller the objects recovered. Tossing fragile bones into water baths or shaking them in screens can cause their destruction, however.

Another variable affecting selection is recognizability. We observed its operation in samples from Andean sites. Some were obtained by sifting the matrix using fine (5 mm.) screens. Others were columns of unscreened matrix brought to the laboratory for examination. The animal bone samples differed in two ways. The first was expected: there were many more bones from small rodents and birds in the samples from the columns, representing fragments too small to be retained by the 5 mm. mesh. The other difference was not anticipated: the column samples yielded much higher numbers of camelid sesamoids (small bones from the feet), despite the fact that they were sufficiently large to have been caught in the screen. The explanation seems to be that the sesamoids are so similar in size and color to the small rocks naturally present in the matrix they were not recognized.

Spatial organization of human-animal interactions in the society represented by a site also affects the samples. The places where animals were killed, butchered, and processed may have been different. To reconstruct these activities, the localities involved must be excavated. Collecting animal bones and inferring human-animal behavior competes with all other concerns of archeological research, however, so that samples almost inevitably suffer the sullegic bias of being the by-product of digging for something else.

To summarize, sullegic processes (1) cull samples from the residue left by other taphonomic processes, (2) reflect procedures employed for excavation, and (3) incorporate errors resulting from poor correspondence between the samples and the spatial arrangement of human-animal behavior during occupation of the site.

### Trephic Processes

One might think that the information associated with a fragment of bone would be relatively safe once the specimen had been collected. Unfortunately, trephic processes, as the curatorial factors associated with sorting, recording, and reporting on bones have been termed, also take their selective toll.

Beyond the occasional clerical errors, such as lost or illegible labels, lie more serious problems. When bones are removed from the ground, their environment is changed and the new wetter or drier, hotter or colder conditions may cause rapid deterioration. Packing and shipping can have other calamitous effects. Every animal bone specialist has had the experience of unwrapping an important fragment, only to find it reduced to dust.

Another category of trephic processes can be labeled "identification." A specimen can be identified as a bone fragment, a hip-bone fragment, a hip-bone fragment from a sheep, a hip-bone fragment from a one-year-old sheep, or a hip-bone fragment from a one-year-old ewe, depending on the attributes preserved. Other things being equal, precision of identification varies with the investigator and the amount of skeletal material available for comparison. It also varies with the range of possible taxa in the biota, the fragmentary remains of animals of similar size being difficult or impossible to differentiate. Finally, precision of identification varies with the character of the literature. Most taxonomic studies published by zoologists identify taxa on the basis of details of the skull, teeth, pelt or feathers—aspects rarely represented in archeological samples. Faced with this problem, some animal bone specialists have developed their own taxonomic keys. Boessneck, Muller, and Teichert (1963) revolutionized the analysis of samples of sheep and goat bones by doing this, but few other taxa have been treated in similar detail.

"Reporting" problems are another important category. Complete inventories of animal bone remains are often not published because of their cost. Their elimination may be justified on the basis that the collections are available for reexamination. Few institutions, however, have the time, money, space, or inclination to allow a constant flow of animal bone specialists access to storage. Moreover, samples are usually stored in a way that makes restudy enormously time consuming. In an effort to alleviate this problem, several animal bone specialists have proposed minimum criteria for the published descriptions of faunal samples (notably, Grigson 1978b, Driver 1981).

In short, not all that is found is reported. Trephic processes select bones for description on the basis of (1) their resistence to loss during shipping and storage, (2) their susceptibility to identification, (3) the adequacy of the taxonomic comparative literature, (4) the quality of the reference skeletal collections, and (5) their relevance to perceived questions of biological and cultural significance.

## EXTRACTING INFORMATION FROM ANIMAL BONE COLLECTIONS

Given the number, variety, and complexity of the processes affecting the completeness and representativeness of samples of animal bones, what can be done to reduce their analysis to manageable proportions? Several procedures can be employed to achieve this goal.

### Identifying Sources of Bias

External information often permits assessing what processes may have affected a sample of animal bones. What predators live in the vicinity of the site? What is the likelihood that fluvial transport redistributed the carcasses? Is there enough water in the environment to permit attritional chemical reactions to take place? Did the ancient inhabitants engage in extensive earth-moving? Do burrowing animals live on the site? Was the excavated matrix passed through a screen? How large was the mesh? Do trees grow on the site? How steep is the slope on which debris was originally deposited? What processes have been identified at other sites in the region or period? There is no way to draw up a complete check-list for the possibilities. The only procedure is to consider each potential source of bias in turn.

The relationship between a sample and the total amount of material incorporated in a site must be kept in mind. Even huge samples may be only a pitifully small representation of what was originally deposited. A. S. Gilbert (1979) has demonstrated this for his sample of 25,000 bones from Godin, a large mound in western Iran. Using conservative figures for the population, meat-eating habits, and duration of occupation, he calculated that the multi-season excavation recovered only 0.015 percent of the animals needed to sustain the number of inhabitants inferred. Clearly, this evidence is insufficient to permit assessing the average diet during any period of occupation. It allows only reconstructing the exploitation of animal products in the portion of the town that was excavated.

### Identifying Specific Biases

Examining the differing toughness of surviving bones may provide clues to the amount of loss from attritional factors. Marks left by teeth, roots, and tools permit assessing the intensity of these sources of attrition. Sorting the bones into several size categories and counting the number of fragments in each can yield evidence of a perthotaxic factor such as fluvial transport or a sullegic factor such as screen-mesh size.

Another broad category of information is spatial patterning. Hunters may butcher large game at the kill site to reduce its weight for transport. Different bones are left at the processing station than are discarded at the camp, creating a strong contrast in the samples.

The most important source of evidence for estimating biasing processes is the archeological context of bone finds. The same or analogous factors that manipulate bones also affect stone tools, pottery, and plant remains. Correlating the distributions of different kinds of debris can reveal patterns of disturbance of a site that are not observable directly (Nance 1983).

Beyond identifying the processes affecting an animal bone sample lies the more difficult task of estimating their intensities. Some attritional factors can be modeled mathematically as decay processes. If the form of a decay process can be inferred from experimental or observational data, then it may be possible to simulate running the clock backwards and to reconstitute the situation that existed before attrition began (Gilbert and Singer 1982).

### Subdividing the Sample

The usual approach to animal bone analysis is to apply each procedure to all units composing the collection from a site. This is probably as misguided as it is common. Dexter Perkins Jr. once related to us an instructive conversation with statisticians working for the Gallup Poll. He had described one of the thorniest areas of contention in animal bone archeology — how to estimate the abundance of animals from a sample of bones — and asked advice on appropriate statistical procedures. Their answer surprised him. "Why," they asked, "are you putting this question to *all* the bones in your sample?" They pointed out that this would merely establish a value in a sample already known to be biased in unpredictable ways and therefore probably an unreliable "informant." Instead, they suggested using locational and morphological attributes of the specimens to subdivide the collection into "audiences" of fragments that could offer "opinions" on each question.

Another factor affecting the decision whether or not to subdivide a sample is the scale of the historical-cultural framework from which it is drawn. Bone data can be manipulated to produce statements such as "pig bones comprise 40 percent of the sample during Period II." This may be informative when the culture represented at the site is localized and homogeneous. To establish that 25 percent of the animal remains deposited in a large city over a 500-year period were sheep, however, is meaningless because of the multiplicity of temporal and cultural variables involved.

Only by subdividing the sample to take account of this variability can useful historical conclusions be drawn.

## Suitability of a Sample for Study

It may seem heretical to suggest that some bone collections should not be studied. It is possible, however, that evaluation of the probable sources of bias and evidence of alteration will indicate that massive distortion from the original physical-consequences population has occurred. If a huge amount of corrective manipulation is required to "clean up" a sample, then the project director/archeologist and the animal bone specialist must decide whether the statistically weak information that will be produced warrants the time and money that will have to be spent to obtain it. The complexities of both the human-animal relationship and the record it leaves behind must be understood if the correct decision is to be made.

# 4    Nature and Terminology of the Vertebrate Skeleton

## COMPOSITION AND DEVELOPMENT OF BONE

### Constituents

Bone is a complex integration of organic and inorganic constituents. About 90 percent of the organic fraction is a kind of protein known as collagen; the remainder is non-collagenous proteins and amino sugars (Ortner and Putschar 1981). The collagen forms long twisted strands, often gathered into bundles. The inorganic fraction is largely hydroxy-apatite crystals composed of calcium phosphate. These tiny rod-shaped crystals are arranged parallel to the collagen fibers, a combination that possesses considerable rigidity without being brittle. Other minerals occur as additions or substitutions, and these are often informative about past biological conditions (Parker and Toots 1980).

### Ossification

Bone is produced either by endochondral ossification or by inter-membranous ossification. The first process is responsible for the development of such elements as long bones from a cartilage model. The second process, typified by the development of the skull, omits the cartilage step.

Three types of bone cells are involved in the growth, maintenance, and gradual remodeling of the skeleton. Osteoblasts accomplish the deposition of bone, osteoclasts its resorption, and osteocytes its maintenance. Evidence of their activities is recorded in the micromorphology of the collagen-mineral matrix. Bone is constantly remodelled during an animal's lifetime; thus, the morphology of a fragment provides information on its experience as well as its genetic heritage.

Ossification proceeds in a geometrically describable pattern from a number of centers. A typical long bone (Fig. 24) contains three centers. One is in the middle of the shaft, termed the *diaphysis*. The other two are in the ends or *epiphyses*. The parts of the diaphysis nearest the epiphyses are called *metaphyses*.

In a growing animal, the zone between the metaphysis and the epiphysis consists of cartilage. Formation of this cartilage and its gradual ossification allows the long bones to expand longitudinally. Eventually, cartilage ceases to be deposited and what remains is ossified, joining the epiphyses firmly to the diaphysis. The fact that this process of fusion follows a fairly regular time-table within a species provides a basis for estimating the age of an animal at death.

### Structure

Bone has two distinctive structures. Cortical bone is a smooth dense layer that surrounds each part of the skeleton. Cancellous bone has a porous appearance, produced by intersecting small bone plates (trabeculae), and is found in varying amounts in different parts of different bones (Fig. 25). The proportions of cortical and cancellous material in a bone reflect mechanical stresses involved in supporting body weight; in providing a framework for attachment of muscles, ligaments, and tendons, and in forming a protective enclosure for certain organs. The optimum combination provides maximum strength and minimum weight.

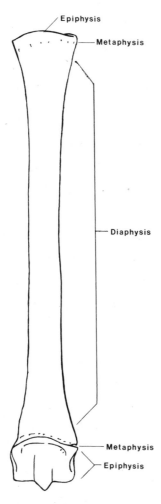

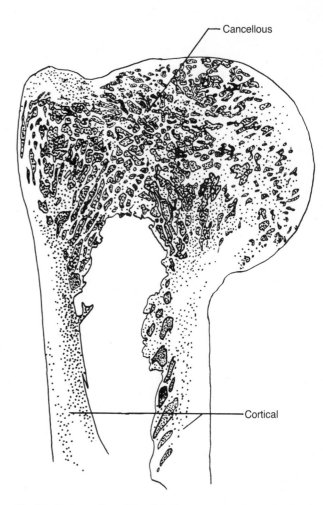

Fig. 24. Schematic donkey metapodial illustrating the main zones and the centers of ossification.

Fig. 25. Cross section of the distal humerus of a sheep showing the locations of cortical and cancellous bone.

An example of this principle is provided by the femur. A longitudinal section of this long bone shows the trabeculae aligned along the planes of stress that would be generated during support and transport of the animal's bulk.

## Teeth

Teeth are among the more resilient parts of the skeleton, largely because of their simple solid structure (Fig. 26). A thin hard layer called the enamel encapsulates the projecting portion. A layer of dentine separates the enamel from the pulp cavity and the root canal, which contains the nerve.

Animal teeth are remarkably variable in number

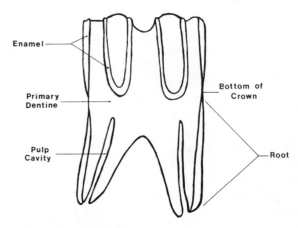

Fig. 26. Schematic tooth of a herbivore.

and form, making them useful for classificatory distinctions. The fact that they are worn away gradually through use makes them important sources of other information. The degree of wear can be used to estimate age at death, and the microscopic form of the marks can reveal the nature of the foods consumed.

## GENERAL SKELETAL TERMINOLOGY

### Principal Divisions of the Skeleton

The vertebrate skeleton is divisible for convenience into two main parts: (1) the axial skeleton, composed of the skull, vertebrae, ribs, and sternum, and (2) the appendicular skeleton, consisting of the hip and shoulder girdles, limbs, and extremites (Fig. 27). A minor third category consists of the visceral or splanchnic bones that occur in various soft tissues. An example is the hyoid bone, which supports the tongue and parts of the throat. Although not large, it is frequently encountered archeologically. Hyoids of cattle, sheep, and goats are often scarred by butchering marks (Fig. 28).

The vertebrate skeleton is bilaterally symmetrical. A slice along the front-to-back axis produces halves that are mirror images. The angle of this slice is called the *median sagittal plane* and anything parallel to this plane is said to be oriented sagittally. For example, the bony crest on the top of a gorilla's head is called a sagittal crest (Fig. 29).

**Fig. 28.** Fragments of hyoid bones of cattle from Tell Jemmeh with cut marks made during butchering.

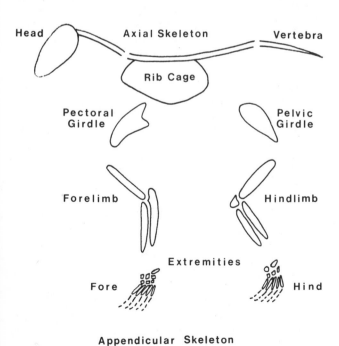

**Fig. 27.** The principal divisions of the vertebrate skeleton. The axial skeleton includes the head, spinal column, rib cage, and sternum. The appendicular skeleton consists of the girdles, limbs, and extremities.

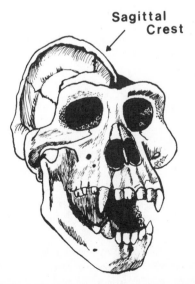

**Fig. 29.** Gorilla skull. The bony development on top of the cranium is the sagittal crest. Features parallel to this plane are said to be oriented sagittally.

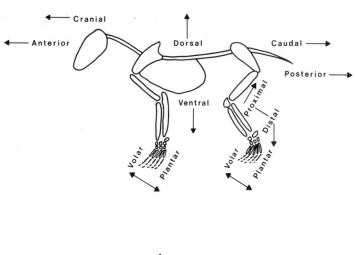

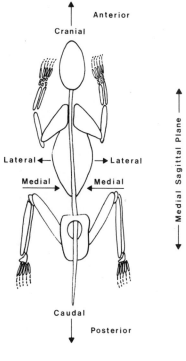

Fig. 30. Terms of position in the animal skeleton.

body. These are: (1) *ventral,* oriented toward the belly, (2) *dorsal,* toward the back, (3) *cranial,* toward the head, and (4) *caudal,* toward the tail. The often-used alternatives — inferior, superior, anterior, and posterior — can be ambiguous since they describe the orientation of a bone in terms of an animal's normal stance. Consequently, the ventral border of the clavicle (shoulder blade) is superior in cattle and anterior in humans.

## Extremities

The hand and foot are termed extremities to distinguish them from the rest of the appendicular skeleton and given special positional designations. *Palmar* and *volar* identify the front and back of the hand; *dorsal* and *plantar,* the top and bottom of the foot.

## Teeth

A special set of terms is employed to describe teeth (Fig. 31). The jaw is pictured as straightened rather than U-shaped; in this position, the tooth surface closest to the sagittal plane is called *mesial;* that farthest away, *distal.* The side of the tooth facing the tongue is called *lingual;* that facing the lips, *buccal.* The surfaces that meet during chewing are *occlusal.* A view from the root is called the *radical* aspect.

## Positional Terms

Parts of a skeleton are described with reference to the median sagittal plane. When the axis of a structure is at a right angle to the median sagittal plane, its orientation is *transverse.* When it is closer to the plane than some other skeletal structure, it is referred to as *medial;* when farther away, it is said to be *lateral* (Fig. 30).

A second pair of relative positional terms uses the vertebral column as the point of orientation. A structure is *proximal* if close to and *distal* if far from this feature. Four other positional terms identify a structure in terms of its proximity to the extremes of the

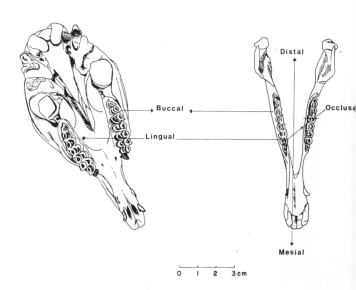

Fig. 31. Terms of position in the dentition.

## SPECIFIC BONES AND THEIR CHARACTERISTICS

Their common evolutionary heritage makes the bones of vertebrates roughly analogous, though individual elements have often been altered remarkably to meet particular needs. This underlying homology makes it possible to discuss both in general and in specific terms the kinds of bones likely to be encountered archeologically.

Biology provides the terminology for the bones of the vertebrate skeleton. The following vocabulary applies primarily to mammals. Specific details on amphibians and reptiles are provided by Olsen (1968).

### Skull

Vertebrate skulls can be visualized as having three components or areas of organization: (1) the cranium, (2) the face, and (3) the mouth.

*Cranium.* The cranium encapsulates the brain and is composed of rugged curved plates (Fig. 32). The *frontals* form the anterior and dorsal parts of the brain case. In such animals as antelope, gazelle, sheep, and cattle, they are modified by the presence of horn cores, the structures on which the horns develop. In deer, the analogous structures are pedicels, the bony eminences on which the antlers develop seasonally. Posterior to the frontal bones are the *parietals,* which form the sides of the brain case. The caudal portion is occupied by the *occipital,* a complex structure containing four morphological zones. It surrounds the *foramen magnum,* the large perforation through which the brain is linked with the spinal cord. In some species (such as rodents), an *interparietal* intervenes between the parietals and the occipital. The sides of the brain case are completed by the *squamosal* bones (in many mammals termed the *temporals*), which incorporate the auditory apparatus and the points of articulation with the lower jaw. The ventral portion of the cranium consists of part of the occipital and the *sphenoid* bones, which lie in the median sagittal plane. Even as fragments, these bones are often recognizable because of their bilateral symmetry (Fig. 32). The boundaries between the cranial bones, known as *sutures,* are irregular lines that become gradually obliterated as the animal ages.

Among birds, the bones forming the brain case are seldom visually distinct. The dorsal and part of the ventral portion of the skull is usually encountered in

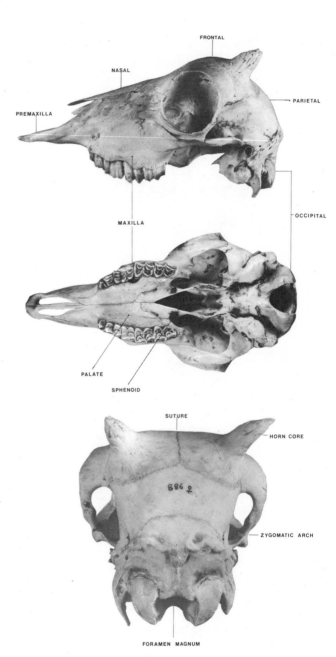

**Fig. 32.** Three views of a sheep cranium: lateral (top), ventral (middle), and posterior (bottom).

fragmentary condition. Because the surfaces of the fragments are smooth and curved, and the cross sections show compact layers separated by coarser material, they may be confused with fine pottery.

Distinctive morphological attributes on the frontal bones are the horn cores and pedicels, and the ridge that forms the dorsal border of the eye socket (orbit).

OCCIPITAL CONDYLE

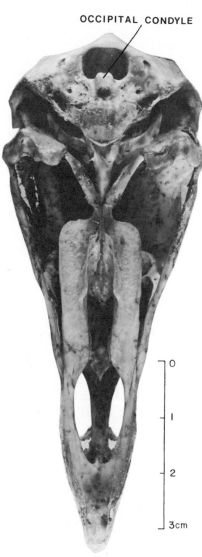

0
1
2
3cm

**Fig. 33.** Ventral view of a bird skull.

0        1        2        3cm

**Fig. 34.** Petrosal bone from *Bos taurus*, encountered at Tell Jemmeh.

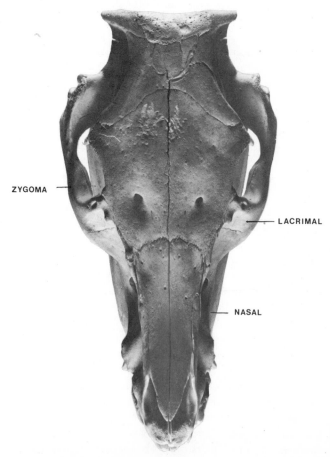

ZYGOMA

LACRIMAL

NASAL

**Fig. 35.** Dorsal view of a pig cranium.

On the occipital, pillow-like lumps, known as occipital condyles, form the point of articulation between the head and neck. Birds have a single condyle (Fig. 33). The bony masses associated with the ears are frequent finds, particularly the convoluted chunks of extremely compact bone known as *petrosals* (Fig. 34).

    *Face.* The anterior of the cranium forms the posterior of the face or rostrum. The long slender *nasals* are located along the median sagittal plane and articulate with the frontals between the orbits. Lateral to the nasals and also joined with the frontals are the *maxillary bones,* which hold the non-incisor upper teeth and form part of the cheeks. The rest of the cheeks are built around the *zygomatic* arches, curves of bone that link the face to the sides of the cranium. Fragments of these arches are common finds, made recognizable by their curved form (Fig. 35).

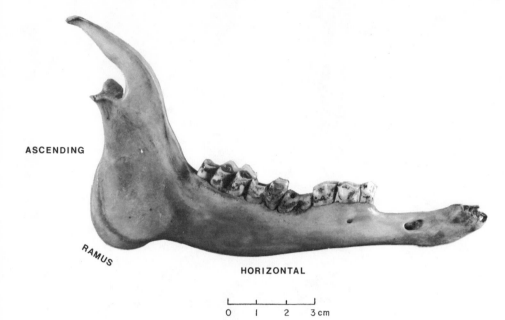

**Fig. 36.** Dentary bone of a gazelle.

ASCENDING

RAMUS

HORIZONTAL

0   1   2   3 cm

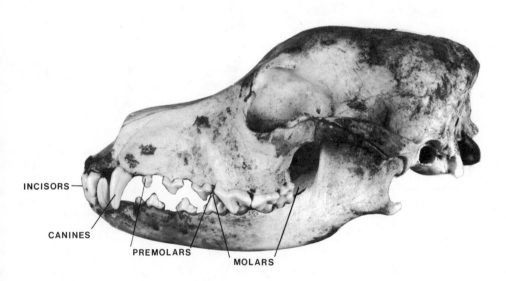

**Fig. 37.** The four types of mammalian teeth.

INCISORS

CANINES

PREMOLARS

MOLARS

The front of the face is composed of the *premaxillary bones,* which hold the upper incisor teeth. These bones have a distinctive "golf-club" shape and lack teeth in artiodactyls, such as sheep and goats (Fig. 32). In addition to the maxillary and premaxillary bones, the roof of the mouth contains the *palatine bones,* which are posterior to the maxillae and connect with the sphenoids. Within the facial cavity are fragile elements called *turbinate bones* and a midline structure called the *vomer.* The orbits are formed by the frontals and maxillae plus small bones called *lacrimals,* which contain the tear ducts. Among birds, the eye cavity is enclosed by a *sclerotic ring.*

The facial bones are in general much more fragile than those of the cranium. They are also distinct morphologically in different species. Readily identifiable fragments include the maxillary areas with holes (al-

veoli) for teeth and parts of the zygomatic arch. Diagnostic features of the palatine and nasal bones are their flatness and the regularity of their medial border.

**Mouth.** The palatine, maxillary, and premaxillary bones form the roof of the mouth. The *mandible* or lower jaw is composed of two *dentary bones* that meet at the anterior ends and ultimately fuse in most mammals. Each dentary bone is composed of a *horizontal ramus,* which holds the lower teeth, and an *ascending ramus,* which articulates with the cranium (Fig. 36).

**Teeth.** Because they are a primary element in adaptation to the environment, teeth vary considerably among mammals. This makes them important clues to identification.

Four types can be distinguished moving from front center to back: (1) *incisors,* (2) *canines,* (3) *premolars,* and (4) *molars* (Fig. 37). The number of teeth

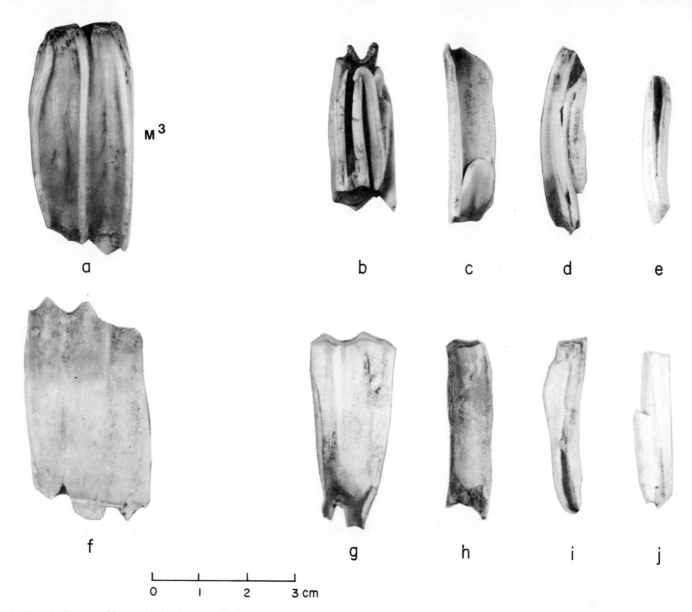

M³

0    1    2    3 cm

**Fig. 38.** Pattern of fracture in herbivore teeth. Eight fragments are arranged next to two complete sheep or goat third molars.

of each type differs widely as a consequence of evolutionary modification (actually a reduction) of the ancestral pattern characteristic of marsupials: 5 upper and 4 lower incisors, 1 upper and 1 lower canine, 3 upper and 3 lower premolars, and 4 upper and 4 lower molars. This pattern is expressed as a formula:

$$\frac{5\ \ 1\ \ 3\ \ 4}{4\ \ 1\ \ 3\ \ 4}$$

For many placental mammals, the formula is:

$$\frac{3\ \ 1\ \ 4\ \ 3}{3\ \ 1\ \ 4\ \ 3}$$

For sheep, however, the formula has been modified to

$$\frac{0\ \ 0\ \ 3\ \ 3}{3\ \ 0\ \ 3\ \ 3}$$

and for rats, it is

$$\frac{1\ \ 0\ \ 0\ \ 3}{1\ \ 0\ \ 0\ \ 3}$$

Most mammals have two sets of teeth during their lives. The first set, the *deciduous* or milk teeth, is gradually replaced by *permanent* teeth as the individual matures. An extensive terminology has developed to describe the morphology of the *crowns* or exposed parts, and the *roots,* concealed in the bone. For instance, DeBlase and Martin (1974:24) define 66 terms for describing rodent teeth. The following terms are most commonly used:

*Brachydont.* Low-crowned teeth found in animals with omnivorous or soft-food diets.

*Bunodont.* Teeth well adapted to crushing, characteristic of bears, pigs, and humans.

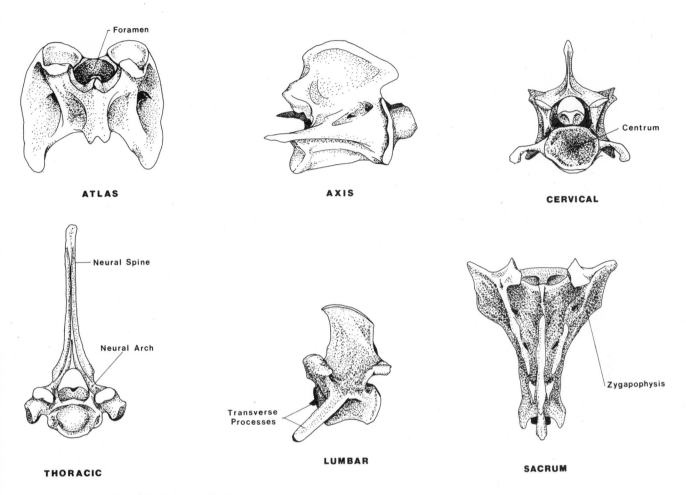

**Fig. 39.** Sheep vertebrae showing typical features.

*Carnassial.* Shearing tooth found in carnivores such as dogs, where cutting is performed by the last upper premolar and the first lower molar.

*Diastema.* A large gap between the incisors and premolars characteristic among animals lacking canines.

*Edentulate.* The congenital absence of teeth (as opposed to loss during life or after death).

*Hyposodont.* High-crowned teeth found in many herbivores that depend on coarse diets.

*Lophodont.* Teeth with complex patterns of ridges of enamel on the occlusal surface, associated with herbivores. When these patterns are crescent-shaped, as among deer, the tooth is described as selenodont.

*Secodont.* The cutting teeth of carnivores, on which the cusps are modified into longitudinally connected ridges useful for slashing meat.

Fragmentary teeth are frequently found in archeological sites. Fracturing often follows the planes of interface between dentine and enamel. In animals with lophodont dentition, the fragments are columnar and seldom identifiable to species (Fig. 38). Much of the shattering seems to occur after burial, so that parts of a single tooth may not be widely scattered. Reconstructing is simplified if small units have been employed in excavation, and the effort is justified by the amount of information a complete tooth can yield.

## Post-cranial Axial Skeleton

The bones of the post-cranial skeleton have three main functions: (1) protecting the spinal cord and providing a structure for suspension of the internal organs and the appendicular skeleton, (2) surrounding the chest cavity, and (3) forming the ventral axis of the chest.

*Vertebral Column.* The first function is accomplished by the vertebral column or spine, composed of a series of bones possessing a central opening through which the spinal cord passes (Fig. 39). The ventral portion of each bone, called the *centrum,* is drum shaped and has epiphyses on both the anterior and posterior surfaces. A curve of bone called the *neural arch* arises from the dorsal surface of the centrum and completes the bony ring around the spinal cord. Atop the neural arch in most mammals is the *neural spine,* a knife-shaped development that may be quite elongated. On the lateral surfaces of the neural arch are *transverse processes* and *zygapophyses* (articular facets), which assume distinctive forms at different locations along the vertebral column. Because of structural weakness, vertebrae are often found broken into fragments corresponding to their four components—centrum, epiphysis, transverse process, and neural spine—making it necessary to be familiar with these shapes as well as that of the intact bone.

The vertebral column is conventionally divided into five zones (Fig. 40). The vertebrae of the neck are termed *cervical.* The first cervical, which articulates with the occipital condyles of the skull, is called the *atlas* (Fig. 39). The second cervical, the *axis,* has a tongue-like protrusion on the anterior surface of the centrum called the *odontoid process,* which articulates with the atlas.

The second zone is composed of the *thoracic* vertebrae. They frequently possess large neural spines and always have knoblike transverse processes that articulate with the ribs. The third zone consists of the *lumbar* vertebrae. Articular facets are absent and transverse processes are often large and wing-like.

Posterior to the lumbar vertebrae is the *sacrum,* composed of several sacral vertebrae fused into a rigid structure. The *caudal* vertebrae or tail bones constitute the fifth zone. Their features are weakly developed and they look like small segments of a thin rod.

The number of vertebrae in each zone is variable among mammals, as the following ranges illustrate (Lawlor 1976): cervical—generally 7; thoracic—12 to 15; lumbar—6 to 7, but sometimes more than 20; sacral—3 to 5, but may reach 10; caudal—extremely variable.

**Rib Cage and Sternum.** The second group of bones in the post-cranial axial skeleton is the *rib cage.* The ribs are curved, with a cross section similar to an airplane wing. The *head,* at the end nearest the vertebrae, bears two articular facets, which are the points of contact with two adjacent thoracic vertebrae. The ventral portion of the *shaft* terminates in cartilage that connects the rib with the third functional section, occupied by the *sternum.* The latter, whether a group of bones or a single bone, commonly consists of flat segments recognizable because of their bilateral symmetry (Fig. 41).

Bird sterni deserve special mention. Since this bone provides the rigid structure for attachment of massive breast muscles used in flight, it is a very large element in the avian skeleton. It is typically composed of three extremely thin plate-like structures. Two broad curved surfaces extend laterally from the median sagittal plane, which bears a prominent keel. Most of the sternum is fragile; what usually survive archeologically are the thicker portions around and including the most anterior part, known as the *manubrium.*

### Appendicular Skeleton

The appendicular skeleton consists of the hip and shoulder girdles, the fore and hind limbs, and the extremities (Fig. 27). Most of these bones may be classified into three categories of shape: (1) flattened bones with sockets that provide an anchor for large muscles and serve as a point of attachment for limbs; (2) tubular bones with expanded and often rounded ends that make up most of the length of the limbs, and (3) small chunky bones that act as shock absorbers in the wrist and ankle.

**Pectoral Girdle.** The proximal portion of the anterior appendicular skeleton is called the pectoral girdle. The primary bones of this structure are the *scapulae,* one on each side of the vertebral column. This

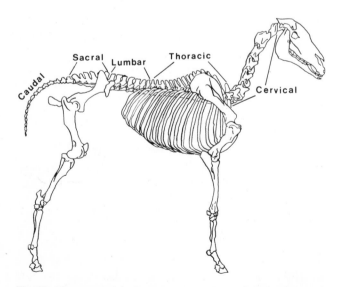

**Fig. 40.** The zones of the vertebral column, illustrated on the skeleton of a horse.

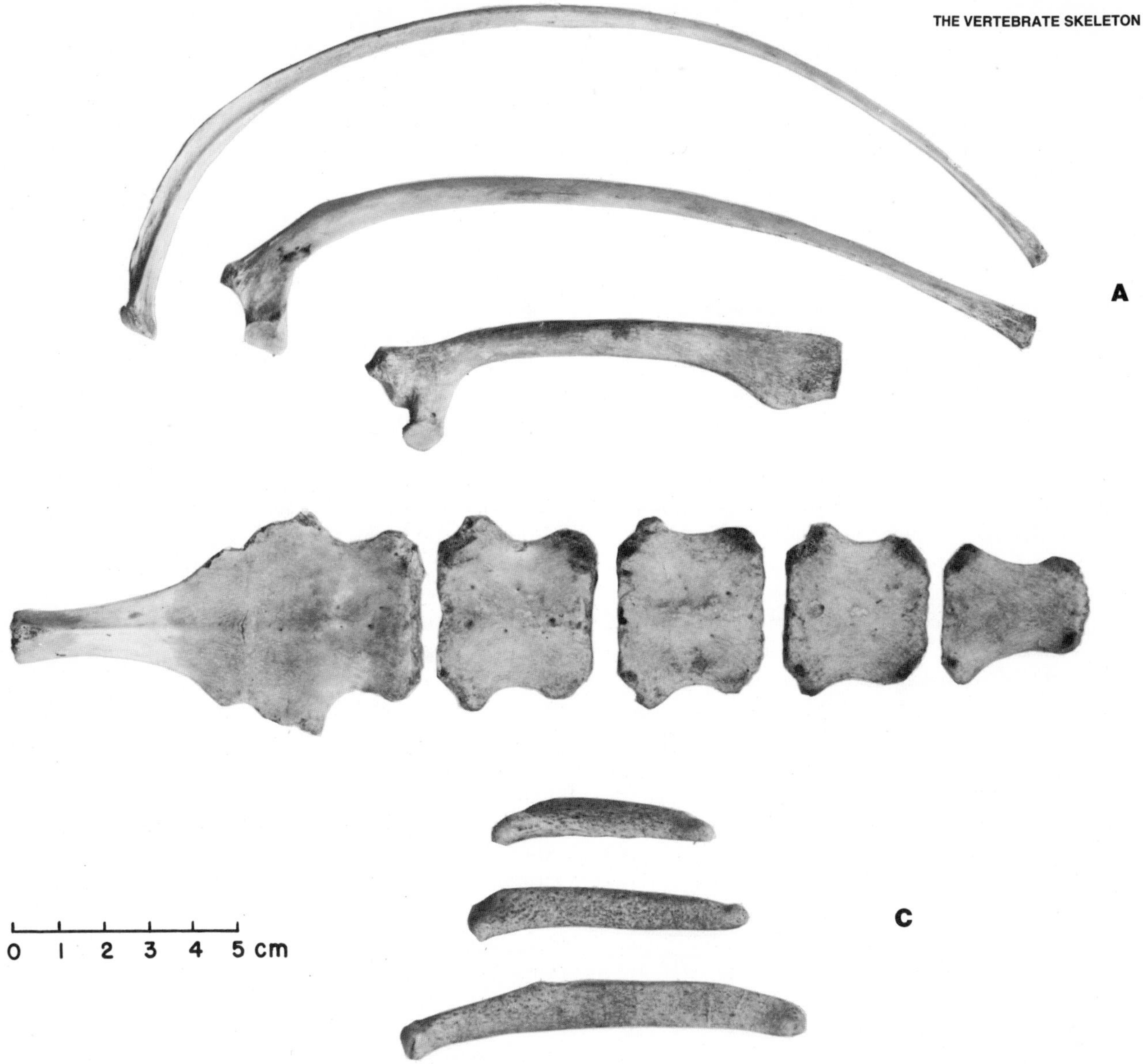

A

B

0  1  2  3  4  5 cm

C

**Fig. 41.** Parts of the axial skeleton of a sheep. **a**, Ribs. **b**, Sternum. **c**, Cartilage fragments.

plate-like bone usually has a well developed spine and terminates distally in a cuplike socket called the *glenoid fossa* (Fig. 42). Much of the scapula consists of thin compact bone that breaks easily, so that it is seldom found intact. Typical archeological remains include the glenoid cavity and portions of the adjacent neck, sections of the anterior and posterior margins of the blade, and fragments of the spine.

In many species (such as sheep, deer, and cattle), the scapula is the only bone in the pectoral girdle. It is not connected to the axial skeleton, but is held against the rib cage by muscles and other fibrous tissues. In some animals, however, a second bone, the *clavicle,* connects the scapula with the sternum. This straight or sinuous rod-shaped bone is best known among primates, insectivores, and bats. Among birds, the clavicles are fused to form the *furcula* (commonly called the wishbone).

The cranial margin of the glenoid fossa, referred to as the *coracoid process,* serves as the anchoring point for the *coracoid,* another bone linking the scapula with the sternum. Among mammals, it occurs only

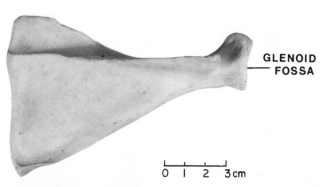

GLENOID FOSSA

0  1  2  3 cm

**Fig. 42.** Scapula of a gazelle.

in the echidnas and the platypus, but is a very important component of the pectoral girdle among birds.

**Pelvic Girdle.** The pelvic girdle is composed of two *innominate bones,* which are fused dorsally with the sacrum and ventrally with each other (Fig. 43). Each innominate consists of three bones, which fuse into a rigid structure as an animal matures. They are in contact at the *acetabulum,* the cup-shaped socket that articulates with the hind limb.

The anterior bone of the innominate is the *ilium,* a flattened element that adjoins the lateral surface of the sacrum. Extending caudally from the acetabulum is the *ischium,* which forms the foundation for the rump. Extending medially from the acetabulum are the *pubic bones,* which join at the median sagittal plane. The caudal portion of the ischium also extends medially and joins the pubic bone to form the roughly circular margin of the large *obturator foramen.* The tripartate structure of the innominates is often reflected in the kinds of fragments encountered in archeological sites. Fragments that include part of the acetabulum are particularly useful for identifications.

Among birds, the pelvic girdle is part of a complex of fused bones. All the posterior thoracic verte-brae are fused to each other and to the lumbar, sacral, and first caudal vertebrae to form the *synsacrum.* The innominates lie lateral to this structure and are joined with it by a series of ridges. Viewed dorsally, the whole complex has a vaguely helmet-like appearance. Since the pubis is weakly developed, the obturator foramen is close to the ventral margin of the innominate. The acetabulum is a ring-like structure in the center. Caudal to the acetabulum is a large opening called the *ilio-ischial fenestra.* Fragments of the synsacrum and the fenestrated area, including the acetabulum, are frequently encountered archeologically.

In some mammals, notably the dog, there is a splanchnic ossification called the *os penis.* It is recognizable by its bilateral symmetry and deep ventral groove, but is seldom encountered in archeological sites.

**Long Bones.** The bones of the limbs are collectively termed long bones. All have cylindrical shafts (the diaphyses) capped proximally and distally by expanded areas that provide articular surfaces. In accord with their weight-bearing function, the shafts are extremely strong columns of compact bone. They are often found fractured, however, because the dia-

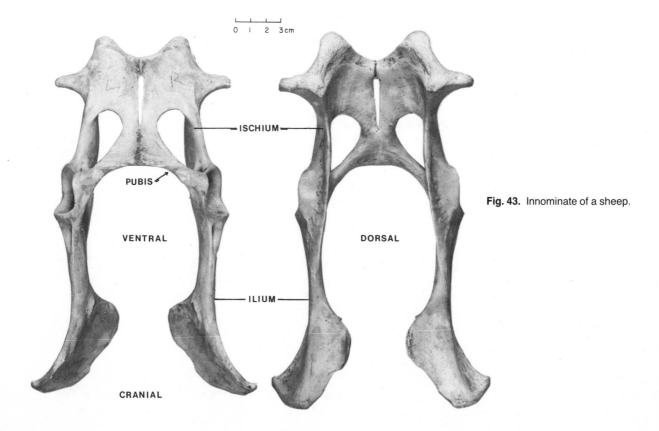

**Fig. 43.** Innominate of a sheep.

PROXIMAL

0  1  2  3 cm

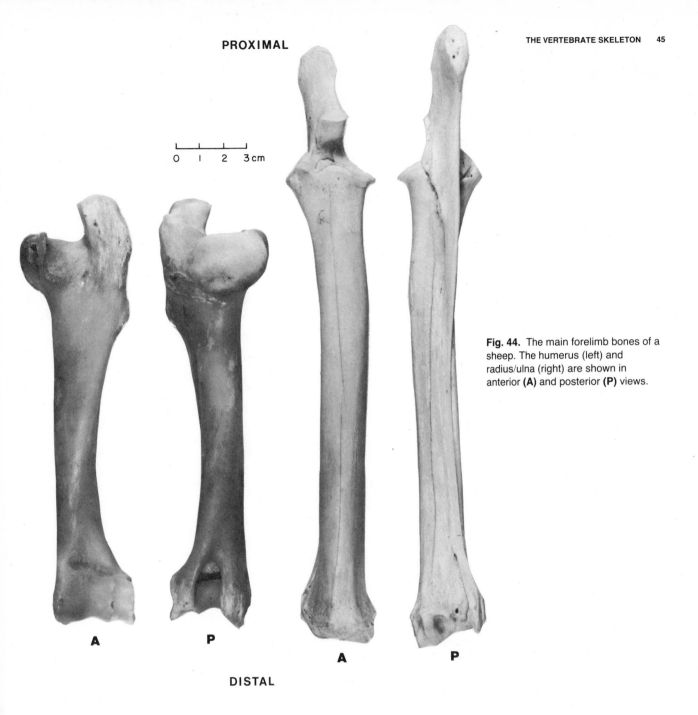

A       P

A       P

DISTAL

**Fig. 44.** The main forelimb bones of a sheep. The humerus (left) and radius/ulna (right) are shown in anterior (**A**) and posterior (**P**) views.

physis is broken during processing a carcass to extract the fat-rich marrow from the medullary cavity. For purposes of identification, it is useful to think in terms of five categories of fragments. The three principal segments are the proximal end, the distal end, and the mid-shaft section. Two additional categories are characteristic of skeletally immature animals, in which the epiphyses have not fused to the diaphysis and are encountered as separate bones.

*Forelimb*. The bones of the mammalian forelimb are the *humerus*, the *radius*, and the *ulna* (Fig. 44). The proximal end of the humerus, which articulates with the glenoid fossa of the scapula, has a rounded surface (the head) bordered by proximally projecting tuberosities. The distal end is often shaped like a lon-

gitudinal section of an oil drum with sagittally oriented grooves and ridges. The distal end articulates with a cup-shaped surface composed of the proximal ends of the radius and ulna.

The ulna has a prominent proximal end called the *olecranon process,* which lies posterior and dorsal to the proximal end of the radius. Among goats, cattle, and deer, which have restricted ability to rotate their forelimbs, the ulnar and radial shafts are partially fused and the shaft of the ulna is often so reduced that it resembles an awl. The distal ends of the radius and ulna present rounded aspects with complex topographies for articulation with the wristbones.

Bird wings have the same basic structure. The proximal end of the humerus is bulbous and flattened

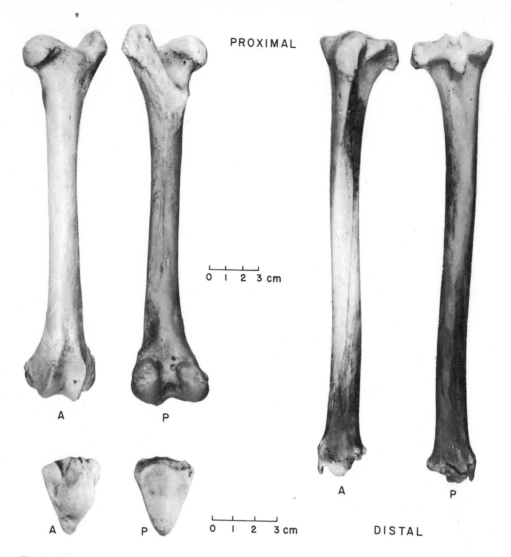

PROXIMAL

0 1 2 3 cm

A      P

A      P

0 1 2 3 cm

DISTAL

A      P

**Fig. 45.** The main hindlimb bones of a sheep. The femur (left), tibia (right), and patella (lower left) are shown in anterior **(A)** and posterior **(P)** views.

in a medial-lateral direction. The lateral margin frequently exhibits a prominent crest. The distal end possesses a cluster of closely packed lumps. The radius and ulna articulate only at their proximal and distal ends, rather than along the shafts as among mammals. The ulna is further distinguished by small lumps along the outward curving part of the shaft, which serve as points of attachment for feathers.

*Hind Limb.* The upper bone of the hind limb is the *femur* (Fig. 45). The rounded proximal portion is called the head or *caput*. Projections or *trochanters* may occur lateral to the head (the *greater trochanter*), posterior and distal to the head (the *lesser trochanter*), or on the lateral shaft (the *third trochanter*). The distal end of the femur has two large bulbous surfaces that articulate with the triangular surface of the proximal end of the *tibia*, one of the bones of the lower limb. The tibia shaft is triangular in cross section, becoming quadrangular toward the distal end, which has a square cupped articular surface. A pointed projection *(malleolus)* on its medial portion contributes to the

ankle joint. The *fibula* lies lateral to the tibia and is sometimes fused with it. In many herd animals exploited by humans, the fibula is reduced to a thumbnail-shaped bone with a small proximal projection (all that remains of the shaft) and a distal cup-shaped articular surface.

Differences in cross section assist in identifying shaft fragments of commonly encountered artiodactyls (deer, antelope, sheep, goats). The tibia is triangular, the humerus and femur nearly circular, and the radius semicircular.

Among birds, the primary bones of the hind limb are the femur, which is similar to mammilian examples, and the *tibiotarsus*. The latter is a straight cylinder adjacent to and sometimes fused with the fibula. The proximal end of the tibiotarsus has a lumpy flat surface with a crest *(cnemial crest)* at its anterior margin. The proximal side of the shaft bears a ridge *(fibular crest),* which is usually prominent. The articular surface of the distal end is characterized by two prominent rounded condyles separated sagittally by a

---

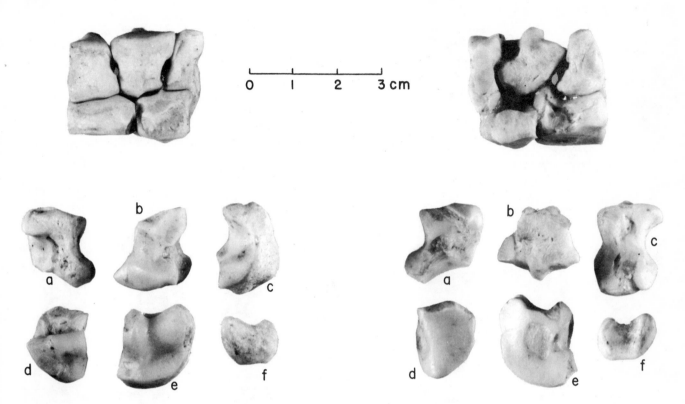

**Fig. 46.** The wrist bones of a sheep. The left carpals are articulated (top) and the right carpals are disarticulated (bottom). Both are shown in anterior (left) and posterior (right) views. **a,** Radial. **b,** Intermediate. **c,** Ulnar. **d,** First. **e,** Second and third. **f,** Accessory.

deep groove *(sulcus)*. This area is analogous to the astragalus among mammals.

　Both mammals and birds possess a bone in the knee, termed the *patella,* which has a lumpy polyhedral form and a smooth volar surface (Fig. 45).

　***Wrist and Ankle.*** The general ancestral pattern of the mammalian wrist contains eight bones or *carpals* arranged in two rows of four each (Fig. 46). The proximal row articulates with the radius and ulna; the distal row, with the *metacarpals*. The terminology for these bones is quite variable (Cornwall 1956:146–7). We recommend the terms proposed by Sisson and Grossman (1953:92) because they have been used for domestic animals and thus have wide applicability in archeological collections. They can be defined diagramatically:

Proximal

Radial　　Intermediate　　Ulnar　　Accessory

Medial　　　　　　　　　　　　　　　　Lateral

First　　Second　　Third　　Fourth

Distal

All of these bones are small blocky solids, hard to recognize during excavation or screening. Since they often bear cut marks, and in some cases are distinctive taxonomically, efforts should be made to insure their recovery.

　Among birds, the structure analogous to the mammalian wrist is composed mainly of the proximal end of the *carpometacarpus*. Two bones remain independent, however; the ulnar and the fused radial and intermediate carpals *(scapholunar carpal)*.

　The mammalian ankle may be composed of up to seven bones, divisible into two complexes (Fig. 47). The proximal complex consists of the *astragalus* and the *calcaneus;* the distal row of the *navicular,* the *cuboid,* and three *cuneiform* bones. The astragalus is a blocky bone that articulates proximally with the distal end of the tibia. The calcaneus articulates with the lateral side of the astragalus. It is elongated caudally and has an epiphysis, the *tuber calcis,* that serves as a point of origin for the Achilles tendon, the major tendon of the foot. In herd animals, the navicular and cuboid are fused into the naviculo-cuboid, which is shaped similarly to the distal epiphysis of the tibia.

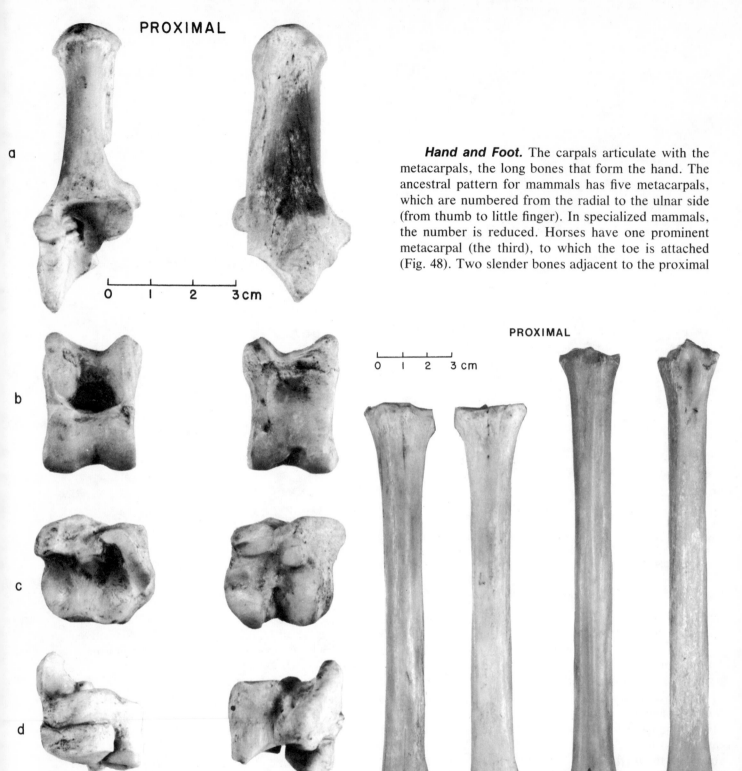

PROXIMAL

a

b

c

d

e

f

DISTAL

*Hand and Foot.* The carpals articulate with the metacarpals, the long bones that form the hand. The ancestral pattern for mammals has five metacarpals, which are numbered from the radial to the ulnar side (from thumb to little finger). In specialized mammals, the number is reduced. Horses have one prominent metacarpal (the third), to which the toe is attached (Fig. 48). Two slender bones adjacent to the proximal

PROXIMAL

A    P    A    P

DISTAL

**Fig. 47.** The ankle bones of a sheep. **a,** Calcaneus. **b,** Astragalus. **c,** Naviculo-cuboid. **d,** Naviculo-cuboid. **e,** Fibula. **f,** Cuneiform.

**Fig. 48.** Equid metacarpal (left) and metatarsal (right) in anterior **(A)** and posterior **(P)** views.

Since mammalian metacarpals and metatarsals are difficult to distinguish, the ambiguous term *metapodial* is often employed. A frequently encountered metapodial fragment is the distal epiphyseal condyle.

The terminal bones of the extremities are the *phalanges*. These are arranged in groups called *digits*. Among mammals, the general pattern is five digits with three phalanges on digits II through V and two on digit I. The first and second phalanges are small tubular bones with epiphyses at both ends, resembling miniature long bones (Fig. 50) The third phalanx is often drastically modified into such disparate structures as a horse hoof and a cat claw. In four-footed (*tetrapodal*) animals, the fore and hind digits are similar.

**Fig. 49.** Metapodial 2 or 4 from an equid, a natural bone that may be misinterpreted as a tool.

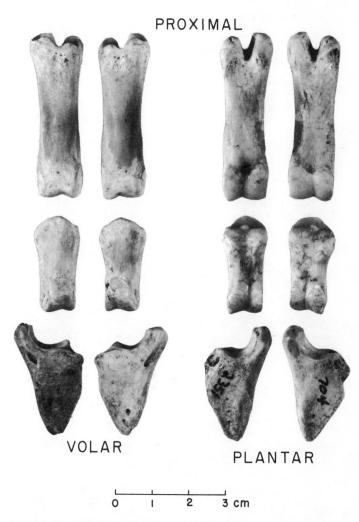

**Fig. 50.** Sheep phalanges in volar and plantar view.

surface along the palmar medial and lateral margins of the horse forefoot are the reduced metacarpals II and IV (sometimes called splint metapodials). Their form makes them easily mistaken for tools (Fig. 49). In other herd animals, the metacarpal is often reduced to one bone, produced by longitudinal fusion of metacarpals III and IV. This is sometimes called the *cannon* bone.

The analogous structure among birds is created by fusion of metacarpals I, II, and III. It is easily recognized by its similarity to an archer's bow.

Among mammals, the *metatarsals* form the foot. Among birds, the analogous structure is the *tarsometatarsus,* easily recognizable because it usually terminates distally in a trilobed articular surface.

Among birds, the three digits of the wing are all distinctive. Digit I consists of the *pollex,* a splinter-like bone connected to the carpometacarpal near the proximal end. Digits II and III articulate with the distal end of the carpometacarpal. Digit II has two phalanges, the first cleaver-shaped and the second spike-like. Digit III has a single small pointed phalanx.

The bird foot has four digits. The first has two phalanges; the second, three; the third, four, and the fourth, five. All except the terminal digit are small tubular structures resembling mammalian toes. The terminal digit is modified to hold the talon and may be confused with the analogous bone in mammalian carnivores. Distinctive for birds, however, are the flat palmar surface and the absence of a bony sheath at the proximal margin (Gilbert, Martin, and Savage 1981).

**Sesamoids.** The final category of bones from the extremities consists of sesamoids, of which the *patella* or knee-cap is the most significant and common (Fig. 45). These bones are formed by ossification centers within tendons and ligaments. Among sheep, cattle, and horses, they form near the distal (plantar)

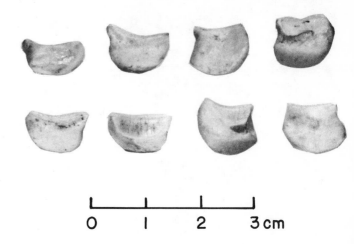

**Fig. 51.**  Sesamoid bones of a sheep.

end of the metapodials and the plantar area of articulation between the second and third phalanges. Their small beanlike appearance makes them easily confused with pebbles and thus overlooked (Fig. 51).

# 5    Collecting, Recording, and Conserving

This chapter reviews the kinds of information that a project director/archeologist must provide an animal bone specialist to insure a fruitful collaboration. The discussion of the categories of assemblages identifies the principal types of analytic problems the projected study is likely to encounter and the kinds of contextual information needed to solve them. The sampling, collecting, recording, and processing procedures permit accurate answers to the following questions: (1) How large is the collection (number of fragments, weight, volume)? (2) How fragmentary is the collection? What is the critical size? (3) What are the main archeological contexts? (4) Generally speaking, what kinds of finds were recovered? (5) Were field preservation techniques used? (6) What collection techniques were employed and how are they related to item 3? (7) Is the collection organized so that the most important questions can be answered first?

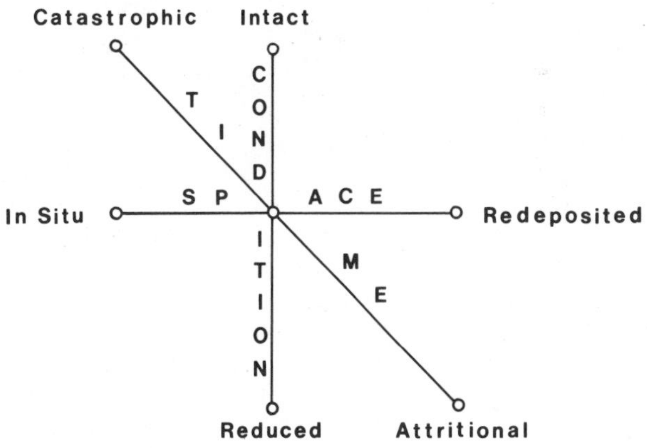

**Fig. 52.** Three axes of variability in animal bone samples. The temporal axis ranges from attritional (slow) to catastrophic (rapid); the spatial axis from in situ (articulated) to redeposited. The condition varies from intact (complete) to reduced (disintegrated).

## CATEGORIES OF BONE ASSEMBLAGES

Skeletal elements can be broken in so many ways that no manual can hope to illustrate even a fraction of the categories of identifiable fragments. Fortunately, the number of species in most archeological contexts is small. Thus, even a few hours spent at a museum of natural history examining the skeletons of the most common forms from the region where the sites are located would be well invested. If the expected taxa include domesticated animals, much insight can be gained by simply examining the meat on one's dinner plate. These zoological and anatomical distinctions are cross-cut by archeological criteria, which provide a matrix for categorizing animal bone remains.

### Temporal Variability

In considering the basic kinds of bone finds, it is useful to think of three intersecting axes of variability (Fig. 52). One axis specifies the duration represented by the accumulation. While the contrast between catastrophic and attritional mortality may be strong, the boundaries between these categories can be hazy. How many animals have to die for the process to be labeled catastrophic? A useful way to solve this problem is to stipulate that the catastrophically killed group be a behavioral unit, such as a bachelor band or nursery herd, whose mortality was purely a function of location. Being in the wrong place at the wrong time bone representing short events widely spaced in time, might be called a catastrophically constituted attritional sample.

Several criteria can be used to establish the position of a sample along the catastrophic-attritional continuum. One is to observe the degree of similarity between the sex and age categories among living populations and those of the same species in the bone sample. The closer the correspondence, the greater the probability that mortality was catastrophic. Another is to estimate the age at death of the individuals in the sample and note any evidence of seasonal concentration in mortality. These two analyses also provide the data for assessing two cultural questions: (1) how selective was the kill or cull? and (2) how were the activities of hunting and slaughtering scheduled?

## Spatial Variability

The second axis of variability specifies the spatial characteristics of a find. The perthotaxic space is the size and shape of the area over which the parts of a single carcass are distributed prior to burial. Taphic (or taphonomic) space incorporates the additional factors that intercede between burial and excavation. If the taphic space is relatively large, the sample of bones in an excavation unit is likely to derive from a large number of different animals. When the taphic space is small, the number of animals represented is likely to be small, although the number of bones collected may be the same.

The polar positions on the spatial axis are easy to distinguish. At one extreme is the in situ find, in which all the bones belong to a single or several animals, and their skeletons are complete. At the other extreme is the redeposited find, in which all the bones derive from different animals. Most archeological samples fall somewhere between, creating a situation known as *interdependence*. Interdependence is the probability that when one bone from a particular carcass is found, another from the same skeleton will be present. Species to species variations in interdependence become a significant factor when analysis focuses on estimating the relative abundances of different animals in a sample.

Several kinds of evidence can be used to estimate the location of a sample along the continuum from in situ to redeposited. The most powerful criterion is the frequency of articulation (Fig. 53). How many bones preserve their anatomical relationship? Are whole

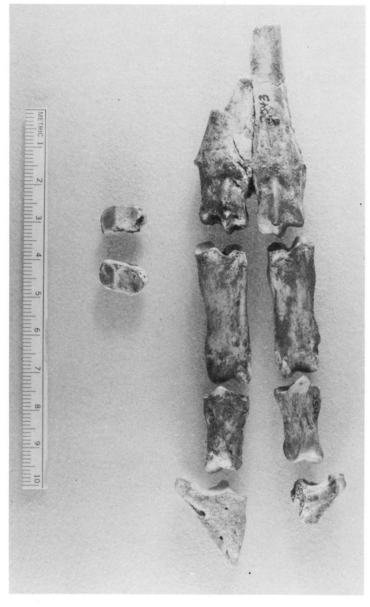

**Fig. 53.** Sheep foot bones found in articulated position at Tell Jemmeh.

completely outweighed an individual animal's talent and physical equipment for survival.

Second, how long is "all at once" — an hour, a day, a week? Or, viewed from the opposite perspective, how regular and prolonged does mortality have to be to fit the definition of attritional? As an instance of the difficulty of categorization, consider that mortality might occur sporadically, perhaps seasonally. The resulting accumulation, composed of large lots of skeletons articulated or only joints? If joints, are they usually the same ones?

A second criterion is the relative frequency of each skeletal element. Without disturbance, the ratios will correspond to those in the living animal. For example, every right femur of a horse should be accompanied by one right radius and two right first phalanges. Although this assemblage could occur in a randomly redeposited situation, the fact that redeposition is almost always patterned makes the usual result a strong divergence from the anatomical ratio.

Bone ratios are likely to be distorted by a host of destructive processes, to which different elements offer differential resistance. One means of minimizing this distortion is to use sample-wide ratios rather than anatomical ratios as a basis for comparison, on the assumption that the whole sample represents an area larger than the biggest taphic space. If so, subsample variations from the site average could reveal internal patterns of redeposition.

A third criterion is the location of cuts produced during butchering. If bones with cut marks are those articulating with bones missing from the sample, the bias probably stems from redeposition after butchering.

A final criterion is the orientation of bone fragments. The effects of many natural processes of redeposition vary with the weight and shape of the bones. Currents of water tend to sort small knubby bones and to align the long axes of splinter-like bones. Concentrations of bones of similar sizes or fragments pointing the same direction can be evidence of this process.

## Bone Condition

The third axis of variability is bone condition and the polar opposites are intact and reduced. Again, the extremes are distinct: whole bones versus bone dust. Most samples lie somewhere between. Their position on the continuum may have important practical or theoretical implications. In the latter area, for instance, the intensity of bone reduction has been linked to environmental and subsistence stress among aboriginal Australian groups (Gould and Watson 1982).

Condition affects the excavator's choice of recovery system and the analyst's ability to make identifications because reliable collecting and confident classifying are both crudely related to the sizes of the specimens. A useful measure of the degree of reduction can be generated by examining the pattern of fragmentation for each bone element of each taxon.

Experience has taught us that, within a site or even a region, the bones of abundant taxa tend to fragment in characteristic patterns. For example, the metapodia of sheep and goats are frequently split longitudinally, producing a medial and a lateral proximal fragment, assorted shaft splinters, a medial and a lateral distal fragment, and (in immature specimens) a medial and a lateral epiphysial condyle. Tabulating this information is useful in identifying what part of a sample deserves analysis and the amount of work that will be involved.

## Combinations of Categories

These three axes produce a cube composed of eight compartments, each representing a different combination of factors:

| Time | Space | Condition |
|------|-------|-----------|
| Catastrophic | In situ | Intact |
| Catastrophic | In situ | Reduced |
| Catastrophic | Redeposited | Intact |
| Catastrophic | Redeposited | Reduced |
| Attritional | In situ | Intact |
| Attritional | In situ | Reduced |
| Attritional | Redeposited | Intact |
| Attritional | Redeposited | Reduced |

The problems posed by these combinations can be exemplified by three comments.

Attritional samples reflect a melange of behaviors. A collection from a hunting-gathering site is likely to represent an unknown number of "hunter's bags," which may or may not reflect uniform procedures (Wilkinson 1976). Attritional samples also merge time. If the period represented is too long, a description of the assemblage may have little cultural meaning.

Redeposited samples merge numerous animals, each represented by minimal information. Combining them analytically obscures the variability in strategies that might have been employed for their acquisition and processing. Failure to consider that the area over which a carcass is redeposited may be different for each species will seriously compromise efforts to estimate species abundance.

Reduced samples are hard to collect and difficult to identify because they embody an unknown mix of cultural and natural information.

The above points underscore an extremely important axiom of animal bone archeology: the excavator must record information in the field about the circumstances and condition of animal bones if reliable information is expected from their analysis.

## SAMPLING STRATEGIES

### Identifiability

In an influential paper, Binford and Bertram (1977:125) state: "In training students to observe and record faunal material, we have always taken the position that there *is no unidentifiable* bone. All bones, even the smallest fragments, may be identified with sufficient training in osteology" (emphasis in the original). The key question is: identifiable as what? Only as a bone, or as something more specific, such as "a mammal bone," "a mammal humerus," "a deer humerus," etc.? Each category in this sequence requires more detailed information about the bone fragment. Where should one say "identifiable" begins? The solution is to assert that the modifier is appropriate when a bone can be placed in a category that is useful for some kind of analysis (Fig. 54).

There is no set of universal criteria for differentiating identifiable from unidentifiable bones. Failure to appreciate this point has led to endless misunderstanding and even rancor between archeologists and animal bone specialists. An analogy from another

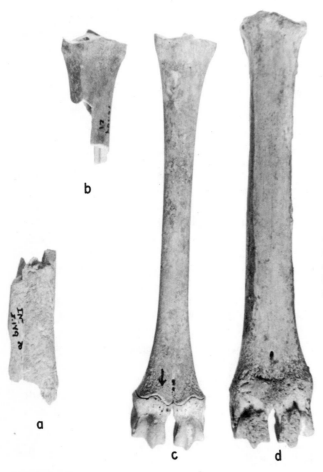

**Fig. 54.** Degrees of specificity in identification. **a,** Fragment of a metapodial from a sheep or goat; neither species nor age nor fore or hind limb can be ascertained. **b,** Fragment of a metapodial identifiable as the left metatarsal. **c,** Left metatarsal identifiable as sheep and as relatively young (epiphysis not fused to diaphysis). **d,** Left metatarsal of a relatively mature goat (epiphysis fused); the robustness of the distal end suggests the sex may be male.

0    I    2    3 cm

class of material can clarify this situation. A routine procedure employed on many large sites in the Middle East is called a "pottery reading." This involves examining the sherds collected each day and dividing them into diagnostic (rims, handles, bases, decorated) and non-diagnostic (everything else, including mainly plain body sherds) categories. The non-diagnostic portion may be stored, but is usually discarded. The amount thrown out can be impressive. At one large excavation, we watched truck loads on their way to the dump, surely what would have been a painful sight for a ceramic specialist aware of the amount of potential information being destroyed. Routine intensive collection can be equally unproductive. As a spokesman for the paleobotanical community once remarked, modern archeologists can generate samples so huge that no botanist would attempt their study. How can an archeologist steer a path between losing information and drowning in potential data?

## Multiple Strategy Approach

A solution to this dilemma has been suggested by Meadow (1980), who recommends applying a battery of collection techniques to a site. Some areas get screened, others not. Some screens have fine mesh, others coarse. In some areas, excavation proceeds slowly enough to record the position and orientation of every fragment; in others, the matrix is rapidly shoveled away. In some areas, bagged samples of matrix are collected for subsequent examination in the laboratory. Each procedure takes varying amounts of time and effort and project directors rarely know in advance how expensive each technique will be. The following data can be helpful in reaching a decision.

1. Estimate the extent of the site you hope to excavate in a given field season.
2. Conduct experiments to establish how much matrix per man-day can be removed using each procedure, remembering that experimenting with rapid techniques is destructive.
3. Estimate the amount of material you can transport and store for future study.
4. Estimate the amount of bone produced under each procedure per day per team member.
5. Use the following equations to estimate how much effort can be put into each method of collecting by juggling the A's, B's, C's, etc. until a feasible combination is achieved.
Equation 1. A (Matrix per Day per Excavator using Collection Technique 1) + B (MDE using CT2) + C (MDE using CT3) + . . . . = Total Amount of Site to be Excavated × Total Number of Days of Excavation × Total Number of Excavators.
Equation 2. A (Bones per Day per Excavator using Collection Technique 1) + B (BDE using CT2) + C (BDE using CT3) + . . . = Total Bones Storable × Total Number of Days of Excavation × Total Number of Excavators.

Converting A, B, C, etc. into percentages establishes the proportions of each method that can be employed per field season within the constraints of time, funds, and personnel.

After the management decision has been made, each technique can be appropriately employed using the following criteria:

1. Samples from small, intensively collected, randomly assorted excavation units are almost always more informative than those from large trenches.
2. Intensive collecting procedures should be employed in each different archeological context represented.
3. A compromise can be achieved between intensively sampling a whole excavation unit and rapidly excavating it by screening every n'th bucket of matrix (the interval depending on the size of the unit, quantity of bone, etc.).
4. Some portion of the matrix should be collected for laboratory examination to establish whether certain types of bones are being missed during excavation or screening.
5. The collecting technique used to gather each sample must be recorded, noting mesh size of screens, difficulties in screening, color contrast between dirt and bone, and the existence of other finds superficially similar to bone.
6. All bone fragments found in the units sampled must be saved.

## Maximizing Analytic Accuracy

Another solution to the sampling problem returns us to the concept "identifiable." In Chapter 2, we emphasized that the analytic units in animal bone archeology are cultural as well as zoological. In 19th-century North American sites, for example, a common find is a ring-like segment of long bone. Often it is difficult to establish with confidence which domestic

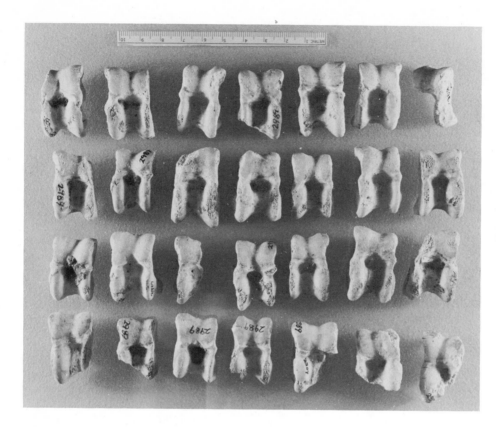

**Fig. 55.** Sheep and goat astragali used as artifacts, found in a cache at Tell Jemmeh, Israel. Some have been shaped by grinding (e.g. first bone in the third row).

animal is represented, making the fragment unidentifiable by species. Because the cut of meat has socioeconomic significance regardless of species, however, the ring is identifiable in a cultural sense. As a further instance, because the morphological distinctions separating the genera *Ovis* (sheep) and *Capra* (goat) are restricted to parts of the skeleton and these elements may not survive, the bulk of such remains are assignable only to a residual sheep-goat category. Fragments identifiable to genus tend to be bigger than ambiguous bones. Hence, getting a true picture of the broader (sheep-goat) category requires that the relative frequencies of many small fragments be established and more intensive methods of collection be employed to obtain a reliable sample.

Establishing the kind of collection procedures to employ using the criteria of identifiability involves the following steps:

1. List the important categories of animals expected to be encountered.
2. Identify the distinctive morphological features of the bones of each category.
3. Identify the smallest diagnostic feature.
4. Make a test excavation employing techniques appropriate for retrieving the smallest categories, and also to see whether unanticipated taxa are present.

5. Adjust the collecting technique to insure that fragments of the size typical of the smallest useful morphological feature are being reliably collected.
6. Use this collecting technique in parts of the site to be intensively processed.

## COLLECTING PROBLEMS

### Recognizing Specimens

What shapes are readily identifiable as specimens? The answer varies enormously from site to site and archeologist to archeologist depending on (1) the experience of the excavator, (2) the pace of excavation, and (3) the condition of the specimens. An extreme example of bias in recognition comes from Çatal Hüyük in Anatolia. Although the excavation was done by very experienced workmen, some lots of bone contain astonishing concentrations of one element: the astagulus of cattle (D. Perkins Jr., pers. com.). Because astragali have been used as dice for centuries, the workmen apparently recognized them more readily as items worth saving (Fig. 55).

## Articulation

Probably the most important observation to be made on exposure is articulation, either of a joint or a whole skeleton. The following procedures should be employed before removing articulated remains.

Make a labeled sketch of the group of bones on a separate record form that can be delivered to the animal bone analyst. This drawing should show the anatomical orientation of the parts (flexed or not flexed) and their spatial orientation (e.g., resting on medial or lateral surface). Further, it should note the relationship of the articulated specimen to any nearby features, such as walls, floors, pits, and artifacts (Fig. 56).

The selection of elements for detailed in situ photography depends on the research design and the fragility of the remains. Complex articulations and those including elements providing important measurements should always be photographed (Fig. 57). Whenever possible, the photograph should be taken from above rather than from an oblique angle. A scale must be included and should be placed parallel to each critical dimension of the find. The importance of this cannot be overemphasized. Had Petrie (1931, 1932) used scales in his record of the equid burials at Tel el Ajjūl, we would now be a lot closer to understanding the history of interaction between man, donkey, horse, and onager during the Bronze Age in the Mediterranean region.

When the bones in an articulation are exposed, they are in danger of deterioration because of changed conditions of light, temperature, and moisture. Many excavators like to leave their finds in situ on pedestals as they proceed across an excavation unit. This may be safe with stones and pottery, but it is risky with bones unless considerable care is taken to protect them or exposure is brief. Protection can be accomplished in two ways. The easiest is to recover the bone with dirt, taking care to mark the buried location. Covering with boxes or plastic is undesirable because such materials create ovens or steam baths, accelerating the rate of destruction. The best procedure is to mark the location and remove the specimen, but this can be done only if it is in a relatively good state of preservation. An articulated unit should be bagged separately from the rest of the finds from the excavation unit.

If the articulated bones are fragile, a decision must be made about field consolidation. This is a lengthy and tedious process, so the question must be asked, Is it worth the effort? The answer depends on the potential the fragments have for future study. If the bones are measurable, the answer is almost always "yes," because one of the most useful and least common kinds of information is the correlation between measurements of different bones of the same skeleton. A second consideration is whether additional study is likely to improve the field identification, an assessment that only the animal bone specialist can make. A third factor is that field consolidation produces chemical alterations. If the find is to be used for radiometric dating or trace-element studies, dust may be more useful than the consolidated bone.

## Screen Collecting

Screens are not the fail-safe collecting methods they are sometimes thought to be. True, they trap fragments above a certain size, but only objects recognized as significant are usually saved. Small specimens encased in lumps are likely to be missed. One solution is to wet-screen the matrix, but care is required since bone may be destroyed by water. Another problem was encountered at Tell Jemmeh in Israel. There, bricks were made using mud from earlier midden, often incorporating bone. Thus, brick fragments had to be carefully broken to recover the enclosed specimens.

Since the matrix is passed through the screen sequentially, the opportunity exists to catch articulations missed in situ. Personnel who remove materials from the screens should search for elements that go together, such as joints or limbs. The larger the excavation unit, the more critical this attention is.

The biggest decision to make concerning screen collecting is the size of the mesh. Watson (1972) provides two useful criteria. One is the minimum size of an identifiable fragment. How small can a bone fragment be and still be identifiable at the level of specificity required? This value tends to correlate with the size of the animal, identifiable cow-bone fragments being larger than their sheep analogs. The other criterion is the minimum size of a reliably recoverable fragment. This can be defined geometrically as any fragment that exceeds the mesh-size in two of its three dimensions. In practice, this definition is probably too restrictive, since most long splinters are unlikely to slip lengthwise through the screen. A suitable screen size can be selected by experiment. A few small identifiable fragments can be passed through a nested set of graded screens. Observation will establish the mesh size likely to insure capture of the desired proportion of identifiable fragments.

ANIMAL FIND ARTICULATION

Site Name _Tel Miqne___         Field __ _I NE_____

                                   Square___ _4_____

                                   Locus # _4321_____

A. Species: ___ _Sus_____

B. Bones Present: _Humerus, radius, ulna __ - Left_____
_All bones lying on medial surface_____

C. Description of Articulation:
    1. Narrative: (orientation, condition of bone, points of
    articulation: _Extended, proximal end to North, articular_
_Surfaces Not quite touching, condition of bone - good_

    2. Osteological Measurements: (following von den Driesch)
_Not required - removed intact_____

D. Association:
    1. Features: (walls, floors, pits, ovens, etc.) _found in_
_Pit L.4301_____

    2. Objects: __ _Not Applicable (NA)_____

    3. Pottery Reading: _Iron I_____

E. Drawing #: ___ _NA_____

F. Photograph #s: _NA_____

G. Dates Cited in Notes: __ _16 July '84_____

H. Associated Plans and Sections: _NA___ _See top Plan for_
_16 July_____

**Fig. 56.** Form for recording data on articulations in the field. The form requests basic information about the context and provides a space for making a sketch of the skeletal relationships. This form, designed for the recording system at Tel Miqne, can be modified to fit other requirements.

Most bone collections are not gathered using systematic criteria. Instead, they are accumulated while excavating for other kinds of remains. Watson (1972) suggested a method for assessing the bias this introduces. He assumed that the sizes of fragments representing a species have distributions of abundance approximating a logarithmic curve. That is to say, abundance decreases steadily with decreasing size. Comparing the lengths of fragments from a number of sites showed that the large-size categories followed the logarithmic curve, but the small-size categories did not. At some point, instead of increasing steadily as predicted, they began to tail off, producing a roughly bell-shaped curve. Watson considers the point at which the divergence begins to be the critical size. All specimens larger than this are being reliably recovered; all those smaller are not (Fig. 58). This observation makes it possible to specify the sullegic bias of a collection with some precision. If the critical size is larger than the identifiable fragments required for

I. Sketch of Articulation: (The sketch should utilize the space available in the square provided. This drawing is not intended as a top plan of the square in which the articulation was found since the regular top plan should include the location of this find.)

          )  3.0 meters                     North
North/South Grid Line

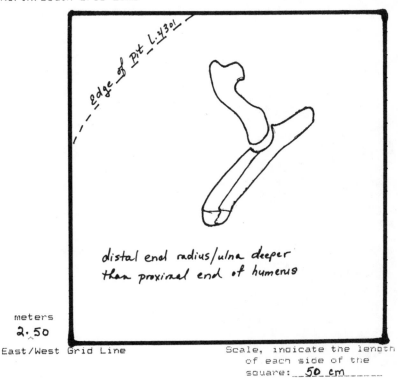

distal end radius/ulna deeper
than proximal end of humerus

meters
2.50

East/West Grid Line

Scale, indicate the length
of each side of the
square: __50 cm_____

J. Location, center of articulation is:

    1.  __2.30__ S. of North Balk    2.  __2.20__ W. of East Balk
    3.  Top Level __101.56__    4.  Bottom Level __101.48__

analysis, a collection has limited utility. However, since most samples contain an array of species and minimum identifiable sizes vary by species, portions of the collection may provide useful information.

## THE ANALYTIC IMPORTANCE OF CONTEXT

Information about the context and association of bone finds provides the infrastructure for analysis and interpretation, but this is seldom available to the animal bone specialist at the beginning of the study. Perhaps the archeological decisions necessary to assemble this information are difficult. Sometimes, however, we feel our work routine is considered to begin with identification and tabulation, making the information about context and association relevant only after these tasks have been completed. Although this approach is acceptable with collections numbering a few hundred specimens or from few contexts, it

**Fig. 57.** Articulated donkey skull and forelimb in situ at Tell Jemmeh.

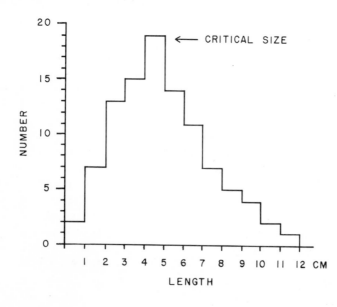

**Fig. 58.** Establishing the critical size for an animal bone collection. The size of the smallest fragment reliably collected by the screening method employed can be estimated by plotting the frequencies of different bone sizes, here measured as greatest lengths. Above the critical size, the plot of frequencies takes on a logarithmic form; below, it drops irregularly toward zero. Comparing the size of the specimens in a category to the critical size provides an indication whether the frequency of that category is a trustworthy indicator of abundance.

is very inefficient with large sets of data. The animal bone specialist requires contextual information to determine the order in which information should be extracted from the sample, as well as for making appropriate decisions about storage. Three cases will exemplify this point.

## Tepe Ganj Dareh

Just over 50,000 bone fragments were identified and tabulated from a sample ten times that large recovered from the Neolithic village of Tepe Ganj Dareh in Iran by fine-mesh screening. The primary goal was establishing whether goats or sheep (or both) were wild or domesticated. Mesh size was fine enough, however, to capture reliably most of the identifiable fragments from animals the size of hares and partridges. The sample consisted of more than 1600 lots, each representing an excavation unit. Each lot had a label showing: (1) provenience number identifying the field-record sheet, (2) square and depth, (3) date of excavation, and (4) identity of the excavator.

The analysis focussed on change through time rather than horizontal variability. Unfortunately, the stratigraphy of the site, composed of the tumble-down remains of a succession of cellular mud-brick dwellings, was so complex that many excavation units could not be assigned confidently to one of the main layers, designated A, B, C, D, and E. The first requirement was therefore to provide a context confidence value for each excavation unit. A numerical rating from 1 to 5, indicating whether the unit represented a floor deposit, an erosional deposit of uncertain temporal ascription, or some intermediate context, was appended to the layer letter. The context confidence could also be expressed by mixed designations: A/B, A/B/C, B/D, etc., indicating durations of varying lengths. This approach made it possible to control provenience with precision. The Ganj Dareh system also made it possible to combine sequentially sub-samples of gradually decreasing temporal reliability to create lots of sufficient size for statistical treatment.

While these confidence gradations were available only towards the end of the analysis of the Tepe Ganj Dareh sample, they provide a useful model. If available at the beginning of analysis, they would permit selecting for study the most reliable samples and leaving the problematic ones for subsequent examination as needed.

## Tell Jemmeh

The animal bone finds from Tell Jemmeh, a large mound in Israel occupied during the second and first millennia B.C., were intended to be used to evaluate a broader spectrum of questions than were examined at Tepe Ganj Dareh. Further, the considerable functional variation in architectural features at the site suggested associated horizontal variability in the samples, which had to be identified before temporal patterns could be proposed. Finally, the long-term nature of the project introduced the possibility that changes in personnel might account for certain kinds of sample differences. For these reasons, a more complex approach was taken to identifying context.

Each sample was from an excavated square. The square identification provided a rough estimate of time period and functional context, as well as the names of the field supervisors responsible for identifying contexts and setting unit boundaries. These data are important because excavators introduce significant "personal signatures" into the collections. Comparing the horizontal and vertical dimensions of the excavation units at a Near Eastern site revealed enormous differences among the six similarly trained and experienced excavators digging adjacent squares. In sites dug following "natural" stratigraphy, the variability can be dramatic.

The temporal assignments for more than 3000 lots of bones were made by the excavator working with the animal bone specialist over several weeks, during which the excavation-unit descriptions were read, locations were matched with profiles, and associated ceramic finds were assessed. The result was a carefully estimated temporal spread for each lot, measured in centuries or parts of centuries. More than 30 categories were generated for the 16+ centuries of occupation of the site. These could be grouped and regrouped into periods of varying durations.

The final component of the Tell Jemmeh context identification was the functional/depositional assessment. About 90 categories were distinguished using observations about architecture, features, associations, and sedimentation. These, too, could be grouped in a variety of ways for analysis.

## Tel Miqne

The procedures employed at Tel Miqne, a Philistine occupation in central Israel, deserve emulation. The excavators, Trude Dothan and Seymour Gitin, publish a descriptive volume after each field season that provides stratigraphic and artifactual assessments for each excavation unit, together with a tentative reconstruction of sedimentary history. These listings can be used to correlate the variability of animal bones with other categories of material remains during the course of their analysis.

## Recommended Procedures

The project director/archeologist should separate animal bone samples according to the reliability of their contextual/stratigraphic association. Then, a cross-cutting classification should be made based on major discontinuities in horizontal disposition and chronological sequence. This matrix of information can be used by the animal bone specialist to decide where to begin the analysis and in what order to proceed.

At least one excavator treated our collaboration as a double-blind experiment. He sent us a collection accompanied by minimal identification and suggested we look for patterns in variability of bone remains across the lots. The groupings we generated would then be compared to some other stratigraphic or architectural partitioning of the sample. Such an approach cannot be recommended. It makes unrealistic assumptions about the linkage between cultural-historical variables and bone frequencies and attributes. Further, few bone lots are sufficiently extensive to provide useful statistical input.

To repeat, animal bone archeology is a cooperative venture. Nowhere is that cooperation more necessary than in the sharing of archeological information and the establishing of context groupings for analysis.

## FIELD PROCESSING TECHNIQUES

### Cleaning

A question frequently posed to animal bone specialists is: "Should I wash the bones before I send them to you?" As with other questions, the answer is equivocal. In certain circumstances, washing can be terribly destructive. Immersion can exert pressure on invisible flaws, causing the bone to fall apart. Or, water can soften the surface. Scrubbing even gently can produce or obliterate scratches and polish, changes that play havoc with analysis. Shipping dirty

bone can have equally disastrous effects. Jiggling during transport can grind beautiful specimens to powder. Dirt trapped inside a braincase may shrink on drying into a hard rough sphere that batters the interior of the skull. Washing prevents such damage and is necessary if any of the analytic methods to be used depend on weight.

Experiments should be conducted on a few specimens to identify potential problems before washing routinely. Specimens with crystalline growth should not be washed because the crystals will expand and shatter the bone. Scrubbing should be minimized. If a bone needs extensive cleaning, the correct procedure can be selected in the laboratory. Allow to dry in shade to retard evaporation and minimize exposure to changes in temperature. Use metal or heavy wooden tags marked with waterproof ink (laundry markers work well) to label the drying bone. Few things are more depressing than chasing airborne labels or watching writing dissolve.

### Sorting

As a back-up information base, some field description of animal bone samples should be undertaken. Every excavator should be familiar with the skeletal-fragment categories for the most common taxa likely to be encountered (Fig. 59). Additionally, any spectacular or unusual specimens should be noted. It is important to do this recording near the excavation so subsequent examination can reveal the degree of post-excavation damage a collection has suffered.

### Recording Volume and Weight

Sample volumes should be measured immediately after washing, since this insures the bones will be only wetted once. The sample is transferred from the washing screen to a bucket or similar container provided with a scale indicating fluid content. Volume is measured by displacement on this scale.

After the bone lot has dried thoroughly, it should be weighed before packing. This is a good time to segregate fragile fragments needing consolidation.

### Numbering

Should identification be marked on the bones, and if so what information should be included? Labelling is

Sample Identification (provenience):_____

| Category: | Size | | |
|---|---|---|---|
| | Small | Medium | Large |
| (1) Teeth | | | |
|     Loose | | | |
|     In mandible/maxilla | | | |
| (2) Skull | | | |
| (3) Vertebra | | | |
| (4) Rib | | | |
| (5) Shoulder | | | |
| (6) Hip | | | |
| (7) Long Bone | | | |
|     With articular surface | | | |
|     Splinters | | | |
| (8) Wrist/ankle | | | |
| (9) Fingers/toes | | | |
| (10) Undetermined | | | |

Total number of fragments_____
Sample weight_____
Sample volume_____

**Fig. 59.** Categories of skeletal fragments for field description. Sizes can be expressed as small, medium, and large, with the dimensions standardized for each category.

a time-consuming and potentially damaging procedure. It is, further, likely that unnecessary fragments will be labeled. Labelling does provide the best insurance, however, that context will not be lost.

What should the label be? Many excavators use elaborate mnemonic devices that are useful but do not make it easy to establish what part of a collection has been processed. In most cases, we have transformed such codes into a sequential numeric label of the following type, making sure to have multiple copies of the table of correspondences:

Site Acronym + Excavation Unit
+ Specimen Number
Example: TJ-236-27

Numbering should be done with ink (Fig. 60). After the label dries, try to read it (or have a coworker try). If a bone is too tiny or too dark to be numbered legibly, place it in a vial or small plastic bag. If the container is opaque, indicate what the specimen is on the label (e.g. a small tooth). Covering labels with varnish is usually undesirable, although this may protect the number from being eroded away on crumbly surfaces. A better procedure is to pack such specimens independently.

**Fig. 60.** Preliminary sorting and numbering fragments in a field laboratory.

## Packing and Shipping

Bone collections should be organized for packing (Fig. 61). If several containers are required to hold fragments from a single excavation unit, this information should be provided on the label (e.g., 1 of 3, 2 of 3, 3 of 3). Most animal bone archeologists do not have sufficient lay-out space to unpack a large collection all at once. Thus, it is important to segregate major analytic units for packing. Try to combine lots of similar weight and volume. Pack delicate specimens in a separate container. The contents of each box or crate should be listed on the exterior (or abstracted, if the list is long). A complete list should be placed inside and a copy sent separately to the animal bone specialist. A third copy should be kept for the project files.

Collections have been successfully packed and shipped to us in plastic bags, paper bags, cloth bags, and cardboard boxes. Each has advantages and disadvantages. Plastic bags allow one to see the contents without opening the package, permitting special categories to be located without extensive labor. Unless the bones are very dry, however, mold will grow inside a plastic bag. Also, plastic bags are difficult to label permanently. Finally, the closures on zip-lock bags are not always reliable; such bags should not be too full to insure secure closure. A label should be placed inside unless the bones have been numbered.

Paper bags are cheap and strong, but difficult to close securely and disastrous if the collection gets wet. Bone fragments are often sharp and may cut paper during shipment. Paper is also vulnerable to consumption by a variety of pests. Cloth bags are more expensive, but can be reused. They can be numbered permanently, are not easily cut, and maintain strength when wet. They are permeable, preventing a deleterious damp environment from being established inside. A useful combination is to pack paper bags from related excavation units together in medium-sized cloth sacks.

Finally, boxes can be used. These are doubly effective, since they provide ready-made containers for the sorting process that begins an animal bone analysis. Further, they allow organized storage of the collection in the laboratory when placed on shelves with labels facing outward. Glue-on paper labels can be used to enter contextual information (Fig. 62). On the negative side, extensive internal packing is necessary to prevent movement of bone fragments. Cost is higher and the volume shipped is enlarged by this procedure. If cushioning is required, cotton should be avoided unless the bones are isolated from contact

**Fig. 61.** Boxes containing fragments sorted into provisional broad taxonomic and skeletal categories prior to packing for shipment.

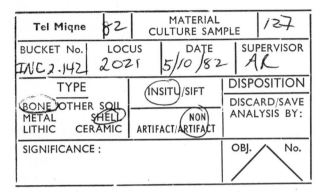

| Tel Miqne | 82 | MATERIAL CULTURE SAMPLE | 127 |
|---|---|---|---|
| BUCKET No. INC2.142 | LOCUS 2021 | DATE 5/10/82 | SUPERVISOR AR |

**Fig. 62.** A paper label used by the Tel Miqne project.

with it. Horn cores, immature epiphyses, and fragments of spongy bone become hopelessly entangled in cotton fibers.

After the lots of bone have been packed using one or several of the procedures described above, they should be placed in sturdy cartons or wooden crates no heavier than can be lifted by one person. If shipment is overseas, it is advisable to use wooden crates. Make sure labels are printed on the side of each crate. The rule is simple; do not assume that boxes stacked together will stay together during shipment.

### Storing

Some agreement should be made prior to analysis about final storage of the collection. Beyond the question of where it will go lies to the problem of organization. Two polar options exist. The material can be stored by excavation unit or by zoological designation. The choice is determined by anticipated use. Are future investigators likely to focus on the collection as artifacts, with non-zoological information the goal? Or are they likely to consult it to answer taxonomic questions? Since this is usually hard to predict, we suggest the following organizational structure, which inconveniences everyone a little but no one too much.

I.   Rare or Singular Species
 Taxon 1.   Bone type 1, Bone type 2. . . . .
 Taxon 2.   Bone type 1, Bone type 2 . . . .
II.  Archeological Context 1 (structure, period, etc.)
 Complete skeletons
 Articulations
 Taxon 1.   Bone type 1, Bone type 2 . . .
 Taxon 2.   Bone type 1, Bone type 2 . . .

III.  Archeological Context II (repeat subheadings)
IV.   Archeological Context III (repeat as needed)

## CONSOLIDATION

If the decision is made to consolidate a find in the field, the following procedures are appropriate. They are abstracted from suggestions developed by the Conservation Laboratory, Department of Anthropology, Smithsonian Institution. Additional discussion and alternative methods can be found in Baumgartner and Lanooy (1982), Brown (1976), Huelsbeck and Wessen (1982), Robinson (1981), Szilvassy (1979), and Webb (1982). The *Art and Archaeology Technical Abstracts* are an up-to-date source of experiments and techniques. In applying any of them, the most important rule is to try to do things that are reversible.

### Supplies

The following chemicals and tools will suffice for resolving most problems of conservation in the field:

Polyvinylacetate (PVA or PVA-AYAF). This is available in a variety of grades and forms (beads or chunks) from chemical suppliers.

Acetone. If unavailable, ethanol may be substituted, but dissolving PVA in this solvent can be very difficult.

Polyethylene bags (4 mil thickness)
Spray bottles
Dental tools
Soft brushes. The variety of sizes usually used for excavation; soft, because stiff bristles can produce scratches that may mislead the analyst.

Plastic containers with lids, in a variety of sizes to hold bones of different dimensions.

Enema bulb
Eye dropper
Gauze or cheesecloth
Rubber gloves
Plastic wrap
Polyethylene sheeting
Wooden spoon

### Consolidating Solutions

The standard impregnating solution consists of 100 grams of PVA (about 120 ml or half a cup) mixed with 1 liter (1+ quart) of acetone. Dissolution of the PVA takes 24-36 hours, so the mixture should be prepared in advance of excavation. Acetone evaporates rapidly. Therefore, if the container holding the solution must remain open for extended periods, it will be necessary to add more solvent occasionally.

In areas of the world where PVA or acetone are difficult to obtain or import, a less satisfactory procedure is to use a solution of white glue (carpenter's glue) and water. The disadvantages are inferior penetration and drying from the surface inward, which can seal water in the bone.

Another useful and rapid technique is applying Duco cement or other acetone-reversible commercial product. This is particularly relevant for mandibles, in which the teeth are often loose or partially fragmented and may be separated prior to examination. This can be a real problem with finds such as the cheek teeth of equids, since the molars and premolars in the center of the row are very hard to identify in isolation and their locations can be critical for making taxonomic decisions. In such cases, it is advisable to place a bead of cement along the gap between teeth and bone, allow it to dry, and package the mandible separately (Fig. 63). A similar procedure can be employed when unfused epiphyses and diaphyses are encountered. If they fit together, they can be glued to prevent inadvertent

separation after removal and insure survival during transport. Alternatively, epiphysis/diaphysis pairs can be wrapped separately from other bones.

## Applying Consolidating Agents

Some bones can be lifted from the matrix and submerged in PVA solution. The strength of a bone should be tested before immersion because superficially strong specimens may crumble under the pressure of liquid infiltration. Use a dropper to squirt the PVA solution on a non-diagnostic portion. If this seriously softens the bone, it should be consolidated in situ.

*After Removal.* If the bone is dry, clean the surface by whisking gently with a soft brush. Then place the specimen on a rack in a waterproof coverable container or plastic bag and submerge it in the 10 percent PVA solution. Tightly cover the container or place a twist tie on the bag and allow the bone to soak until all bubbling ceases. Make sure that a label specifying the provenience is placed with the soaking bone. After soaking, lift the bone with the rack and allow it to drip dry. For final drying, place the bone on polyethylene sheeting, positioning it to minimize points of contact. Excess PVA and dirt can be removed with acetone.

If the bone is damp or wet when discovered, the initial procedure is slightly different. Cleaning should be done using a water spray and brushes. Place the cleaned specimen on the rack as before and submerge it in a 95 percent solution of acetone for at least one minute if damp or two minutes if wet. Then immerse it quickly in the 10 percent PVA solution and treat as described above.

*In Situ.* If the bone is too fragile to move, preliminary consolidation must be done in situ. First, carefully isolate the specimen on a low pedestal of dirt. This can be a serious problem if the matrix hardens after exposure. At Tepe Ganj Dareh in Iran, for example, the soil rapidly became much harder than the bones, making it necessary to remove the matrix very carefully with dental picks and leave a thin casing of dirt around the bones.

After isolating the bone, brush the surface delicately or use a gentle air spray (the enema bulb) to remove loose dust. If the specimen is dry, spray it with a diluted solution of PVA and acetone (increase the proportion of acetone about one-third) until it is thoroughly saturated. Cover loosely with polyethylene sheeting and erect a shade to retard evaporation during drying. After the fragment is dry, excavate the

**Fig. 63.** Sand box for supporting glued fragments during drying.

pedestal, invert it, and carry out the same procedure on the under side. If the specimen is wet, clean it first with a water spray and then spray it *thoroughly* with acetone. After waiting about two minutes, proceed with the application of PVA solution as above.

If the bone is still too weak to be moved safely, it can be covered with sheets of cheesecloth or gauze and painted with a thickened solution of PVA. The mesh structure provides additional support.

### Jacketing

If a whole skeleton or articulation is to be removed as a unit, it will be necessary to "jacket" it with plaster of Paris. The process is relatively simple, as is the equipment. A plastic bucket is convenient for mixing the plaster of Paris, since the dried residue is easily dislodged. Strips of cloth or old rags can be used, but those previously saturated in turpentine, cleaning fluids or other flammable and oily substances should be avoided. The thickness of the fabric may range from sheets to feed bags or terry-cloth towels, providing it is flexible. If rags vary in thickness, layering should begin with the thinnest, working outward to the thickest. If no cloth is available, newspaper can be substituted in emergencies, but it affords less protection than hardened fabric. A wooden stick is useful for mixing the plaster of Paris with water, but hands work equally well.

If it is necessary to provide a platform for the specimen to insure safe removal, industrial grade cardboard or (preferably) thin wood should be used. In some instances, it is desirable to place a narrow frame around the lower edge of the specimen and incorporate it into the plaster casing. We have done this when the articulation is small enough to be removed with an underlying block of earth, which acts as a platform. The width of the wooden slats composing the frame depends on the size of the specimen. They may be nailed together, but this is not vital and should not be done in place or near the specimen because of potential disturbance by the vibration of hammering. Three sides of the frame may be joined before it is placed around the block and the fourth side constructed of plaster. The frame acts as an additional stabilizer and shock absorber, particularly during shipment.

The specimen should be as clean and dry as possible before being jacketed. As much dirt should be removed from the surface as safety allows. Then brush it and let it dry until any dirt adhering or inside

no longer feels damp. If the exposed remains are in bright sun, they should be shaded while drying. If they were treated with preservative, the latter must be *absolutely dry*, not tacky to the touch.

The plaster of Paris must be mixed at the site and is best made in several batches, since it hardens quickly during standing. Put some of the powder into a bucket and begin adding water, mixing until you get a lump-free, thick liquid resembling thick pancake batter in consistency. Let it set a minute or two and then immerse the cloth strips, a few at a time, until they are saturated. Allow the excess to drip off before applying to the specimen.

Plaster-soaked cloth should not be in contact with the bone. The first layer should be a slightly padded, protective filter consisting of several layers of gauze, fine cheesecloth, thin fabric or newspaper. Apply the initial dry layer over a small area, somewhat larger than will be immediately covered with plaster-soaked cloth, add the latter and smooth it out. Repeat this procedure, overlapping adjacent cloths, until the desired surface is covered.

When the specimen is encased in its first plaster layer, let it dry for several minutes or until the plaster is putty-like. Then apply a second layer, again overlapping the edges of the rags, and allow to set. The number of layers depends on the condition of the specimen, the method of removal, the time available, and other variables. Enough layers should be applied to afford protection without creating excessive weight. Depending on thickness of the cloth, five to seven layers generally suffice. Once all the layers are in place, let them dry until the plaster is hard and has a hollow sound when tapped.

Often, the whole specimen need not (or cannot) be encased in situ. If one or more areas remain exposed, they should be allowed to dry several days in shade. Often, more dirt can be brushed away after additional drying. If the bottom can be freed easily from the matrix, lift the whole thing onto a temporary platform, such as a plywood board. Should this jeopardize the specimen, leave a supporting platform of earth attached.

At camp, let the specimen dry further in a safe place, away from direct sun if parts are still exposed. Some additional cleaning or removal of dirt may be possible prior to completing the jacketing. If part of the top is still open, begin there. When the layers are dry and you feel it is safe to turn the whole specimen over, do so. Clean away the dirt clinging to the bottom, let dry, plaster, etc. This last step is desirable

**Fig. 64.** Donkey skull inverted after the exposed side was encased in plaster for protection during transport.

only if the specimen is not large and heavy, and if much of the underlying dirt was dislodged in the field. If you have removed the specimen with an earth plat-form, turning it over introduces the risk that the weight of the dirt will crush the bones. To avoid this, hold or prop the specimen on its side until the bottom has been cleaned. You can then decide whether to

plaster the bottom or ship the specimen with three sides encased. This is a safe option if top and sides have been jacketed properly (Fig. 64).

The specimen is now ready for shipment in a strong box, preferably of wood because of its weight. It orientation should be clearly marked on the exterior.

# 6    Analysis of Single Bone Finds

## TAXONOMIC IDENTIFICATION

Bones are looked at as individual finds before being grouped into taxonomic categories based on the cultural-biological or biological-environmental questions being posed. For reasons of convenience and mutual intelligibility, identification employs zoological nomenclature.

### Degree of Precision

The first problem is to place zoological labels on the bones. The question immediately arises: How precise should be identifications be? The answer can determine whether the analysis will require months or years to complete. At Tell Jemmeh, for example, molluscan remains were sorted initially into general categories. Joseph Rosewater of the Smithsonian was able to classify samples into zoological families in a few days, and warned us that more specific identifications would require lots of effort. His words were prophetic. Additional work by several specialists has gradually refined his results, but a great deal of time has been involved. Meanwhile, the initial classification proved exceptionally useful because it showed where additional effort would be most informative.

### Guidelines

Several criteria can be employed to determine where to place taxonomic emphasis:

1. Rare species may be extremely important. For example, the Araucanian chicken, which lays blue eggs, has been cited as evidence for transpacific con-

tact. It is unlikely to occur in large quantities in western South American sites, yet its discovery in a firmly dated context would be invaluable.

2. All morphological distinctions between closely similar species are not equally pronounced. For instance, the contrast between the calcanei in sheep and goats is relatively strong, whereas that between the distal tibiae is not. If potential differences occur on fragments smaller than the critical size (the minimum dimensions reliably captured by a collecting technique), it will not be profitable to expend much energy attempting to identify them.

3. Several taxa may tell the same tale. For example, the season of occupation of a site may be documented by the presence of migratory species. The identification of a few duck species may establish this point without laborious examination of all avian bones.

4. General categories may be adequate for estimating diversity. A frequent concern is how many kinds of animals were killed and in what relative frequencies. It may be sufficient to establish that five taxa of birds of prey are present, leaving precisely which ones moot.

5. Certain skeletal elements provide several kinds of information; others only one. The pelvic girdles of sheep and goats exemplify this point. Not only can the two species be differentiated from fragments of these bones; age at death and sex can also be established.

6. One pass through a collection is never enough. As more material is handled, earlier distinctions can be refined or even overturned. For this reason, a research design should approximate in some rough way the order in which identifications are to be tackled. A flow-chart (Fig. 65) shows a solution to this problem.

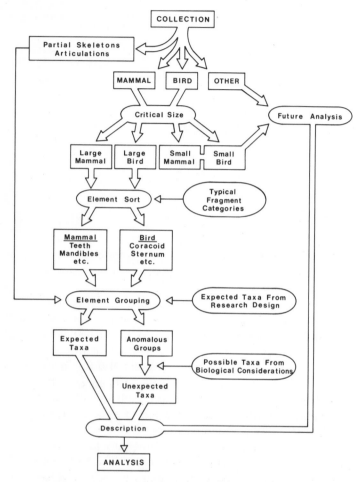

**Fig. 65.** Flow chart of the process of sorting in animal bone research. The double lines indicate the movement of material and the single lines the movement of information.

## AIDS TO IDENTIFICATION

Identification is most commonly made through visual comparison, though measurements and other analytic procedures are occasionally required. The principal kinds of sources of information are archeological collections, publications, field reference collections, and museum reference collections.

### Archeological Collections

Previously analyzed animal bone collections from sites in the same region are ideal for several reasons. First, the types of fragments are likely to be similar to those being studied. Second, the bones in the reference material are likely to be extremely similar morphologically to the taxa in the new sample. Uncertainties resulting from comparing a recent skeleton from a distant or unknown locale to ancient samples are circumvented. Third, the criteria of identification can be employed consistently. As new archeological material is identified, it should be interfiled with previously studied finds so that assignments can be reevaluated as sorting progresses.

Balanced against these advantages is the danger of consistent misidentification if the initial identification was wrong or the boundaries of the categories shift as the sorting procedes. Many animal bone archeologists like to retain the collections they have studied for future reference. This is a mixed blessing, however, since few have adequate facilities for storage and restudy.

### Publications

The explosion of interest in animal bone studies has led to the publication of a number of guides to archeological osteology. The classic work is Cornwall (1956), which contains an extensive key for making initial diagnoses of skeletal-element and taxonomic identifications.

The series by Olsen (1964, 1968, 1979, 1982) covers a wide range of taxa from North America. Other useful sources include Lawrence (1951), Gilbert, Martin, and Savage (1981), and Gilbert (1980). Identifying Old World collections, particularly those from Europe, is facilitated by consulting Schmid (1972), Pales and Lambert (1971), Lavocot (1966), and Gromova (1950). Bird remains are covered in five German publications (Bacher 1967, Ebersdobler 1968, Fick 1974, Kraft 1972, Woelfle 1967). Remains of domesticated animals are discussed by Sisson and Grossman (1953) and Boessneck, Müller, and Teichert (1964). Animal bone reports often include illustrations of exceptional or typical finds, which can be culled to produce an informal key.

Relevant data may be found in some paleontological and neontological reports, such as the publications of Tchernov (1968) on Pleistocene faunas of the eastern Mediterranean, but many discuss a limited number of species or focus on specific morphologies. One problem with the neontological literature is its emphasis on complete skeletal elements (such as skulls), rarely found intact archeologically, and on pelage or plumage, rarely found at all. Nevertheless, many field guides and faunal surveys include details of cranial and dental anatomy that can be useful. Some, such as the review of Chilean mammals by Reise (1973), provide a key for identification. Other relevant sources include the *Zoological Record, Biological Abstracts, Journal of Mammology, Wildlife Review and Abstracts, Bibliography of Fossil Vertebrates,* and *Mammal Species of the World.*

### Field Reference Collections

Some thought should be given to acquiring reference material for use in the field. One solution is to bring copies of publications. Another is to create a photographic file of the bones of expected species. Before our first field trip to South America, we spent several days in the Divisions of Mammals and Birds at the Smithsonian photographing species we anticipated would be common, based on a review of the literature. The prints proved invaluable in producing provisional taxonomic groupings.

A third solution is to create a comparative reference collection during fieldwork. Mark Druss obtained a hunting license and collected a small sample of avian and mammalian skeletons in northern Chile. These are now in the Museo Gustavo LePaige in San Pedro de Atacama, where they can be consulted by future researchers. Systematic collecting is, however, an intensive and time-consuming activity best left to those zoologists with the training to carry it out properly. Numerous legal codes restrict who can kill what animals when and the need for a field reference collections seems to us insufficient justification, by itself, for killing animals.

Several alternatives to direct collecting exist. One is purchase from local markets. While particularly useful in building a reference collection of fish skeletons, this is often a source of rodents and birds, as well as domestic species. Hunters may provide the postcranial elements of game animals, since they are primarily interested in the pelts and heads. Establishing a relationship with such individuals may also elicit information on local ethnozoological categories. Finally, when laws allow, road kills can be salvaged.

The question that a project director must ask is how this assembled pile of purchased, presented, and scavenged animal parts is going to be cleaned. Chaplin (1971) discusses procedures of skinning, gutting, dismembering, and cleaning whole carcasses the size of deer. A number of publications describe various solutions to skeletonizing smaller animals (e.g. Feduccia

1971, Gross and Gross 1966, F.C. Hill 1975, Ossian 1970, Somer and Anderson 1974).

We have used the following techniques with reasonable success. Larger specimens are cleaned of the majority of their soft tissue, taking care not to cut the bone. They are then taken some distance from the site and exposed to the elements under a screen firmly staked to the ground. Some of these layouts are ransacked by scavenging animals, but most are collectable. After exposure has eliminated the majority of the rotting tissue, the bones are either simmered in soapy water or (when conditions are hot enough to raise the temperature to about 110 degrees F) allowed to bake in the sun in a solution of enzyme detergent. Plain soap or enzyme detergent solutions are changed when they appear or smell unpleasant. For small animals, the soaking techniques are used without previous exposure.

These procedures do not produce museum-quality specimens. The surface of the bone may be leached of all its organic constituents, leaving a chalky and crumbly specimen, if the soaking continues too long. Further, the cartilaginous zone between epiphysis and diaphysis in immature specimens is destroyed and the bone parts separate. If specimens are needed for field identification, however, the result is satisfactory.

Sorting bone involves the examination, reexamination, and subdivison of categories. There are many points at which some of the material is segregated and stored (or even discarded) on the assumption that further study is unlikely to be rewarding. In situations where a number of similar-sized species are present, long-bone fragments lacking articular ends and vertebral scraps will be referrable only to general categories, such as sheep/goat, camelid, or medium artiodactyl.

Cleaning long bones and partial carcasses of major food animals eaten during fieldwork is highly recommended when the same taxa occur in the site. Such table scraps provide rough and ready reference material that may permit assigning splinters and chips to skeletal areas, thereby documenting the process of reduction of the carcass.

### Museum Reference Collections

All fine identifications of archeological animal bone fragments require access to museum reference collections. How much effort should be put into this procedure depends on the research design. Just because a bone fragment can be identified does not mean that it has to be done immediately.

For those researchers who do not have ready access to museum reference collections, several comments are in order. It is rarely feasible to transport large samples of fragmentary remains to museums. The simplest procedure is to divide the problematic specimens into taxonomic groups, select representative examples from the various skeletal-element categories that require identification, and make several trips. Common courtesy demands that arrangements be made in advance with the curator or collection manager in charge of the reference material. An alternative approach is to try to borrow specimens. In processing the Tell Jemmeh collection, we had to check the possibility that the addax (Addax nasomaculatus) was present. Fortunately, the Field Museum of Natural History in Chicago was able to arrange a short-term loan of one of their skeletons.

Since museum reference collections are established primarily to meet the needs of zoologists, they may be organized in ways that make their use by animal bone archeologists laborious. Generally, organization is taxonomic, which can mean that considerable distance separates the storage locations of specimens needed for comparison. Also, skins and skulls may be stored separately from post-cranial elements. In such cases, it is generally profitable to identify dental and cranial fragments first. Not only are the details of these areas of morphology better documented, but it is likely that a much broader range of forms will be represented than among post-cranial elements.

Caution should be exercised in using museum material that has old or fragmentary documentation. Taxonomy is an ongoing scientific enterprise and collection-management staffs can seldom find time to update labeling to match the latest revision. The problem is illustrated by sheep (Ovis), which have been studied by a number of authors since 1873 (Valdez 1982:11, Table 3). The classifications range between recognizing 17 species and no subspecies to recognizing 1 species and 37 subspecies, with numerous intermediate alternatives. In such instances, the animal bone archeologist can be confronted with a maze of labels, particularly if the reference collection has been built over a period of years. It is important to come equipped with lists of synonyms and discarded names to cope with this situation. The final report should show how the taxa in the reference collection correlate with the classification employed in the analysis, whenever there are conflicts.

Finally, the animal bone archeologist should keep in mind that animals from zoos make up a significant part of museum collections. Not only is the provenience in the wild usually unknown, if indeed the animal ever was wild, but zoo animals suffer a variety of afflictions. Some of these leave marks on the skeleton, so care should be taken when using such samples for comparison. The identifying numbers of all skeletons used should be provided in the final report.

Some museums have an inordinately valuable collection called a synoptic series, in which the bones are grouped by skeletal parts rather than whole animals. Each series contains one representative of the same bone (such as the femur) from a number of major taxonomic categories. Synoptic series can be used to reduce rapidly the range of possibilities for an unidentified fragment. Once the family has been identified, the zoogeographic literature can be consulted to select the most likely forms within that family. Individuals of those species can be located in the general collection and compared.

## DESCRIBING ANIMAL BONE FINDS

The specific approach to describing a bone fragment depends on the analytic categories formulated in the research design and the methods employed for handling the data. Nevertheless, there is a core of information common to all analyses that we will briefly outline.

### Species

It may seem obvious that a taxonomic assignment is a necessary part of an animal bone description. Ideally, ascriptions are made on the basis of the similarity in morphological landmarks between the archeological find and a reference specimen. In practice, however, many identifications involving choices among similar forms are influenced by the context. In many archeological situations, the historical or environmental circumstances severely limit the taxa likely to be represented within some biological grouping. In others, experience in analyzing collections of the same culture or period indicates that certain taxa are overwhelmingly common, whereas closely related forms are not likely to be present. For example, many

0    1    2    3 cm

**Fig. 66.** Y-shaped spinous processes of bovid thoracic vertebrae, diagnostic of the presence of humped or zebu cattle in Levantine archeological deposits.

descriptions of Near Eastern collections employ the category *"Ovis/Capra"* for large numbers of fragments, most of which are from domesticated sheep or goats or, perhaps, their wild ancestors. It is recognized that ibex, tur, barbary sheep, tahr, and markhor may also occur, but most types of fragments do not permit distinguishing these rare species. Thus, the *Ovis/Capra* category is the minimum group suitable for analytic purposes.

This situation makes it essential that taxonomic labels be accompanied by a notation describing the method of identification. This should explain how the range of potential species was reduced, if it was, and what kind of errors may exist. Taxonomic labels should be arranged hierarchically, and higher-level terms should specify the lower taxa included. Zoological nomenclature should be employed, particularly at lower levels, and reference to the zoological literature should be included where taxonomic disagreement exists.

For many identifications, it is important to specify the morphological criteria employed. When a character is unmistakable, reference to the specimen used for comparison is sufficient (Fig. 66). In knotty problems, such as distinguishing sheep from goats or the various forms of camelids from one another, it is not. In these cases, the features deemed diagnostic must be specified. In separating sheep and goat scapulae, for example, the shape of the glenoid fossa, the form of the posterior border of the neck, the size of the tuber scapulae, and the position and angle of the spinous process are all useful in one degree or another. In recording, each sample should be evaluated

separately as sheep-like or goat-like for each criterion, rather than given a summary estimation.

## Element

The second requisite of an osteological description is specifying the skeletal element. This information has two components. One is identification of the specific bone of which the fragment is a part (such as right humerus, left radius, etc.). It may not be always possible to determine the exact skeletal location. The first phalanges of the fore and hind feet of sheep, for example, are nearly impossible to segregate with certainty where males and females of different ages are present. In these cases, which include such other body parts as ribs and vertebrae, the range of possibilities should be specified.

The second component is description of the part of the bone recovered. At a minimum, the morphological zone of each fragment should be recorded. The more the effort that is expended, the less the difficulty that will be encountered during the statistical manipulations of bone counts required in the later phases of analysis.

Fragmentation of many bones, particularly among large animals, is structured by the locations of points of weakness. Long bones frequently are reduced to three types of finds: (1) fragments of the proximal end, (2) fragments of the distal end, and (3) fragments of the shaft (Fig. 24). Each type is characterized by the presence or absence of the appropriate epiphysis or metaphysis. Vertebrae tend to be broken into centrum fragments, epiphyseal discs, transverse processes, and spinous processes. Ribs are often divisible into proximal segments (those with articular surfaces) and distal fragments (those consisting only of the blade).

Mandibular and dental fragments are usually difficult to categorize compactly. Large fragments of teeth are generally assignable to their position in the dental arcade, but small fragments of the cheek teeth of herbivores are frequently indeterminate. Often, all that can be said is that the fragment belonged to an upper or a lower tooth. Most mandibular fragments can be placed into one of three categories: (1) parts of the ascending ramus, (2) parts of the bony structure encasing the cheek teeth, and (3) parts of the symphysis region holding the incisors.

Cranial fragments are notoriously difficult to identify. Usually, all that can be specified is the whole bone of which the fragment is a part. The fact that the

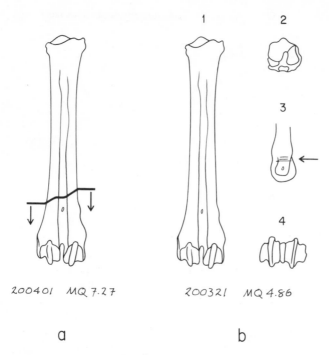

200401  MQ 7.27          200321  MQ 4.86

a                              b

**Fig. 67.** Stencils used to record preserved portions of bones and locations of cut marks. **a,** Complete goat metatarsal, dorsal surface; arrows indicate the portion preserved. **b,** Four views of the metatarsal; **1.** dorsal surface; **2.** proximal surface; **3.** distal end, medial or lateral surface, showing cut marks; **4.** distal surface. The locus number of the specimen is provided on each stencil.

sutures fuse as the animal matures introduces the complication that many fragments may incorporate parts of more than one bone, a condition that should be indicated when observed.

Bones of the shoulder and pelvic girdles are oriented around cup-like structures, the glenoid fossa and the acetabulum. For many species, notably herd animals, the presence or absence of these structures can be used to define categories of fragments.

More time consuming, but more accurate, is to make a visual record of the fragments in each category (Watson 1979). For example, we have made stencils of many of the bones of common species in our collections and indicated on these illustrations the particular portion of the bone present (Fig. 67). This procedure can reveal if some portion of a bone is regularly missing. Among mature long bones, for instance, a proximal or distal portion will include part of the shaft. Comparing the portion of the shaft represented by these fragments with that assigned to the shaft category will show whether parts of the bone are not being recognized or were destroyed during the reduction of the carcass, perhaps by the gnawing of scavengers.

## Maturity

Identification of osteological maturity is the first step in characterizing the age at death of the animal

represented because bones fuse according to a species-specific schedule (Todd and Todd 1938). Although the biological research necessary to link each fusion process with chronological age is spotty, the timing of events is sufficiently well documented for some animals to be used for estimating the pattern of mortality. Bogan and Robinson (1978:59–65) offer a useful bibliography for many species encountered in North American collections, and B. Gilbert (1980) has summarized the data for a number of animals. The primary sources for Old World collections containing wild and domesticated species have traditionally been Habermehl (1961), Schmid (1972), and Silver (1969). Wilson, Grigson, and Payne (1982) have published a more recent survey of the problem, focussing on domesticates. For the mammals of Latin America, the literature is sparse except for camelids (Wing 1972, J. Kent 1982).

Several kinds of criteria are useful for estimating patterns of mortality. Each has weaknesses and we urge the reader to consult the primary literature before elaborating interpretations.

**Epiphysis-diaphysis Fusion.** Although this process is gradual, it can be divided into two periods: either the epiphysis is firmly joined to the diaphysis or it is not. Looking at the process in this dichotomous way has certain benefits, the most important being consistent classification. Bones can be scored as fused or unfused by attempting to separate them *gently.* Because this distinction is clear, it is the only characterization of maturity in post-cranials that we recommend for field description. More precise subdivision of the process should await the sorting of the collection, when a number of examples of the pattern of fusion can be examined and consistent categories established.

Consistency in application has to be balanced against difficulties in interpretation (Watson 1978). Fusion requires several months to accomplish. As a result, fused and unfused examples may be assigned overlapping ages — i.e., a fused specimen may be said to be 18 months of age or older, whereas an unfused example may be tagged 24 months of age or younger. To grapple with this problem and permit more precise estimates of age at death, some workers have subdivided the fusion process. The following scheme employs five stages.

A.   Small fragile-appearing bones with unfused epiphyses and poorly defined metaphyseal areas; such specimens represent fetal, neonatal or very juvenile individuals.

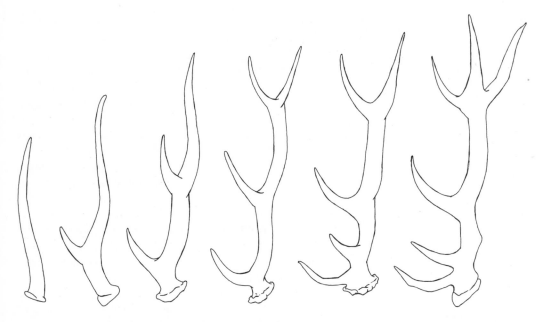

**Fig. 68.** Annual growth in deer antlers. Each replacement is larger and more complex, providing a basis for estimating age at death.

B.  Unfused bones of nearly mature proportions, the metaphyseal zones of which have
sharply defined topographies; depending on
the bone, these characterize juvenile or sub-
adult individuals.
C.  Partly fused bones where some portion of
the metaphysis has ossified.
D.  Completely fused bones where the metaphysis remains visible as a line.
E.  Completely fused bones where the metaphysis is obliterated.

We must caution that these stages are relative. Among
improved breeds of domestic stock raised under ideal
conditions, they may match actual chronology fairly
closely. In all other situations, however, the pace of
fusion is governed by numerous external factors.
Consequently, specimens graded B, C, or D could
easily derive from animals of identical ages, some of
which were well fed, some starved, and a few cas-
trated.

The stage of fusion must be specified in the description. Though this may seem obvious, there are
numerous published examples where a collection is
described as containing some proportion of "unfused" elements. This observation is nearly useless.

***Antler and Horn Development.*** The antlers of
deer increase in size and complexity with each yearly
replacement (Fig. 68). The horns of members of the
sheep and goat family grow throughout life. Age can
be estimated from the number of rings on the horn,
which are laid down annually in many cases (Schaller
1977), and from the size of the horn core and the cavity
within it (Fig. 69; Hatting 1975).

Detailed work on the horns of cattle has shown
that the surface of the core changes in texture and appearance as aging proceeds (Armitage and Clutton-
Brock 1976). Patterns in the distribution of textures
are associated with age stages. The six stages of surface change proposed by Armitage (1982:38 and Fig.
1) have the following characteristics:

1.  Soft spongy bone, light in weight. Many large channels formed by nutrient foramina. Surface pitted by numerous minute pores. Stage of actively growing bone.

2.  Soft porous bone. Channels leading into nutrient
foramina are less conspicuous than in Stage 1. Numerous
minute pores present. Stage of actively growing bone.

3.  Porous bone. Nutrient foramina appear mostly as
large spherical or elliptical pits which are arranged closer
together than in Stage 2. Numerous minute pores present.
Stage of growing bone.

4.  Bone becoming more compact but surface still feels
rough to the touch. Appearance of nutrient foramina as in
Stage 3, but more scattered. Many minute pores present.
Stage of growing bone.

5.  Compact bone with scattered nutrient foramina.

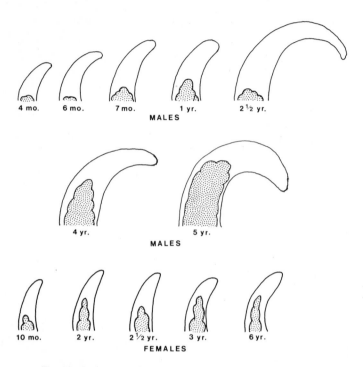

**Fig. 69.** Developmental sequence in horn cores of male and female sheep, useful for estimating age at death (after Hatting 1975).

Only very few minute pores present. Stage in which growth of bone is virtually completed.

6. Smooth, compact bone. Very few nutrient foramina and minute pores are present. Stage of senescent bone.

**Tooth Eruption.** The sequence of dental eruption is more or less well known for many mammals; consequently, the age of mortality can be estimated from the state of eruption and wear of each tooth. The following simple classification, worked out by Eubank, Phillipson, Whitehouse, and Higgs (1964), is applicable to a wide range of animals:

C    The tooth has not broken through the mandibular bone, but a small hole is present in the dorsal surface.

V    The tooth is visible in its crypt, but has not emerged above the dorsal margin of the bone.

E    The tooth has emerged above the bone.

1/2  The tooth is half erupted.

U    The tooth is at full height, but the cusps are unworn.

W    The cusps are beginning to show wear.

The same publications recommended for the

chronologies of epiphyseal union can be consulted for schedules of tooth eruption.

Although tooth eruption is a fine measure of age, it applies mainly to juveniles and sub-adults. Exceptions include elephants, kangaroos, and manatees, most of whose cheek teeth emerge from the posterior portion of the mandible as the anterior teeth are worn away, and species with incisors that are rootless and continue growing throughout life.

**Tooth Wear.** Particularly for the study of domestic species, eruption is an inadequate criterion since it is the mortality of the older age classes that informs about the management they received. Therefore, considerable attention has been directed toward tooth wear in some of the barnyard species. These investigations reveal distinctive patterns of enamel and dentine wear that can be used to estimate relative age. The categories developed by Grant (1975, 1978, 1982) for sheep/goat, cattle, and pig are shown (Fig. 70). Payne (1973) and Deniz and Payne (1982) have refined the wear sequence for sheep and goats. Using animals managed by Anatolian pastoralists for their data base, they have been able to assign age ranges to their stages and produce mortality estimates for single teeth and for mandibles. Crabtree (1982) has extended the method to the upper cheek dentition of these species. Similar wear sequences have been documented for horse incisors (Sisson and Grossman 1953) and camel teeth (Rabagliati 1924). Wheeler (1984) has published on New World camelids. Further examples can be found in the literature on game management.

**Dentine Deposition.** Although the methods are too elaborate for detailed description, this technique needs to be mentioned because it provides narrow estimates for age at death and even season of death, when specimens can be sacrificed for the analysis and time and money can be devoted (Bourque, Morris, and Spiess 1978, Higham 1969). It involves counting the annually deposited layers of dentine or cementum on the roots and in the secondary dentine of mammal teeth (Klevezal and Kleinberg 1969). These layers are reminiscent of tree rings and, after proper sectioning and preparation, appear as dark or light bands. Broad or "summer" bands contain large numbers of active cells called cementocytes, intermixed with calcium salts. Narrow or "winter" bands consist almost entirely of the latter material (Stallibrass 1982). A number of factors, including diet, nutrition, sexual activity, and environment, combine in complex and poorly understood ways to create the layers.

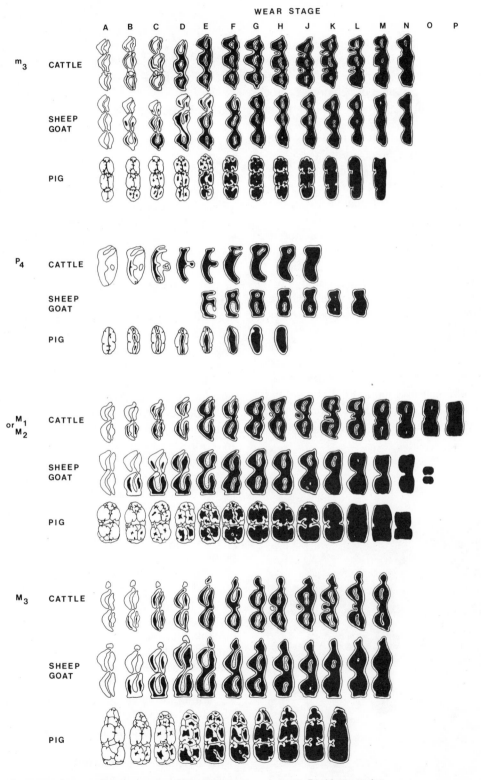

**Fig. 70.** Stages of tooth wear in cattle, sheep/goat, and pig. **m,** Deciduous molar.
**M,** Permanent molar. **P,** Premolar (after Grant 1982).

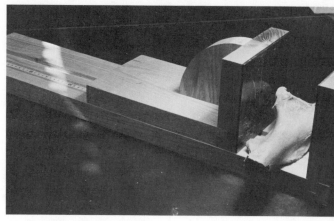

**Fig. 72.** Measuring box in use.

## Osteometry

***General Considerations.*** Although measurements contribute to a host of issues important to archeological interpretation, bones are difficult to measure and a vast number of possible dimensions can be recorded. The repeatability of many measurement procedures is suspect, making the reliability of published data uncertain, particularly when the landmarks and techniques are not precisely described. A basic text in zoology recommends strongly that measurements be taken more than once to establish the investigator's consistency of performance (Simpson, Roe, and Lewontin 1960). We echo that exhortation and further suggest that measurements be taken during intensive osteometric sessions rather than sporadically throughout the process of sorting and recording.

Within the field of animal bone archeology, two basic philosophies guide when and what to measure. One advocates making as complete an osteometric documentation as possible. Historically, this position has been supported by those who come to animal bone collections with a zoological perspective or who are interested in the animal's response to human control. The other argues that measurements should be limited to those for which a link can be demonstrated with some specific question. This disagreement can be re-

**Fig. 71.** Dial calipers in use. These are more suitable for laboratory than field measurement.

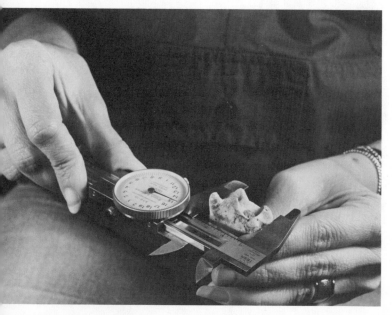

solved by acknowledging both positions to be wrong. There is no way that all dimensions can be recorded, particularly since new relationships between sizes and zoological or cultural categories are constantly being discovered; equally, it is irresponsible to ignore the pattern of reporting in the particular subfield to which one contributes.

Until recently, most animal bone studies focussed on a site or region. Internal variability in the sample was the primary concern. Between-site syntheses were constructed at an abstract level that seldom made direct reference to the bones. Now, the focus has shifted to problems, such as interpretation of bison remains from the North American plains, animal husbandry in Britain and Europe, and domestication in southwest Asia. The analytic phase of such research cuts across many sites, making comparability in reporting essential.

A number of publications are of great assistance in selecting appropriate measurements. The monumental classic on mammals is by Duerst (1930). For purposes of animal bone archeology, German workers have streamlined his daunting list of measurement possibilities and established the confidence that can be placed on the accuracy of each dimension. The results, published by Von den Dreisch (1976), form a useful starting point for compiling a list of routine measurements, particularly for domestic animals and their ancestors. Wing (1972) provides diagrams of possible measurements for South American camelids. For birds, Howard (1929) has published suggestions, which are incorporated in the manual by Gilbert, Martin, and Savage (1981).

Although most measurements are made in the laboratory (Fig. 71), there are circumstances where they must be done in the field. For this reason, it is wise to have available a large pair of non-dial calipers (with divisions in the metric system), a measuring box (Fig. 72), and a manual for reference. All fragile specimens, particularly candidates for consolidation, should be measured prior to treatment. All complete bones should have their maximum dimensions recorded prior to packing and transport because overall length is often the most telling variable. A bone measured in the field that subsequently breaks may not have to be laboriously reconstructed.

Measurements require documentation of three kinds. First, the landmarks used must be precisely specified. Reference to a published example or a simple drawing of what was done will suffice. Second, the procedure of measurement must be described. How many independent attempts were made? What kind of equipment was used? Third, the condition of the specimen should be noted. Since heat can dramatically alter the size and shape of bones, evidence of burning or baking should be recorded (Coy 1975, Fig. 1).

***Uses of Measurements.*** Measurements can be critical for taxonomic decisions. For example, sheep and goat calcanei can be distinguished by the length of the articular facet relative to the overall length of the lateral process (Boessneck 1970). Bactrian camels can be separated from dromedaries on the basis of the proportions of the depth and width of the distal metapodials (Wapnish 1984). A battery of measurements is required to separate the various forms of the genus *Equus* (Eisenmann 1980, Groves and Willoughby 1981). Generally speaking, the closer the taxonomic relationship, the greater the probability that measurements rather than morphological features will provide the basis for differentiation.

Measurements can be used to estimate the size of the whole animal represented by the specimen at hand. In Europe, much effort has been devoted to calculating the height at the withers of domestic stock from various osteological dimensions (Zalkin 1960, 1961). These data are valuable for detecting the presence of breeds or varieties within a species and for comparing ancient stock with modern counterparts.

Extensive experimentation has produced algorithms that allow carcass size to be predicted from osteometric data (Wing and Brown 1979; Reitz and Honerkamp 1983, Reitz and Cordier 1982). While work of this sort has been painstaking and extensive, the algorithms should be applied with considerable caution in archeological settings far removed from the context of the modern data used to create the equations.

Because many species are dimorphic, it is possible to use bone dimensions to estimate sex. The goat bones from Near Eastern Neolithic sites illustrate this point. Measurements taken on a long series of distal humeri cluster in two groups that correlate with the values in a series of modern goat skeletons of known sex. Interpretation is complicated by the possibility that castrates are incorporated in the archeological sample; depending on the animal's age when the procedure is done, neutering can have variable effects on growth and development of the skeleton. Some dimensions may be intermediate between male and female, whereas others may exceed the male mean. Higham (1969) has resolved this problem in his study of European cattle remains.

Measurements can also be used to estimate age. Ducos (1968) has linked an index based on crown height and basal thickness in cattle molars to age (Fig. 73). Levine (1982) has produced similar curves for equid remains (Fig. 74).

Finally, the wild or domestic status of a specimen may be inferred from its size. Zeuner (1963) uses the increase in femur length of the domestic chicken as such an indicator. More commonly, the change in status is correlated with a decrease in size. Wild and domestic pigs can be distinguished by differences in the length of the molars. It is important to remember that criteria of this kind usually overlap considerably.

**Fig. 73.** Relationship between age and size in cattle molars. The index is the ratio between crown height and basal thickness for each molar (after Ducos 1968).

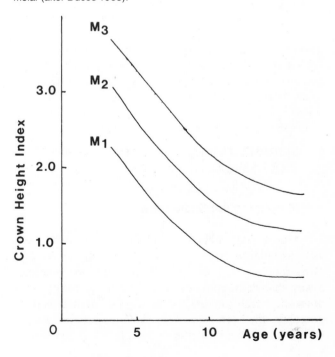

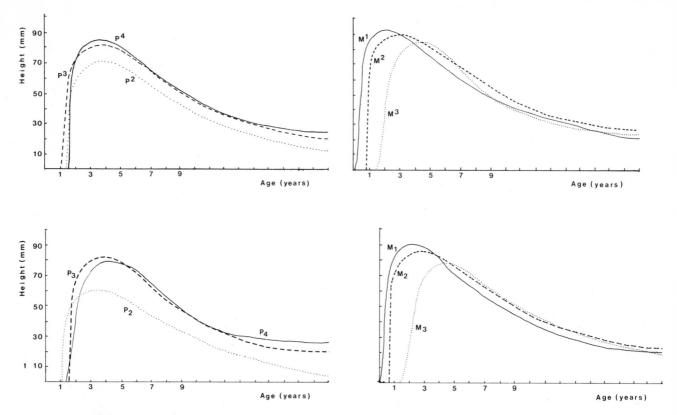

**Fig. 74.** Relationship between age and size in equid teeth. **p,** Deciduous premolar. **P,** Permanent premolar. **m,** Deciduous molar. **M,** Permanent molar (after Levine 1982).

In the case of the pig, a series of threshold values has been developed for southwest Asia and Europe. Any specimen above one threshold is wild and any specimen below another is domestic. These two thresholds are separated by a "gray area" where positive determination for a single specimen is impossible (Boessneck, Müller, and Teichert 1963).

## MORPHOLOGICAL, HISTOLOGICAL, AND BIOCHEMICAL ATTRIBUTES

### Morphological Characters

Morphology may be evaluated qualitatively as well as quantitatively. Zeuner (1955) classified the cross sections of horn cores of contemporary goats in a way that documents evolution from the wild to the domestic condition. As the process of domestication proceeds, the horn core changes from a scimitar shape with a quadrangular cross section to a twisted shape with a medially flattened or teardrop cross section. Although the range of variation among wild populations needs refinement, these morphological categories have been applied to archeological specimens (Fig. 75).

Morphological characters may identify breeds, races, and strains within species. A well known example is Grigson's (1974, 1975, 1976, 1978a) classification of cattle crania. Jourdan (1976) has distinguished three races among pig remains of late Roman and early Christian date excavated from sites in northern France on the basis of the degree of anterior-posterior compression of the face and skull (Fig. 76).

How an animal was used may be assessed from qualitative morphological criteria. Since bone is in a constant state of remodelling, stress gradually modifies the relative position and shape of bony structures. The distal radii of cattle are affected by use for traction; in particular, the two anterior facets on the distal articular surface are shifted to an even more anterior position (Ghetie and Mateesco 1977).

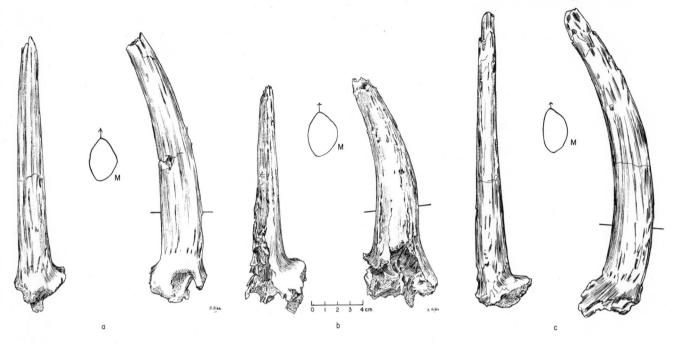

**Fig. 75.** Three goat horn cores from Tepe Ganj Dareh exhibiting morphology intermediate between wild and domestic forms.

## Histological Studies

Microscopic examination may provide diagnostic attributes. Petrographic thin sections of the articular surfaces of weight-bearing bones of wild and domestic sheep, goats, cattle, and camelids reveal strong differences in internal architecture, both in the shape and organization of trabeculae and the patterns of deposition of hydroxy-apatite crystals (Drew, Perkins, and Daly 1971; Pollard and Drew 1975; Hecker 1975). These conclusions are controversial (e.g., Watson 1975; Zeder 1978), but the principle that the activity and diet of an animal should be reflected in the mi-

crostructure of its bony architecture seems sound and worthy of further investigation.

Medullary bone is an important osteological attribute among birds (Driver 1982). This osseous material, granular in appearance, is deposited in the normally hollow shafts of female birds in the weeks just prior to egg-laying, apparently as an extra supply of calcium for shell making. The presence of medullary bone can thus be used as an indicator of sex as well as season of mortality. The long bones of species that deposit medullary bone should be examined either by careful drilling into the cavity or by controlled fracture (after pertinent measurements have been recorded).

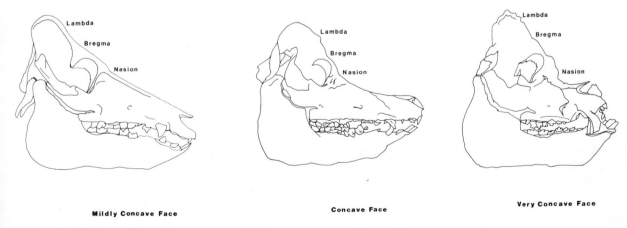

**Fig. 76.** Varieties of facial morphology differentiating three races of pigs in sites of the late Roman and early Christian periods in northern France (after Jourdan 1976).

## Biochemical Attributes

Biochemical attributes are useful sources of culturally relevant information. For instance, strontium levels in animal bone and dental enamel reflect the relative quantities of meat and plants in the diet. The strontium proportion also distinguishes between predominantly browsing and predominantly grazing herbivores. Potentially, this distinction can be used to infer the characteristics of the ancient pasturages cropped by different groups of animals (Parker and Toots 1980).

The ratio of the stable carbon isotopes, 12C and 13C, can be used to characterize ancient plant environments. The two main tracks of photosynthesis, C3 and C4, are associated with different types of grasses, the latter being most common among plants of hot arid lands. These tracks are, in turn, associated with different rates of uptake of the two isotopes in living tissue, providing a means of detecting aspects of diet not directly observable archeologically (Burleigh and Brothwell 1978).

## PATHOLOGY AND TRAUMA

The study of pathology and trauma has been an appendix of even appendix-style animal bone archeology for several reasons. First, bone pathologies are extremely difficult to link positively with specific diseases and developmental disorders. Second, since much of the impetus for the study of abnormal features has come from researchers interested in the history of disease, each case has been treated for its own intrinsic interest. Third, many diseases have no impact on the skeletal system or affect it too late in the course of the affliction to leave clear evidence. Fourth, the rates at which disease affects wild and incipiently maintained animals are poorly known. Some effort has been made to develop average rates empirically. For instance, Baker and Brothwell (1980:91) report that summing the information from a diverse spectrum of British sites showed premortem fracture to occur in about 0.043 percent of the specimens. Samples that deviate widely from this value deserve investigation.

## Cultural Implications

The kinds and frequencies of abnormalities can shed light on cultural behavior. Many wild animals die from disease, accident, and starvation, and human hunters who scavenged would routinely accumulate a larger than normal proportion of pathological and battered animals. The importance of scavenging probably has been underestimated in reconstructing ancient societies (Shipman 1984).

In pastoral societies, many animals are selected for slaughter because of infirmity. Major causes include (1) overcrowding, which increases the likelihood of disease transmission and the frequency and intensity of violent behavior; (2) overgrazing, which can lead to malnutrition as the quality of forage declines and the pasturage becomes contaminated with parasites; (3) poorly diversified diet, which can produce developmental disorders; (4) selective breeding, which can promote deleterious as well as desirable attributes. The very high mortality among fetal and newborn camelids among archeological remains from Telarmachay, Peru has been attributed to overcrowding, which apparently increased the rate of enterotoxemia (a disease resulting from absorption of a toxin from the intestine; Wheeler 1984).

Awareness among people of the ancient Middle East of the economic effects of pathology and trauma is attested by passages in the Code of Hammurapi (Meek 1969: 176–7):

224: If a veterinary surgeon performed a major operation on either an ox or an ass and has saved (its) life, the owner of the ox or ass shall give to the surgeon one-sixth (shekel) of silver as his fee.

225: If he performed a major operation on an ox or an ass and has caused (its) death, he shall give to the owner of the ox or ass one-fourth its value.

267: If the shepherd was careless and has let lameness develop in the fold, the shepherd shall make good in cattle and sheep the loss through the lameness which he let develop in the fold and give (them) to their owner.

Jewish dietary laws require inspection of carcasses for abnormalities that render the meat inedible. While much of the emphasis is on the lungs, attention is also directed toward osteological abnormalities, such as (1) major defect in the cranium; in some cases holes in the bone; (2) absence of the upper jaw; (3) multiple fractures of the ribs, fractures in certain places in the extremities, and defects in the tendon junction at the tarsal joint; and (4) dislocation in the socket of the femur head (Munk, Munk, and Levinger 1976:39–40). These attributes crosscut the three main pathways leading to osteological abnormality — developmental disorder, disease, and trauma. This is extremely important because it implies that even when the causal agent cannot be specified, identifying abnormality may have analytical significance.

## Identification

Diagnosis of skeletal pathologies is unlikely to be accurate without the advice of a veterinary pathologist. Animal bone archeologists must be able to recognize and describe abnormalities so that specimens can be directed to the appropriate specialist. The immediate goal of this procedure, however, is to assess the frequency of diseased, maldeveloped, and traumatized bones in a sample. The best way to insure that abnormalities are noted is by comparing the specimens in each category of bone.

The following information will permit preliminary identification of the pattern of morphological deformation in a collection:
1. What is the precise location of the abnormality?
2. Is the anomaly a deposition, an erosion, or both?
3. What is the surface texture of the anomaly?
4. Are any other bones involved?

## Dental Malformations

Two kinds of dental malformations are particularly common: (1) one or more teeth are missing or (2) the pattern of wear is unusual. In the first case, evidence should be sought to establish whether the missing teeth were lost and the sockets are closed by osseous growth. If there is no such evidence, the malformation may be genetic. In most cases, loss results from accident or gum disease. Disease affecting the root is sometimes detectable by a "feathery" quality in the root area. Tooth loss in either upper or lower jaw will usually lead to malocclusion. In herbivores, whose teeth are greatly reduced in height through wear, this can produce dramatic distortions in shape (Fig. 77).

## Bone Disease

Also commonly seen in archeological material is evidence of disease of the joints. This may be limited to slight bone projections at the articular margins (not surfaces) and adjoining areas. Sometimes the bony projections are so large as to fuse adjacent bones. In

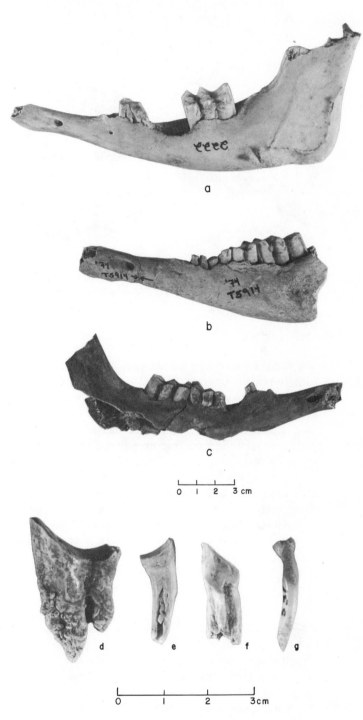

**Fig. 77.** Malformations in sheep/goat teeth from Tell Jemmeh. **a,** Missing teeth. **b–g,** Irregular teeth.

other cases, there is unusual wear at the articular surface (Fig. 78). This often appears as a faceted and burnished area, which might be misidentified as caused by use as a tool.

Bone shafts should be examined to determine if

**Fig. 78.** Arthritic modifications on the articular surfaces of cattle phalanges. Evidence of disease is provided by the presence of exostoses and polishing.

insufficient time to begin bone remodeling) from those that caused death or occurred thereafter.

3. Specimens that are either abnormally bowed or thickened and pitted or noticeably light in weight should be regarded as possible instances of metabolic and nutritional disorders.

4. Features ranging from a localized extra layer of bone to a large swelling with a roughened, pitted surface imply an inflammatory process.

5. Joint disorders are likely to be restricted to the joint area. The joint may show coarse, pitted, destructive changes resulting from infection or have a smoother, osteoporotic, pitted, and "worn" appearance. In old adults, severe joint wear is likely to be manifested by "lipping" or even eburnation of the margins, especially on long bones and vertebrae.

6. Tumors will destroy bone, produce new bone,

any seem swollen or if the exterior surface seems unusually porous or rough (Fig. 79). This last condition can be mimicked by post-mortem factors, but these are usually not limited to a small portion of the surface. Certain diseases can reduce the thickness of the diaphysis wall. Serious fractures that have healed can often be recognized by an overall shortening of the bone or an area where the shaft seems to overlap itself. Less serious fractures may only produce a thickening in the area of the break that is difficult to recognize without X-ray.

### Criteria for Diagnosis

The following criteria and the conditions they reflect are adapted from Baker and Brothwell (1980:197–202). Because numerous variables can affect the identification, the reader is again cautioned to seek the advice of a pathologist (Fig. 80).

1. Deviation in shape and size from morphological norms may indicate a congenital defect. Abnormally small bones could be evidence of a disorder of cartilage growth, resulting in dwarfism. Other signs of early developmental disorders include fused adjacent digits, extra digits, poorly developed acetabula, wedged vertebral bodies, and pronounced malocclusion.

2. Although healed fractures can take odd shapes, they are usually easy to recognize, particularly using X-rays. It is often impossible to differentiate those that occurred just prior to death (allowing

**Fig. 79.** Pathological alterations of the diaphysis portion of herbivore bones. **a,** Long-bone shaft with a spongy, rough-looking area. **b,** Rib fragment with a swollen zone pierced by many tiny holes.

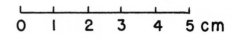

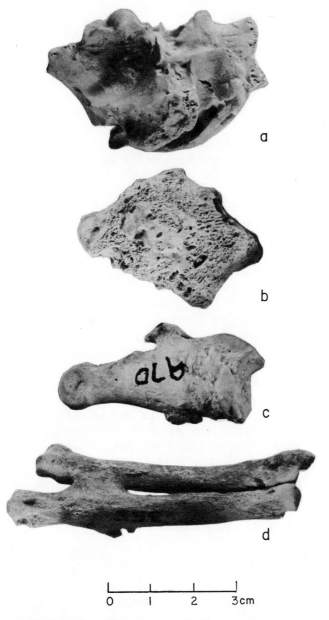

**Fig. 80.** Bones from Tell Jemmeh modified by disease. **a,** Sheep/goat calcaneus. **b,** Cattle phalanx 1. **c,** Sheep/goat phalanx 1. **d,** Fused dog metapodials.

or combine the two processes. In the case of destructive tumors, there is likely to be a marginal area of reaction but no great extension along the bone. When large amounts of new bone are formed, these are likely to possess a spicular or spongy structure distinct from fracture callus.

7. Oral disease may exhibit all the characteristics listed above, as well as such distinct features as peri-dontal recession of the alveolar bone, enamel hypoplasia, and dental caries.

8. Exotic conditions not readily assigned to a general category may occur. It is also possible that conditions and diseases no longer seen may be represented.

## POST-MORTEM MODIFICATIONS

The thorniest area of descriptive work in animal bone archeology is identifying and interpreting post-mortem changes. Habitation sites contain much formal variability usually attributed to human activity, but which can equally or more accurately be referred to the behavior of non-human scavengers and predators. As Binford (1981) has pointed out, we have tended to view bone with the same eyes that we study stone. Since lithics have generally acquired their modifications through human hands, the same logic is applied to breakage and scarification of bones. But humans are not the only animals interested in bones. Large and small carnivores, rodents such as porcupines, and an ever-growing list of other taxa are known to manipulate bones routinely. Moreover, a host of other natural processes act on bone accumulations.

If part of the problem is recognizing multiple causality in the modifications of bones from archeological sites, another is finding reliable rules for inferring cause from effect. Efforts have been made to remedy this situation by observing human and non-human modifiers in action and attempting to generate behaviorally reasonable explanations by replication. The level of analysis in these studies varies from bone to carcass to assemblage. We will discuss only the first two levels.

### Root Marks, Insect Holes, and Polish

The acids released by plant roots can produce spaghetti-like markings that might be misinterpreted as intentional (Fig. 81). Smooth margins and absence of parallel striations in the bed are diagnostic of root activity.

Some insects bore holes in bones (Crader 1983). These can be distinguished from punctures made by carnivore teeth by their larger size and the absence of crushed bone in the bottom.

Soil movement and fluvial action can produce

Fig. 81. Root marks on a cattle phalanx from Tell Jemmeh.

polish, which may destroy important details of cut marks (Shipman and Rose 1983). Plotting the location of polished areas on various types of bone fragments may permit reconstructing their use as tools (Gilbert and Steinfeld 1977). The important datum for differentiating natural from use polish is extent, bones polished by natural circumstances tending to be equally affected on all surfaces. Subsequent breakage may remove some portions, however, and produce a pattern misidentifiable as restricted wear.

These modifications are best described with the aid of schematic drawings, on which the affected areas of polish, puncture, cut or scrape can be defined as accurately as possible. Some excellent examples of the results of this procedure are provided by Binford (1981).

## Cut Marks

Both humans and carnivores attack bone with sharp instruments (tools or teeth) and the effects are often difficult to distinguish, especially in isolation. Cut marks tend to take on meaning when they occur repeatedly at the same skeletal location and when that position is compatible with some human or animal activity. The points of attachment and insertion of tissues serve as landmarks that permit correlating cuts with specific dismemberment procedures. Understanding can be enhanced by familiarity with the basic muscle, tendon, and ligament arrangements of the most common taxa in the sample being studied. A source such as Sisson and Grossman (1953) for domestic animals or a text on general mammalian anatomy is extremely useful for developing explanations for specific kinds of marks.

*Accidental.* Cut marks made inadvertently during excavation are usually easy to recognize (Fig. 82). The color of the cut is distinct from the surface (often lighter) and the edges are unworn. The frequency of such marks is one measure of sullegic bias in a collection. We can safely guess that excavation damage will be greatest in sites where the matrix was resistant, the visual contrast between bone and dirt was weak, and digging proceeded rapidly. The presence of excavation-damaged bone fragments is a signal that extra effort should be directed toward matching broken pieces.

*Tool-made.* Cuts made by ancient bone workers using metal tools are often deep and exhibit a shelf-like appearance. In the Middle East, metal tools became readily available for everyday use only after the advent of the Iron Age. This change is reflected in the nature of the cut marks on bones from debris dated before and after this transition at Tell Jemmeh (Fig. 83). Almost all the heavy cleaver-like damage occurs on the later material; the earlier cuts are the fine multiple incisions associated with stone tools (Ballinger n.d.).

The marks made by stone tools and carnivore teeth are very similar. Simple criteria, such as the greatest width of the marks or the shape of the cross section, have not proved reliable. The following kinds of details are diagnostic of tool use:

Fig. 82. Cut marks on cattle phalanges from Tell Jemmeh, inadvertently made during excavation.

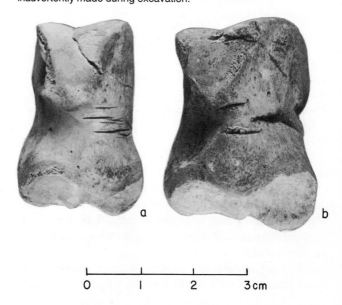

**Fig. 83.** Cut marks produced using metal tools during the Iron Age occupation at Tell Jemmeh.

1. The groove made by a tool is finely striated longitudinally. This criterion is best observed using a scanning electron microscope and procedures described by Shipman and Rose (1983). Unfortunately, relatively slight action by fluvial or other erosional processes can obliterate this evidence.

2. The mark made by a stone tool may be associated with an adjacent parallel mark made by shouldering the cutting implement into the bone. Small backward-directed cuts, called barbs, are sometimes visible at the end of the main incision (Shipman and Rose 1983).

3. The marks made by stone and bone tools can be expected to concentrate in certain locations. All mammals present relatively similar problems of dismemberment because of their shared anatomy. Although the rules of butchery are not universal, they exhibit considerable cross-cultural regularity (Binford 1981). Different solutions relate to the size of the packets of meat desired (Guilday, Parmalee, and Tanner 1962). The larger the animal, the more the parts into which it is likely to be cut.

***Activities Implied.*** In terms of the marks left on the skeleton, animal processing involves four main activities: skinning, dismemberment, meat removal, and tool manufacture. Skinning marks are likely to be found on mandibles, around the bases of horn cores and antlers, and on feet. Dismemberment marks are likely to be located at the major joint capsules, where sharp implements are inserted between articular surfaces to sever tendons and ligaments that hold the skeleton together. Scraping and cutting meat from the bone may leave marks on the shafts or on the flat surfaces of vertebrae, ribs, innominates, and scapulae. The marks associated with tool manufacture are least predictable. Successful identification probably requires understanding the manufacturing sequences of the tools.

Binford (1981) has extensively documented the marks associated with butchering among the Ninamuit of Alaska. It is tempting to use his results as a guide for analysis, but their general applicability remains to be established. Another helpful description was published by Lyman (1977), who studied patterns associated with late 19th and early 20th century techniques, in which a saw was used. His illustrations provide a guide to the locations of the cuts and the shapes of the bone fragments associated with this technique.

***Carnivore-made.*** The marks made by carnivore teeth are likely to be more numerous and less concentrated than human counterparts. They are often associated with multiple punctures (depression fractures) containing crushed bone.

The locations of carnivore cuts are likely to correlate with methods of dismemberment. Carnivores must chew through joints unless the prey is very small. As a result, the articular ends tend to be damaged or missing. They also channel long bones to get at the marrow, leaving marks parallel to the axis of the shaft; human meat-stripping marks, by contrast, are often oriented perpendicularly.

The absence of chewing marks and cuts does not imply absence of carnivore activities. Dogs have been observed to clean the meat from bone leaving few or no traces (Kent 1982).

Since carnivores attack the soft parts of the bones first, their accumulations tend to have high frequencies of shaft splinters. Carnivore damage can be estimated by calculating the ratio between articular ends and diaphysis fragments for each type of long bone.

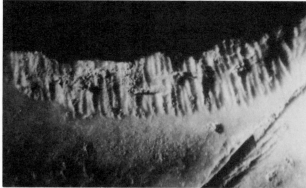

**Fig. 84.** Closely spaced, parallel grooves diagnostic of gnawing by rodents.

### Gnawing

Another confusing category of marks is created by gnawing. Such animals as porcupines and squirrels leave closely packed, subparallel grooves perpendicular to the long axis (Fig. 84). Other animals that gnaw on bone include ungulates (Sutcliffe 1973). The pattern created by sheep is distinguishable from rodent gnawing because the damage looks like a combination of grazing and sawing (Brothwell 1976).

### Burning

Heat alters the dimensions of osteological finds (Coy 1975) and affects the survivability of buried bone. Therefore, some indication of the amount of surface involved and whether the bone was charred or baked should be recorded. Mixtures of burned and unburned bones may indicate that detritus from hearths was combined with other categories of debris. Patterning in burning may permit identifying the cuts of meat that were roasted.

### Weathering

The effects of weathering have been described in five stages (Behrensmeyer 1978):

*Stage 1.* The exterior surface shows some degree of superficial longitudinal cracking.

*Stage 2.* The cracks become more pronounced and flakes of bone begin to lift from the surface.

*Stage 3.* The smooth exterior begins to take on a fibrous quality.

*Stage 4.* The cracks grow deeper and flaking becomes extensive.

*Stage 5.* The bone begins to fall apart.

The rate at which individual bones proceed through this sequence is controlled by such factors as the severity of the climate, the intensity of the sun's radiation, and the degree of mechanical disturbance. Since different bones are likely to weather at different rates, the stages cannot be used for grouping fragments of the same skeleton. The category "weathered bone" may be a useful index for the rate of accumulation of an ancient depositional surface when compared with the proportion of unmodified specimens in a collection. It also may be useful for detecting carcass-utilization patterns, on the assumption that different parts of a dismembered animal are likely to have different discard trajectories.

### Natural Disarticulation

An important research effort is concerned with establishing the pattern in which a typical carcass of a species becomes disarticulated under natural conditions. The best known study was done by Hill (1975), who examined a number of carcasses of topi *(Damaliscus korrigum),* an African antelope. His results, presented in the form of a flow diagram and a table, specify the order in which major portions of the carcass become disassociated and the sequence in which individual joints separate (Hill 1979:741–742). Disarticulation begins with separation of the forelimb, followed by the tail. Then the mandible is divided off and the forelimb begins to disintegrate. Next, the cranium and atlas are disconnected. Finally, the hindlimb is detached. Only after these disarticulations are fairly advanced does disintegration of the ribs and vertebral column begin.

This kind of work provides a template against which cases of potential human activity can be assessed. Hill compared his findings with the Olsen-Chubbock bison-kill data published by Wheat (1972) and concluded that "the disarticulation pattern . . . may differ only slightly from that in circumstances where man has not been involved. It seems that the determining controls of the pattern are inherent in the anatomy of the dead animal itself and thus independent of the agents whereby it is realized" (Hill 1979:744).

Understanding patterns of natural disarticulation has proved valuable in interpreting nearly complete skeletons of equid, gazelle, and sheep/goat from the sites of Tell Jemmeh in Israel, Bab edh-Dhra in Jordan, and Bronze Age tombs in Bahrain. The historical record tells us that animal sacrifice coupled with dismemberment and partial consumption was part of the cycle of ritual activities. The question was whether any of the finds from these sites could be ascribed to such practices. The non-conformation of the remains of the Bab edh-Dhra gazelle and the Tell Jemmeh equid to expected patterns of natural disarticulation is in accord with this interpretation.

A useful graphic way of evaluating carcass finds has been provided by Crader (1983), who shaded the parts of elephant and hippo carcasses she found on schematic drawings of skeletons for use in comparative analysis.

## DATA MANAGEMENT

Intensive methods of collecting have produced vast quantities of osteological material and many animal bone archeologists employ computers to manage the data. Two research-design questions should to be addressed before jumping into the electronic future.

The first question is whether the amount of information recorded need be so large. There is a tendency for animal bone archeologists to identify all the material before formulating problems. Much of this information is not only useless, but slows research appreciably. Unless a site is relatively homogeneous, it rarely makes sense to generate descriptive statistics at the whole-sample level. If the collection is partitioned and those excavation units providing limited archeological information are excluded, the sample sizes become more manageable. A computerized approach may still be necessary, but its application is not dictated merely by the volume of the data. Furthermore, as anyone who has ever entered and verified computerized data bases can attest, the procedure is tedious. Thus, unless generating a catalog is a requirement of the research, it is advisable to divide the collection.

The second question is how to code the informa-

tion. A number of lists have been proposed (e.g. Clutton-Brock 1975, Gifford and Crader 1977; McArdle 1975–1977; Meadow 1978b; Uerpmann 1978) and standardization of data is a powerful motive for adopting an existing system. Analytical programs have also been developed for computing some of the frequently used statistics. These advantages must be weighed against loss of detail that results from standardization and the cumbersome nature of some of the systems. A common approach is to record the zoological taxon, the skeletal element, and the portion of each bone in a collection. While the first two identifications are fairly easy, recording the range of variation represented in the third would require an enormous set of categories. Universal systems consequently rely on zoological or biological categories for their grids, rather than the typological categories that emerge from sorting archeological remains.

We therefore recommend a compromise. Standardization is most important in osteometry and there is general agreement among scholars concerning the dimensions that are important. Fragments reflect processing activities, be they cultural or natural, and these categories should emerge from the sorting. One of the working committees of the International Congress of Archaeozoology is charged with resolving problems of standardization and their results should help alleviate the existing terminological chaos. In the meantime, the various alternatives already published should be examined before an entirely new system of coding is adopted. In most cases, a useful subset of variables can be selected. We have found that creating an ad hoc code is efficient for analyzing many small collections and writing short reports.

A final consideration is the possibility of using a microcomputer. The cost of these machines is relatively low and packaged software permits many of the functions formerly restricted to a mainframe to be done on a personal computer. Of particular note is the development of software "clones" of the standard Statistical Package for the Social Sciences, familiar to many anthropologists. An example is the STATPAC Program developed by Walonick Associates, which runs on a variety of CP/M and IBM compatible hardware. It has the disadvantage of being limited to 2000 or 5000 records, depending on the version, but much larger collections can be analyzed by partitioning the data.

# 7    The Analysis of a Taxonomic Category

## INTRODUCTION

After the descriptive data concerning each specimen in a sample have been collected and recorded, analysis should shift from the specimen to the taxonomic category. This intermediate level of description and interpretation has too often been given short shrift. Category abundance may or may not be estimated using some mechanical (such as weighing) or numerical (such as total number of bone fragments) technique, but interest is always aimed at the variability within and between assemblages. This approach sidesteps an important question: Are the samples representing the taxonomic categories used to compare archeological assemblages really comparable or do they reflect radically different situations? A typical problem of this sort arises when some measure of the abundance of an analytic category (such as a species) is used to assess the rate of mortality. Unless the remains of that species were deposited in similar ways in the cultural units being compared, spurious trends will be reported. Category analysis is thus a crucial inductive step in unravelling the multiple cultural and natural biasing factors that affect materials. It must be combined eventually with deductively derived models of each proposed factor (Schiffer 1983).

Failure to examine carefully the variability of the category is characteristic in reports on samples containing a great diversity of species, none of them abundant. In collections of this sort, the temptation to bypass the category-analysis step is most strong because the quantitative data about each type of bone or species are sparse. Therefore, the reliability of the sample is expected to be weak statistically.

The techniques for analysis at the intermediate level have developed from studying samples dominated by one species. Bison-kill sites in the North American west, white-tailed deer collections in eastern North America, camelid samples from South America, and the remains of domestic stock from Eurasia have all contributed procedural models. No consensus exists, however, on when a category is sufficiently abundant to bear or require analysis.

Two concepts are used in concert to interpret the animal bone record, both at the category and the collection level: (1) taphonomic space and (2) archeological animal. The following discussion provides some guidelines for their application.

## TAPHONOMIC SPACE

### Definition

Taphonomic space is the geographic area over which a single example of an animal category is likely to be dispersed. The concept is applicable at any level. It can be used to refer to the space over which the fragments of a single bone, a single carcass, or all the carcasses of a species or group of species have spread.

It is unreasonable to expect that archeological sampling strategies, even when motivated by animal bone oriented questions, will match the taphonomic space of an analytic unit. Parts of an animal can be distributed among widely separated sites by exchange and by sequential processing, in which larger and heavier bones are left at the kill spot. The problem is to establish what part of the taphonomic space is represented by the sample at hand or, at least, whether those spaces to be compared represent the same segment of the process.

One approach has been developed by Lyman (1979). He notes that a major logical flaw of many analyses of the resources used by a prehistoric group is the assumption that a single bone or fragment implies the whole animal was present. In any situation where the taphonomic space is large relative to the area sampled, the remains are likely to represent parts rather than whole animals. An example is provided by the processing of camelids in Andean South America, where carcass units are redistributed over considerable vertical distances by transhumant societies (Miller 1979). Because this is a common situation, Lyman recommends that analysis focus on butchering units rather than whole carcasses. These units emerge from considering the locations of cut marks, the nature of the butchering process, and ethnohistoric analogies.

## Determining Taphonomic Space

The size and shape of the taphonomic space appropriate for a particular analysis should be established on the basis of a theoretical understanding of the effects of the processes of disarticulation suspected to have been significant biasing agents. Many of these processes will have been identified during analysis of the specimens as single units: Was there evidence of gnawing by scavengers? Were the bone fragments polished by fluvial action? Do cut marks imply the carcasses were segmented by butchering into packets that served as units of redistribution? Other processes can be inferred using ethnographic and experimental data. Unfortunately, only a few studies have attempted to document the relationship between specific processes and taphonomic spaces (Binford 1978, Crader 1983).

*Empirical Methods.* An empirical method was employed by Poplin (1975) to define the space over which the fragments belonging to an episode of trash disposal were scattered. Working with animal bones from an Iron Age site, each fragment of which had been precisely plotted, he searched for joins. When he drew a line between the loci of each pair of joined fragments on a map of the site, clusters emerged that he interpreted as units of animal bone garbage (Fig. 85).

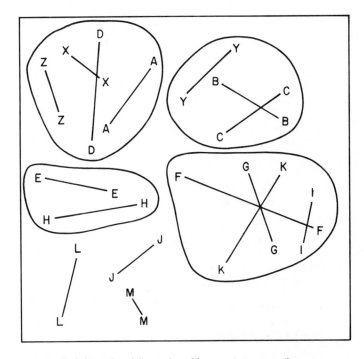

**Fig. 85.** Defining units of dispersion of fragments representing single episodes of discard by identifying old fractures and connecting their find spots. The resulting spaces can be treated as subsamples for analysis.

South (1977) has proposed an index of the process of dispersal of refuse in historic sites in North America:

We assume bone discard behavior can be monitored by ranking pieces of refuse on an 'odorimetric' scale. For example, those odorous remains of refuse, such as bone, would be discarded farther from the structure whereas those less odorous items such as a broken plate, dish, or sweepings from the floor would be thrown nearby, beside the back door or off the end of the porch, front or back, to become scattered throughout the yard by pigs, dogs, chickens, and children. Under these conditions, a higher ratio of bone to artifacts thrown from the house would be found at a distance peripheral to the structure, whereas that refuse thrown adjacent to the house would have a low bone-to-artifact ratio (1977:179).

South's hypothesis suggests several empirical techniques for defining taphonomic spaces for analysis. The ratio of bone fragments to the total number of specimens of other kinds of debris could be used to classify excavation units on South's odorimetric scale. Further, the relative frequencies of different sizes of bone fragments could be used to segregate "primary de facto" debris (material discarded at the

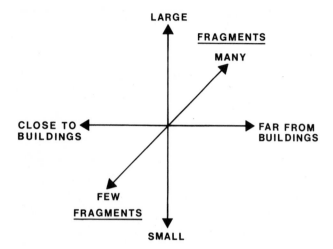

**Fig. 86.** Axes of variability in three factors relevant for identifying spaces within an archeological site that differ in the way bone fragments were accumulated. The factors are: (1) the frequency of bone fragments compared to other categories of debris (diagonal), (2) the relative size of the bone fragments (vertical), and (3) the proximity of architectural features (horizontal).

work area where it was produced) from "secondary" debris (material collected or saved for a time before being tossed out). Ethnoarcheological research suggests that a size threshold separates these two types of garbage (Schiffer 1976). The relationships between fragment size, relative abundance, and distance from architectural features provide a means of classifying excavation units (Fig. 86).

More specific identification of the feature from which a sample was collected than simply its proximity to buildings can be useful. Meadow (1975) sorted his samples from the excavation units at Hajji Firuz, a Neolithic site in Iran, into categories based on the nature of the architectural association. In one instance, building interiors and exteriors were contrasted on the supposition that they experienced different kinds of accumulation. Substantial differences in species abundances were detected in these two groups of samples.

**Preferential Accumulators.** Research on modern communities suggests that certain cultural and natural features act as garbage accumulators. Hayden and Cannon (1983) noted that pits dug for non-garbage purposes are preferential accumulation points. In examining garbage disposal in ancient Egypt, Hoffman (1974) observed a tendency for debris to concentrate in gullies and shallow depressions. It is important to keep in mind that animal bone debris is likely to be deposited well away from habitations, making it difficult to link a body of garbage with social units as small as households unless such units were widely separated.

**Impact of Scavengers.** The effect of scavengers can be tremendous. In the Navaho communities whose garbage accumulations she studied, S. Kent (1982) concluded that scavenging by the large populations of dogs massively biased the process of deposition of bones. The effects were so strong that she suspects any within-site segregation of samples for analysis would detect dog behavior. Information about human activities would be evident only at the level of the community.

Estimating the impact of scavengers on a collection is a major problem in animal bone research. In terms of taphonomic space, a way to proceed is through considering the vulnerability of different archeological features to scavenging. Deep pits and areas not habitable by dogs or other scavengers should be segregated in analysis from courtyards and similar open spaces where animals might den. Some archeological contexts, such as basements of historic buildings, often produce collections attributable entirely to cats and small dogs.

**Grouping Contexts.** The initial step in analyzing a category is determining what archeological excavation units or specimen lots should be combined for comparison with other such groupings. A convenient and common way to accomplish this is to subdivide the collection chronologically and use all the material from each period to generate a summary of the animal activity during that period. Such convenience carries with it serious problems. Pollsters long ago learned that they had to select the population they questioned rather than simply grab whomever was most available. Without controlled selection, there could be no reliable relationship between sequential polls. For animal bone archeology, the samples we compare must also be drawn from analogous contexts for contrasts and similarities to be meaningful.

It is for this reason that so much space was devoted in a previous chapter to procedures for describing the contexts of animal bone finds. If the contexts have been classified, it is possible to hold context relatively constant when comparing animal bone statistics. In many complex sites, where excavation has concentrated on defining stratigraphy rather than exposing large occupational surfaces, recognizing specific contexts may be impossible. Even here, however, the degree of contrast among contexts can be assessed as a basis for interpreting the animal bone data.

## ARCHEOLOGICAL ANIMAL

### Definition

The archeological animal is defined by the frequencies of the types of bones in an analytic category. An archeological animal can be described at the level of a specific bone, carcass part, species, or group of species. The bone frequencies in archeological samples usually vary widely from their values among living examples of the category because of the biases that have affected the remains.

Definition of the appropriate archeological animals may come directly from the research design or may be suggested by regularities in the sample, such as the positions of major dismemberment cut marks on a skeleton. Some archeological animals equate with zoological distinctions; others crosscut or regroup them.

### Description

A straightforward way to describe an archeological animal is to calculate a table of frequencies (or presence/absence information) for each type of fragment in each category. Table 1 presents the archeological animal defined from the category sheep/goat crania in the samples from the early Neolithic site of Tepe Ganj Dareh in western Iran (Hesse 1978). In many cases, it is convenient to express the data as a bar graph, using either numbers or percentages.

Archeological animals also can be depicted using a skeleton. The information can be conveyed either by coloring the bones present or by specifying their frequencies. The camel bones encountered in four chronological contexts at Tell Jemmeh are shown on Figure 87.

Additional descriptions can be generated at other levels. The category of the species is exemplified by Table 2, which shows the types of bones in samples of Chukar Partridge (*Alectoris chukar*) bones from Tepe Ganj Dareh. Instead of being sorted by bone types, fragments can be grouped into carcass parts to describe a species. Table 3 illustrates this approach using red fox *(Vulpes vulpes)* bones from Tepe Ganj

**Table 1.** The archeological animal at the level of the carcass part. The numbers of fragments of each bone in the sheep/goat cranium are shown for each of the five main levels in the early Neolithic site of Tepe Ganj Dareh, Iran.

| | Level | | | | |
|---|---|---|---|---|---|
| Bone | A | B | C | D | E |
| Petrous | 19 | 21 | 8 | 38 | 41 |
| Basilar | | | | 7 | 8 |
| Sphenoid | 1 | 2 | | 3 | 4 |
| Orbit | | | | 1 | 5 |
| Nasal | | 2 | | 17 | 9 |
| Zygoma | 6 | 7 | 2 | 12 | 19 |
| Frontal | 3 | 1 | 2 | 6 | 2 |
| Temporal | 1 | | | 4 | 11 |
| Occipital | 2 | 1 | 2 | 7 | 12 |
| Parietal | 7 | 6 | 4 | 17 | 15 |

**Table 2.** The archeological animal at the level of the species. The numbers of fragments of each bone in the skeleton of the Chukar Partridge (*Alectoris chukar*) are listed for each of the five main levels in the early Neolithic site of Tepe Ganj Dareh, Iran.

| | Level | | | | |
|---|---|---|---|---|---|
| Bone | A | B | C | D | E |
| Sternum | 35 | 70 | 30 | 42 | 59 |
| Beak | | | | | 1 |
| Clavicula | 7 | 16 | 1 | 14 | 15 |
| Fused vertebrae | 1 | 4 | 1 | 2 | |
| Synsacra | 1 | 3 | 4 | 6 | 3 |
| Scapula | 24 | 35 | 22 | 47 | 61 |
| Humerus | 17 | 26 | 13 | 14 | 2 |
| Radius | 1 | 3 | 1 | 3 | 4 |
| Ulna | 1 | 3 | 3 | 4 | 6 |
| Coracoid | 83 | 115 | 49 | 64 | 81 |
| Carpometacarpus | 56 | 89 | 20 | 87 | 22 |
| Innominate | 21 | 28 | 27 | 34 | 34 |
| Femur | 29 | 31 | 14 | 50 | 13 |
| Tibiotarsus | 19 | 7 | 8 | 30 | 5 |
| Tarsometatarsus | 11 | 3 | 5 | 4 | 2 |

**Table 3.** The description of an archeological animal using carcass parts and expressing the results as percentages. The percentage occurrences of the parts of the red fox (*Vulpes vulpes*) are tabulated by levels at Tepe Ganj Dareh, Iran.

| | Level | | | |
|---|---|---|---|---|
| Carcass Element | B | D | E | D/E |
| Neck | | 6 | 4 | 9 |
| Shoulder | 12 | 9 | 6 | 7 |
| Elbow | 33 | 15 | 10 | 15 |
| Wrist | 4 | 3 | 2 | |
| Feet | 18 | 45 | 43 | 34 |
| Hip | 21 | 12 | 14 | 11 |
| Knee | | 9 | | 2 |
| Ankle | 12 | 3 | 22 | 22 |

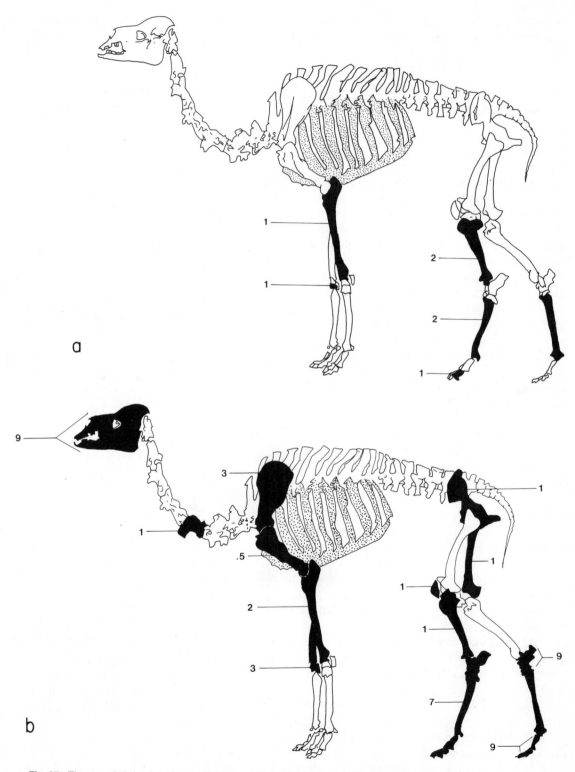

a

b

**Fig. 87.** The use of skeletal outlines to illustrate an archeological animal. The elements of camels encountered in the refuse associated with four periods at Tell Jemmeh are shown in black. **a,** Bronze-Early Iron (1400–800 B.C.). **b,** Assyrian (800–600 B.C.). **c,** Persian-Babylonian (600–400 B.C.). **d,** Hellenistic (400–200 B.C.).

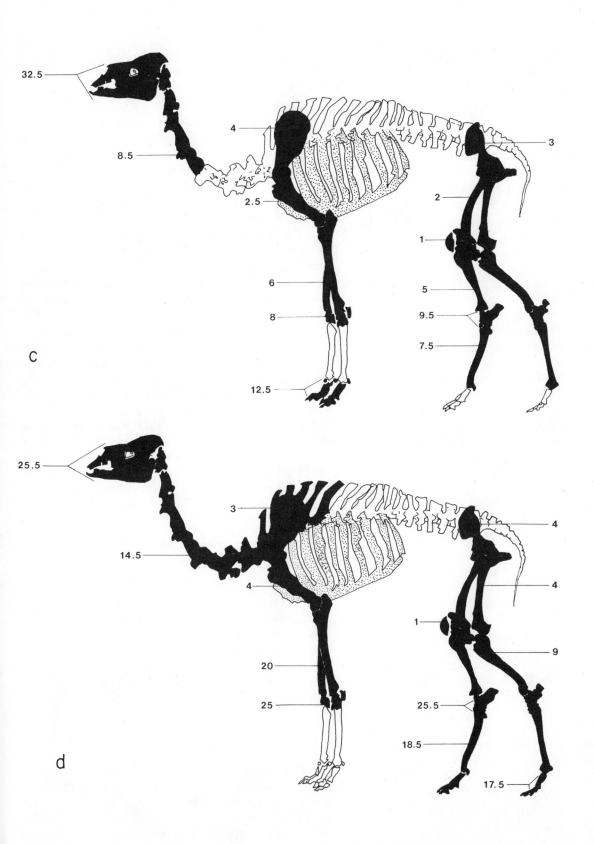

Dareh. This grouping procedure incorporates a condition known as interdependence, which is difficult to detect yet may have a significant distorting effect.

## Interdependence

Interdependence is the likelihood that two fragments will be counted separately despite the fact that both came from the same bone or carcass and represent a single analytic unit. While it might seem that this problem would be easy to resolve, it is devilishly difficult in any situation where the taphonomic space is large or the animal category is greater than a single bone.

If we compare the kind of description provided in Table 2 with that in Table 3, we can see that there is a possibility that interdependence is distorting the frequencies in the latter table. Since all the fragments assignable to the same joint have been combined, there is a chance that two or more specimens are from the same individual. Counting them separately exaggerates the frequencies. For purposes of analysis, this is damaging when the rate of interdependence is different for the different cells (Holtzman 1979) and when the values are compared to an external standard. In the case illustrated, the relatively high percentages of the category "feet" in Levels D and E may reflect survival of several phalanges from the same individuals rather than the true frequency of feet. Four approaches have been used to deal with this problem.

*Appeal to Probability.* In middens, even very large collections are a minute representation of the amount of bone deposited by the ancient inhabitants of the site, estimated from their population size, rates of animal use, and length of occupation. The disparity is so great that it is easy to feel it would be a miracle for one bone of a slaughtered animal to be recovered, let alone two. It is therefore *assumed* that each bone equals a distinct animal or animal part.

*Deposition in Anatomical Arrangement.* During our discussion of recording techniques, we emphasized the importance of recognizing and registering the presence of articulations during excavation. At this point, the information becomes valuable. It not only permits eliminating duplications in grouped categories (carcass units or species), but also makes it possible to estimate the relative rate of such duplications and to factor it into interpretations. A formula for describing the rate might be:

$$\frac{\text{\# of articulated groups}}{\text{total \# of unmatched bones}}$$

*Likelihood of Articulation.* If many of the potentially interdependent bones in a category are measurable, it may be possible to segregate two groups: (1) those where the dimensions suggest articulation would be possible, and (2) those where the dimensions exceed the range of known pairings. To do this requires a large base of data about the morphology of the species in question.

*Degree of Dispersal.* If the findspots of the bone fragments are known with some precision, statistical techniques can be employed to establish whether the anatomical relationships between bone categories are correlated with their spatial relationships. When the strength of the relationship differs for different slots within a category, the rates of interdependence are probably unequal.

If substantial levels of differential interdependence are suspected, there are two possible solutions. One is to carry out the analysis only with those categories not affected by this factor. This approach has been advocated by Binford (1978) and Lyman (1979), who focus on the bone fragment and the resource it represents. Another is to estimate the level of interdependence using the procedures listed above and restrict comparison to categories with similar levels.

## ASSESSING THE SIGNIFICANCE OF BONE-FRAGMENT FREQUENCIES

The concepts of taphonomic space and archeological animal can be clarified by applying them to three typical problems in the analysis of a category: (1) comparing samples from different contexts, (2) comparing archeological animals to external standards, and (3) comparing patterns of distribution among several sites.

### Comparing Samples from Different Contexts

A usual goal of animal bone archeology is to establish the relative frequencies of animal categories in a sequence of cultural contexts. Before that task can be undertaken, it is important to ascertain if the patterning of a taxon is equivalent in each setting. Several procedures can be illustrated from our study of the

**Fig. 88.** Aerial view of the Iranian site of Tepe Ganj Dareh and its environs, showing the extent of the excavations.

goat remains in the early Neolithic site of Tepe Ganj Dareh (Figs. 88–89).

***Establishing Confidence Values for Excavation Units.*** The excavator, Philip E.L. Smith, divided the stratigraphy of the site into five main levels, but the tremendous complexity of the accumulation made it impossible to assign all excavation units unequivocally to one of these levels. This made it necessary to develop criteria for expressing the confidence with which each lot could be allocated to a stratigraphic context. Depositional factors (floor deposit, room fill, redeposition, etc.) were the primary criteria in making these decisions. The following hierarchy of reliability (which should be considered an example rather than a rule) was used to classify the excavation units:

1. In situ; an undisturbed occupational or activity surface.

2. Probably in situ; frequently, an activity surface recognized after excavation.

3. Essentially in situ, but some signs of distur-

bance or contamination (burials, intrusive pits, rodent holes, etc.).

4. Not in situ, but provenience known with considerable certainty (room fill, collapsed rubble, sweepings from ovens.).

5. Not in situ; derived material, but original provenience more or less sure (such as materials washed out from a room or distributed down a slope).

6. Mixed materials from several strata (for example, the interface of several layers, contents of pits or other disturbed loci; also mixtures made during excavation and only perceived subsequently). It was usually possible to allocate such lots to two or three possible levels.

7. Hopelessly uncertain; materials out of context (such as slumped profiles and errors in field or laboratory cataloging).

The question that had to be addressed was whether the goat bones were deposited in each of the levels in equivalent fashion. The analysis had two

**Fig. 89.** Closeup of the stratigraphy at Tepe Ganj Dareh. Much of the accumulation in this early Neolithic site consists of collapsed cellular mud-brick construction, making the depositional sequence extremely difficult to recognize. Prior to sorting and interpreting the animal bones, each excavation unit had to be given a value expressing the degree of accuracy with which stratigraphic position could be identified.

phases. First, the distributions of reliabilities for the excavation units assigned to the main stratigraphic categories were compared to see if there were any serious differences in the way the levels were excavated. These efforts demonstrated inductively the rough similarity of the taphonomic spaces represented. Second, the frequencies of the archeological animals for each main period of occupation were calculated using the procedures described below.

**Establishing Frequencies of Archeological Animals.** In constructing descriptions of archeological animals, it is necessary to evaluate the likelihood that a particular category of fragment represents the whole analytic unit and to adjust the count accordingly. There are two ways to do this. One is to divide the observed frequencies of each category that may occur in more than one skeletal position by the number of possible positions. For example, if right and left sides were not differentiated while tabulating distal humeri, their frequency would have to be divided by two. Further, if fore and hind limb or right and left side of the foot were not recorded for phalanges, the frequencies for goats of phalanx I, II, and III would have to be divided by eight. This procedure usually produces numerous fractional entries in the tables, which may be annoying.

An alternative method is to make the adjustments by multiplication (Table 4). The most common element in the list of categories (here, one of the phalanges) is held constant, and the degree to which it is a multiple of other categories is used to increase the other entries. Thus, the distal humerus count would be multiplied by four (eight first phalanges to two distal humeri) and the axis and atlas counts would be

**Table 4.** The goat archeological animals from the five main levels at Tepe Ganj Dareh. The frequencies of the skeletal elements, listed in decreasing order, are corrected to reflect skeletal proportions. (Initial P = Proximal; D = Distal; RADUL = radius/ulna, etc.).

| Level A | | Level B | | Level C | | Level D | | Level E | |
|---|---|---|---|---|---|---|---|---|---|
| METAC | 184 | METAC | 240 | DHUM | 40 | METAC | 184 | METAC | 184 |
| METAT | 148 | ASTRA | 196 | CALC | 28 | METAT | 180 | METAT | 144 |
| CALC | 140 | METAT | 192 | ASTRA | 28 | ASTRA | 176 | CALC | 128 |
| ASTRA | 100 | CALC | 164 | PH3 | 25 | CALC | 160 | ASTRA | 120 |
| PRAD | 92 | DHUM | 156 | RADUL | 24 | DHUM | 136 | DRAD | 116 |
| DHUM | 92 | RADUL | 108 | DRAD | 20 | DRAD | 96 | DHUM | 108 |
| DRAD | 72 | DRAD | 92 | METAC | 20 | PH3 | 88 | RADUL | 68 |
| PH3 | 62 | PRAD | 88 | AXIS | 16 | PH2 | 75 | SCAP | 52 |
| PH2 | 54 | PH2 | 74 | METAT | 16 | RADUL | 56 | PH2 | 51 |
| PH1 | 52 | PH3 | 72 | PH1 | 15 | PH1 | 43 | PRAD | 48 |
| SCAP | 40 | PH1 | 64 | PRAD | 12 | PRAD | 36 | INNOM | 48 |
| AXIS | 32 | SCAP | 60 | PH2 | 11 | SCAP | 36 | AXIS | 40 |
| INNOM | 32 | INNOM | 44 | SCAP | 8 | PFEM | 28 | PH3 | 39 |
| RADUL | 28 | AXIS | 40 | INNOM | 4 | ATLAS | 24 | PH1 | 33 |
| ATLAS | 8 | PFEM | 16 | | | AXIS | 24 | PFEM | 28 |
| PFEM | 8 | | | | | INNOM | 20 | | |

Spearman's Rho Rank Correlation:

| | Level A | Level B | Level C | Level D | Level E |
|---|---|---|---|---|---|
| Level A | | 0.81 | 0.44 | 0.85 | 0.73 |
| Level B | | | 0.63 | 0.91 | 0.88 |
| Level C | | | | 0.66 | 0.43 |
| Level D | | | | | 0.82 |

multiplied by eight (eight first phalanges to one atlas or axis). These adjusted values are called *corrected frequencies*.

After the corrected frequencies have been calculated, the archeological animals can be described by arranging them in a ranked list. These descriptive summaries can be evaluated by inspection or by using various statistical tools. When the corrected frequencies are converted to percentages and plotted as a bar graph, the results can be examined. In particular, one should be alert for sharp drops in frequency. Since the information is presented in corrected frequencies, the tops of the bars should form a horizontal line if the collection suffered no bias. The degree of deflection from the horizontal is a measure of the intensity of attritional bias. When great differences in attrition are exhibited by different categories of elements, the patterns require investigation. Because nearly all the samples from Tepe Ganj Dareh suffered attrition, the usual pattern is a gently sloping decline across the ranked frequencies.

A number of statistical procedures can be employed to compare ranked lists. Simple application and robust character recommend the Spearman's

Rank Test, the Coefficient of Concordance, and Kendall's Tau (Harshbarger 1971, Thomas 1976). The results of the Spearman's Rank Tests comparing each pair of levels are included on Table 4. Level C stands out distinctly from the others, indicating that the sample should be treated separately in calculating trends during occupation of the site.

**Identifying Factors Affecting Frequencies.** What factors contribute most to the difference between samples is the next consideration. Two are apparent on inspecting the data for Level C. One is the much smaller size of the sample. Level C architecture was built on the ruins of a burned village, which constitutes Level D. It is restricted in area compared to the other periods and may constitute a special activity complex. The second factor is the much reduced relative frequency of recovery of metacarpals and metatarsals. An ad hoc explanation is suggested by the fact that in all periods this skeletal element is frequently cut. Perhaps initial butchering of the carcass involved different deposition of metapodial parts during Period C.

In the Tepe Ganj Dareh material, additional and stronger discordances were found in the samples of fox and hare bones. Bone-fragment categories were grouped into carcass units and each archeological animal was described in the form of a table of percentages (Table 3). In both species, the samples from Level D and Level E, as well as the intermediate Level D/E, contained an excess of foot bones. If the skin and the carcass were distinct units in the processing sequence, the frequencies of these two parts could be expected to vary somewhat independently.

**Intrasite Comparisons.** Graphic approaches can be used to compare archeological animals. Losey (1973) used cumulative frequency diagrams to illustrate the differences between the caribou-bone accumulations in two middens. Schulz and Gust (1983) employed a similar procedure to analyze beef bones from historic contexts in California, but compared categories based on retail cuts of meat rather than types of bones (Fig. 8).

Losey developed an "index of dissimilarity" by expressing the proportion that each type of bone contributed to each sample as a percentage and calculating the differences between percentages in pairs of subsamples. The range of the index is 0 – 200, with higher values indicating greater dissimilarity. We know little about the behavior of this statistic, but it is a way of summarizing variability that might prove useful if more widely applied.

## Comparing Archeological Animals to External Standards

Future progress in animal bone archeology will depend on the development of external standards for interpreting excavated samples. These standards will result from experimental and ethnographic research and will describe the predictable outcome of specific biasing agents and combinations of agents.

The experimental approach is exemplified by Binford and Bertram (1977). They established the density of the bone matrix for a wide variety of skeletal parts in caribou and sheep. They predicted that the greater the relative density, the more resistant a type of fragment would be to attrition from gnawing by carnivores. Since density is partially a function of the age of an animal, and since the species being studied have a distinct season of birth, they were able to use computer simulation to predict the patterns of distributions of archeological animals associated with different seasonal cohorts of victims. In another study, Binford (1978) used extensive data on the behavior of Eskimo dogs to generate expectations for the proportions of different kinds of bone fragments characterizing a collection extensively modified by carnivore gnawing.

Carnivores utilize a procedure for dismembering carcasses that is distinct from human techniques. Specifically, carnivores tend to attack the joint capsule, chewing their way through bone, sinew, and flesh to separate the body of the dead animal into parts. Further, carnivores gnaw on the stripped bone, preferentially destroying the softer ends and leaving the harder shaft fragments split and scarred but more intact. Therefore, collections extensively modified by gnawing are likely to contain substantially higher proportions of shaft splinters compared to articular ends than samples modified exclusively by humans.

Ethnographic data can also be used to construct patterns for evaluating archeological samples. Brain (1967) published the results of a study of the remains of goats found in a modern Hottentot village. Though all the biases were not identified, he concluded that the frequency distributions of the various types of bones reflected "differential durability due to shape and structure, but also . . . the fact that the fusion of epiphyses to shafts occurs at different stages for different ends of long bones" (1967:5), a result in agreement with the density study by Binford and Bertram.

Though it is not possible to control for such important factors as collecting bias, it is interesting to

**Table 5.** Archeological animals (Saxon sheep) compared to ethnographically determined standards (Hottentot goats). Differences between the observed (Obs.) and expected (Exp.) frequencies reveal important limb bones to be missing from the sheep skeletons. ($df = 8$; $\chi^2 = 29.9$).

| Skeletal Element | Hottentot Goats | | | Saxon Sheep | | |
|---|---|---|---|---|---|---|
| | Obs. | Exp. | $\chi^2$ | Obs. | Exp. | $\chi^2$ |
| Humerus | 82 | 70.6 | 1.85 | 29 | 40.4 | 3.24 |
| Scapula | 28 | 35.6 | 1.62 | 28 | 20.4 | 2.83 |
| Radius | 81 | 78.8 | 0.06 | 43 | 45.2 | 0.11 |
| Metacarpal | 39 | 49.0 | 2.02 | 38 | 28.1 | 3.53 |
| Metatarsal | 41 | 53.4 | 2.88 | 43 | 30.6 | 5.02 |
| Tibia | 85 | 77.6 | 0.72 | 37 | 44.5 | 1.25 |
| Femur | 27 | 21.6 | 1.34 | 7 | 12.4 | 2.34 |
| Innominate | 34 | 30.5 | 0.40 | 14 | 17.5 | 0.70 |

apply the Hottentot data — which presumably represent a large part of the basic human taphonomic space — to an archeological sample. A relevant case is Chaplin's interpretation from the distribution of sheep bones in a Saxon site that the "most valuable joints of mutton" had been exported (1969:223). This inference, if valid, would be a useful indicator of interaction by the population at this site with the regional economy. When the bone distributions in the Hottentot and Saxon samples were compared using the chi-square statistic, the value calculated indicated a degree of dissimilarity (Table 5). Much of the difference stems from the relative abundance of metapodials in the Saxon sample and their relative rarity in the Hottentot material. As predicted by Chaplin, the meaty humeri and the femora were relatively rare in the Saxon samples, while the tibiae and radii, which bear little meat in sheep, were near expectable frequencies. The scapulae and innominates were also at expectable frequencies, implying that the carcass was divided at the shoulder and hip girdles for separate processing.

## Comparing Patterns of Distribution at Several Sites

Interesting information can emerge from intrasite comparison of the archeological animals for a category. The abundance of toe bones in the Tepe Ganj Dareh sample encouraged comparison to other Near Eastern collections. The sheep/goat samples from the historic site of Bastam in northwestern Iran (Krauss 1975) and from Ali Kosh in southwestern Iran (Hole, Flannery, and Neely 1969) were grouped into two ca-

**Table 6.** A comparison of the numbers of limb and toe bones from three Iranian sites. Ali Kosh and Tepe Ganj Dareh are Neolithic; Bastam is historic. Note that limb bones predominate at Bastam, whereas toe bones are most frequent at the Neolithic sites.

|  | Bastam | Tepe Ganj Dareh | Ali Kosh |
|---|---|---|---|
| Limbs | 6031 | 8708 | 1709 |
| Toes | 2297 | 12918 | 2571 |

**Table 7.** A comparison of the archeological animals for cattle at the early Neolithic site of Tepe Ganj Dareh, Iran and the early Bronze Age site of Karatas-Semayuk, Turkey. The relative frequencies of wrist and toe bones contrast strongly. ($df = 7$; $\chi^2 = 72.9$).

| | SITE | | | |
|---|---|---|---|---|
| Carcass Element | Tepe Ganj Dareh | | Karatas-Semayuk | |
| | No. | $\chi^2$ | No. | $\chi^2$ |
| Shoulder | 3 | 3.8 | 35 | 1.2 |
| Elbow | 13 | 4.0 | 84 | 1.2 |
| Wrist | 30 | 27.0 | 22 | 8.1 |
| Metapodials | 11 | 4.2 | 76 | 1.3 |
| Hip | 11 | 0.4 | 47 | 0.1 |
| Knee | 7 | 0.1 | 28 | 0.1 |
| Ankle | 16 | 2.7 | 88 | 0.8 |
| Toes | 42 | 13.7 | 61 | 4.1 |

tegories: limb bones and toe bones. The latter predominated in the two Neolithic villages, in contrast to the historic site (Table 6).

A hypothesis might be constructed from this that the processing associated with toes (skinning and preparing hides) becomes segregated spatially from that done to the main part of the carcass when social differentiation exceeds what existed in early Neolithic villages. Alternatively, the difference could be an artifact of the collecting technique, finer screens perhaps being used in the earlier sites. The hypothesis of separation of the two parts of the animal receives some support from a comparison of the frequencies of cattle bones at Tepe Ganj Dareh and Karatas-Semayuk, a Bronze Age site in southwestern Turkey (Table 7). The size of cattle bones makes collecting techniques potentially less significant, yet these sites also contrast in representation of wrist and toe elements.

## ANALYZING VARIATION WITHIN CATEGORIES OF ARCHEOLOGICAL ANIMALS

An archeological animal is often considered to be the result of attritional forces acting on a single population. In fact, the carcass elements may come from several subpopulations of a species. For that reason, it is important to examine differentiation within each category of archeological animal. Two particularly informative approaches are osteometric analyses and mortality patterns.

### Osteometric Analyses

Using measurements to make taxonomic distinctions is relatively straightforward when a series of well documented modern specimens is available for ascertaining the critical sizes that reliably segregate

two morphologically similar forms. Unfortunately, such standards seldom exist. Museum collections are likely to be distorted unless they were gathered with an eye to representativeness of the living populations. Furthermore, large samples are rarely available from the area where the archeological site is located. If reliable critical values have not been established, they can often be generated. The procedure can be illustrated using South American camelids and Near Eastern sheep/goats.

***South American Camelids.*** In Andean South America, the most important large herbivore resources are the camelids. This diverse group includes the domestic llama and alpaca, and the wild guanaco and vicuña. Since they can be exploited in distinct ways, it is important to differentiate them in the archeological record. The matter is complicated by the fact that the four are interfertile and their ancestry is a matter of considerable controversy (Wheeler 1984). Moreover, they are exceedingly difficult to distinguish osteologically. Details of dentition are helpful, but qualitative criteria for the post-cranial skeleton have been slow to appear. Nevertheless, it is possible to recognize two broad size groups, a large one including the guanaco and llama, and a small one lumping the alpaca and vicuña.

This size distinction was used in the analysis of collections from northern Chile (Hesse 1982b). The samples derive from Archaic sites (Puripica-1, Tambillo, and Tulán-52) located along the slopes east of the Salar de Atacama. Though the bones were extremely fragmentary, it was possible to obtain groups of measurements for several osteological dimensions. Each group was plotted as a histogram and examined for

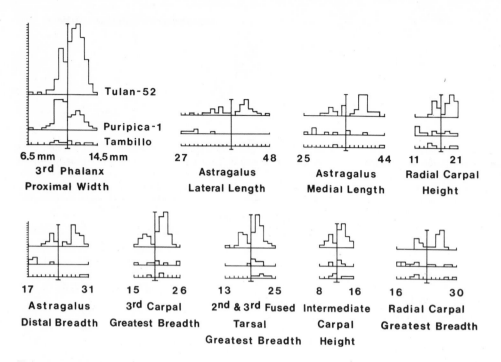

**Fig. 90.** Histograms of measurements on foot bones of camelids from the sites of Tulán-52, Puripica-1, and Tambillo in northern Chile. The range of measurements for each dimension category reflects the actual upper and lower values encountered. The vertical line is a decision point, established by inspection, that separates the distributions into large and small modes. Each "step" is one measurement.

bimodality (Fig. 90). The point that best separated two peaks was selected as the critical value. The sizes of the two modes in each of the univariate diagrams was used to estimate the relative frequencies of the two groups of camelids for each type of bone. Averaging these estimates produced relative proportions for the two species in the three collections. The validity of this procedure is supported by the work of Wing (1972), who published a series of decision points derived from modern skeletons. Only one of the dimensions she analyzed was applicable to the Chilean samples, but that one corresponded to the critical value empirically developed from the archeological material.

***Near Eastern Sheep/goats.*** In analyzing the material from Tepe Ganj Dareh, the primary concern was determining the wild or domestic status of the main herbivore resources. In order to specify the relationship, it was first necessary to establish how each sex was exploited because male sheep and goats are considerably larger than females. The procedure was similar to that used with the camelid samples. Each group of measurements associated with a dimension was plotted as a histogram (Fig. 91). When the number of bones represented by two measurements was sufficiently large, a bivariate plot was generated (Fig. 92). The relative sizes of the two modes permitted estimating the proportions of each sex in the samples from the site.

***Potential Pitfalls.*** Interpreting patterns in measurements for an archeological animal must be approached cautiously. A classic criterion for domestication is changed size with respect to the wild ancestors. A real danger exists that this conclusion will be drawn when the difference in size in two sam-

ples results from differential representation of the sexes in a dimorphic species.

Fairly large numbers of specimens are necessary to detect modality in archeological collections, but little confidence can be placed in critical values obtained by lumping data from several sources until consensus is achieved on standards of measurement.

## Mortality Patterns and Harvest Profiles

***Tooth Wear.*** Some methods of estimating age at death allow fairly precise specifications of the range of time in which mortality occurred. Among these are counting layers of dentine, which may permit designating a year or even a season, and observing stages of tooth wear and eruption, which provide ranges from a few months to several years.

Reconstructing mortality using tooth wear can be illustrated by the data on sheep/goat mandibles from Tepe Ganj Dareh. The estimates were calculated following the procedures described by Payne (1973). All the mandibles and teeth were considered independent, although some undetected overlap undoubtedly exists.

Each horizontal line in the diagram (Fig. 93) indicates the range of age estimates for a single specimen. The distributions of the ranges suggest the pattern of mortality. The lines at the right represent animals dying at advanced ages; those at the left, animals dying young.

To calculate a more precise estimate of mortality, some decisions had to be made. Most of the lines in the diagram span several age categories, implying the animal could have died during any one of them. In con-

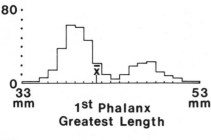

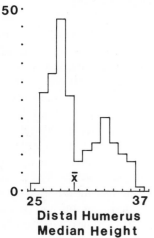

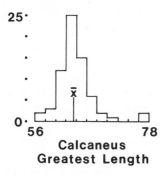

**Fig. 91.** Histograms of three measurements on goat bones from Tepe Ganj Dareh in Iran. The upper and lower limits of each distribution are the maximum and minimum measurements. x̄ indicates the arithmetic mean of the samples measured. In two cases, this value does not correspond to the most commonly encountered measurements because of the bimodal nature of the distribution. The distal humerus fuses earliest, then the first phalanx, and last the calcaneus. The evidence that bones fusing later have smaller numbers of measurements in the larger mode implies that the number of males surviving to mature ages is sharply reduced compared to females. This pattern was combined with information about the relative proportion of mature examples in each element category to estimate sex-specific harvest profiles.

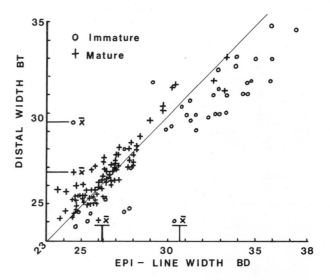

**Fig. 92.** Bivariate plot of two distal widths of the distal metapodials of goats from Tepe Ganj Dareh. In males, which are more robust than females, the width of the epiphysial (EPI) line tends to be greater than the width of the distal end of the trochlear. Most of the circles lie to the right of the diagonal, implying that the immatures include a higher frequency of males. ox̄ = the arithmetic mean of the o's; +x̄ = the arithmetic mean of the +'s for each dimension.

trast, other specimens were graded to only one category. In summing the information, account must be taken of these differences. It would distort the results if the first specimen were assigned a value of one in each of the three possible categories, since this would give it three times the weight of a fragment assigned to only one category. A solution is to partition the first specimen over the number of categories it covers by assigning a value of one-third to each category. The second specimen receives a value of one. This is often the best approach, particularly when stages of wear have not been correlated with chronological age.

After the lines have been converted to series of fractions, the columns of fractions can be added to give a mortality proportion for each age stage and the information presented as a histogram. Alternatively, the values can be converted to percentages and used to construct a cumulative survivorship curve, or what we prefer to call a "harvest profile." Age at death is arranged along the X-axis (here using the age stages) from young to old (left to right). The Y-axis is a percentage scale. At age 0, it is considered to equal 100 percent. The percentage value in each stage (the proportion of animals that died in that stage) is subtracted

·A·B·C·D·E·F·G·H·I·

**MANDIBLES**

**Fig. 93.** Ages at death estimated for sheep/goat samples from Tepe Ganj Dareh from stages of tooth wear on samples of mandibles (top) and individual teeth (middle). Each horizontal line represents a single specimen. Most estimates extend over two or three age categories, implying the animal could have died in any of them. Adjustments to accommodate these differences in precision must be made to produce the cumulative survivorship curve (bottom).

**INDIVIDUAL TEETH**

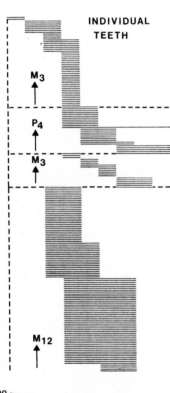

M₃

P₄

M₃

M₁₂

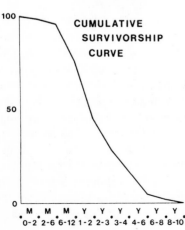

**CUMULATIVE SURVIVORSHIP CURVE**

from the value in the immediately preceding stage. Thus, the percentage in Stage A is subtracted from 100 percent, Stage B is subtracted from 100 percent less Stage A, Stage C is subtracted from 100 percent less Stage A plus Stage B, and so forth. When the final age stage is reached, the value is zero (Fig. 93, bottom).

Two variables affect the reliability of this procedure. The first is the fact that the age stages are not necessarily equal in duration. It is not reasonable to assume that an age stage lasting six months is as likely to be represented as one lasting twelve months. This bias can be overcome when age estimates can be assigned chronological values. The stages can then be converted to months, and the number of months in a stage used to assign a fractional proportion to each specimen.

The second variable is that all stages within an age range estimated for a specimen are not equally likely to be the true age at death. Rather, the distribution probably is more like a bell-shaped curve, with mortality less likely at the extremes than in the middle of the range. If these probability distributions were established, the picture of mortality would be sharper but the computational problem would be greatly complicated. Making the assumption of a flat distribution across the range gives a pattern that is less refined, but not likely to be radically inaccurate.

***Diaphysis-epiphysis Fusion.*** Mortality estimates for archeological animals can also be calculated from the proportions of fused elements in a sample, since the age at which each diaphysis and epiphysis pair becomes united is fairly uniform within a species. Calculating the proportion of fused examples provides an estimate of the ratio of animals that died younger or older than the age of fusion. For example, the distal epiphysis of a sheep humerus fuses at about 6–10 months. If the fused fraction in a sample is 75 percent, then that proportion of the sheep died between the ages of 6 months and about 10 years (the approximate maximum life span of a domestic sheep). There is no indication when during this nine-and-a-half year span the average sheep died; only the range is provided. Conversely, a fused fraction of 75 percent indicates that 25 percent of the sheep died between birth and 6 to 10 months. Fusion fractions are likely to overestimate the number of animals dying in the older age categories since mature bones are more resistent to attrition.

The proportions of fused elements can be arranged in ascending order of age at which fusion is complete. This order is relatively constant among mammals (Todd and Todd 1938). The sequence of fusion proportions then becomes a harvest profile for the animal category, which can be compared within a sample or against an external standard. Because of the differential preservation of mature and immature bones, it is better to rely on the shape of a harvest profile rather than the precise values it includes.

Two equations can be used for calculating the proportion of fused examples (pF) at some skeletal location (E = epiphysis, D = diaphysis, i = immature, m = mature, > = larger):

Equation 1.

$$pF = \frac{\# \text{ mED joins}}{\# \text{ mED joins} + \# \text{ iE} + \text{iD} + \# \text{ iED joins}}$$

Equation 2.

$$pF = \frac{\# \text{ mED joins}}{\# \text{ mED joins} + (> \# \text{ iE or iD}) + \# \text{ iED joins}}$$

In Equation 1, each unmatched epiphysis and diaphysis fragment is counted separately from and added to the specimens that can be matched. This assumes that all unmatched fragments represent different bones, the condition of maximum independence. Equation 2 assumes maximum interdependence. Since loose epiphyses and diaphyses are expected to join, only the category with the largest number of examples is counted and added to the actual matches. Equation 1 may produce too young an estimate for average mortality, while Equation 2 may produce too old an estimate. Deciding which calculation to use involves evaluating the likelihood of drawing erroneous conclusions from estimates that are too high or too low.

When the estimates are compared, the results can be misleading if the rates of interdependence in the samples are different. One method of assessing this is to calculate the proportion of matched specimens to the total number of diaphyses or epiphyses using the following formula:

$$\frac{\# \text{ iD matched with an iE}}{\text{total } \# \text{ iD}}$$

When this value is radically different in the samples to be compared, it is prudent to use Equation 2 even though the result is likely to be biased toward greater age at death.

It is useful to calculate this value for each fusion point used in describing the mortality of an archeological animal because the process of disarticulation is likely to affect them differentially. If this is not done, internal variation in the ways the fusion fractions estimate mortality may produce harvest profiles that are uninterpretable. Krantz (1968) has suggested that a statistic of this sort might index the proportion of recovery achieved by an archeological sampling strategy (cf. Poplin 1981). A critique of his procedure is provided by Casteel (1977).

Another methodological problem is that harvest profiles constructed using fusion information tend to obscure the inaccuracy of this method of age determination. Rates of skeletal development are linked to nutrition, sex, and other biological factors, and experimental data provide a range of estimates for each episode of fusion. Thus, using a line to portray a harvest profile presents a sharper picture than the data support (Watson 1978). An alternative graphic method presents each fusion estimate as a range (Fig. 94). Connecting the high and low ends of the ranges produces a "fat line" description of mortality. The "true" harvest profile should pass somewhere between the extremes.

The possibility of trephic bias must also be considered. The bones of many animals become more distinct morphologically with age so that the probability of assigning a bone fragment to a particular taxonomic category may depend on how long the animal lived. This factor will tend to overestimate age in a harvest profile based on a finely defined taxonomic category, making it inadvisable to compare a harvest profile calculated for a general category, such as sheep/goat, with one developed for one of the subordinate taxa, either sheep or goat.

***Interpreting Harvest Profiles.*** Harvest profiles based on fusion frequencies are often used to compare the pattern of animal exploitation in subsamples from the same site, but this procedure incorporates the

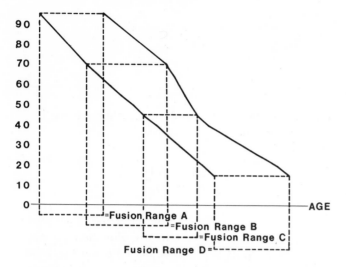

% FUSED (PROPORTION SURVIVING)

**Fig. 94.** "Fat" harvest profile constructed using the ranges of estimates for fusion obtained from four skeletal locations. The "true" harvest profile should lie somewhere between these extremes.

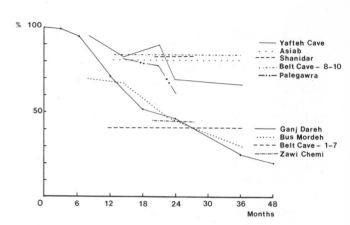

**Fig. 95.** Comparison of the sheep/goat harvest profiles obtained for five late Pleistocene sites (top) and four early Holocene sites (bottom) in the Near East. The lower proportion of mature animals in the more recent samples has been interpreted as evidence for domestication.

questionable assumption that the patterns represent mortality in some well understood population of animals. If individuals of the same species were exploited for different purposes, their carcasses may be represented in a sample by different kinds of bones. Foot bones, for instance, might be segregated as a by-product of skin-working activities and limb bones as a result of meal preparation. Domestic animals of different age and sex might be valued differently as sources of leather and meat. In a complex society, where individuals of high status could command the best animals for each resource, the carcasses that were processed into their garbage might contain the feet of one age and sex category and the limb bones of another. Such selection will distort calculations because the ages of fusion differ according to their position in the skeleton, making a harvest profile derived from the information misleading. The only defense against this kind of problem is to attempt to recognize spatial arrangements of skeletal elements that imply the parts of an archeological animal were differentially deposited.

Harvest profiles may also be compared among sites. This kind of study revealed the replacement of a pattern based on exploitation of mature sheep/goats during the late Pleistocene with one focusing on younger stock during the early Holocene in the Near East (Fig. 95; Coon 1951; Hole, Flannery, and Neely 1969). Though the interpretation of this change as reflecting domestication has been controversial (Hesse 1982c) and the effects of differential preservation, divergent field techniques, and discordant taxonomic identification on the results are unknown, the contrast is sufficiently pronounced to suggest the method may be useful.

Harvest profiles have been generated using contemporary sources of information on animal mortality. Concurrently with his study of tooth wear in Anatolian sheep, Payne (1973) constructed a series of harvest profiles associated with different goals of sheep raising, some directed toward producing meat, others milk or wool. This work has been extended by Redding (1981). The profiles generated by these authors (and others, such as Dahl and Hjort 1976), together with observations by ethnographers on the behavior of pastoral and hunting peoples around the world, provide a body of data useful for comparison with archeological materials.

In general, before ethnohistoric and ethnographic data can be compared with archeological patterns, they must be generalized to depict average behavior over durations analogous to archeological units of time. Much of the diversity in ancient productive strategies becomes invisible when analysis is restricted to animal bone samples. Similarly, much of the variability in modern systems may disappear when performance over decades or centuries is considered.

## COMBINING INFORMATION ON ARCHEOLOGICAL ANIMALS

The insights obtained by combining osteometric information with evidence for age of mortality can be illustrated using examples from Tepe Ganj Dareh and from Tulán-52 and Puripica.

## An Iranian Case

After the distributions of measurements for the sheep and goat bones from the site of Tepe Ganj Dareh were assembled, several patterns emerged. First, some of the immature specimens were larger than the mature ones. The existence of sexual dimorphism suggested the hypothesis that males constituted a larger than normal proportion of the animals dying young, whereas females constituted the bulk of the animals dying after skeletal maturity. This inference was tested osteometrically by plotting the breadth at the distal end of the trochlear (BT) against the breadth at the line of fusion between the distal diaphysis and epiphysis (BD). BT exceeded BD in the mature examples, whereas the reverse was true of the immature examples, supporting the hypothesis (Fig. 92).

Second, the relative proportions of large and small animals estimated using different measurements were not consistent (Fig. 91). When the patterns for several bones were arranged in accord with the age at which fusion occurred, it became evident that among goats larger bones presumably representing males were less and less common in the older age categories. A pronounced contrast exists between the histograms for the distal humerus, which describes the youngest population, and the calcaneus, which describes the oldest (Fig. 91, center and bottom).

This pattern of differential representation by sex in each age category was combined with the information on mortality, using the following steps:

1. The percentage of animals surviving past various ages was estimated from tooth wear.

2. The percentage of animals of each sex surviving past various ages was estimated by the relative sizes of the modes in the distributions of dimensions.

3. The sex survivorship ratio was used to partition the mortality information. For example, if 70 percent of the goats lived past 24 months, but only 25 percent were males, then the value for male mortality in the 24-month and older category is 17.5 percent.

4. These sex-specific mortality estimates were used to create separate harvest profiles for male and female goats.

This analysis revealed two distinct modes of exploitation of goat resources at Tepe Ganj Dareh. In the earliest (basal) periods, the occupants harvested similar frequencies of mature and young (pre-adolescent) females. The combination of male and female mortality produced a picture of relative maturity among the harvested animals (Fig. 96, left). With the development of mud-brick architecture implying year-round occupation of the site, the villagers harvested a higher proportion of younger animals (Fig. 96, right). This general shift involves a complex rearrangement of mortality foci. Very young animals of both sexes were less common, as were mature females. Mature males increased their contribution to overall mortality by a very small fraction. When combined with harvest profiles from other nearby and contemporary sites, this evidence suggested a shift from hunting to herding during the occupation of Tepe Ganj Dareh.

## A Chilean Case

A second example of the process of integration of osteometric and mortality information is the analysis of samples of camelid bones from the sites of Tulán-52 and Puripica in northern Chile. Osteometric information was used to calculate the relative proportions of two size categories of camelids (perhaps guanacos and vicuñas). A problem arose, however, when the information on mortality derived from fusion frequencies was examined. The sample from Tulán-52 fit the expected pattern, the harvest profile curve descending as elements fusing at higher ages were incorporated. In the material from Puripica, the fusion information

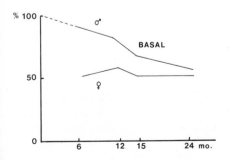

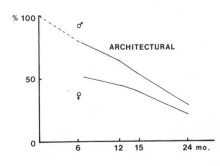

**Fig. 96.** Harvest profiles for male and female goats during the basal (left) and architectural (right) periods at Tepe Ganj Dareh. Lower mortality among adults during the latter period is one indication of a shift from hunting to herding during occupation of the site.

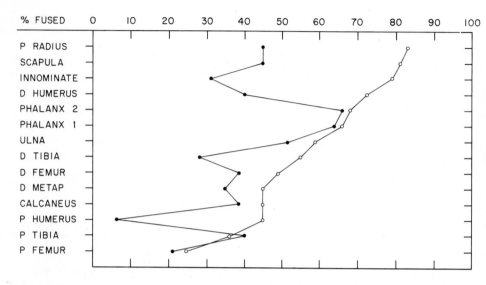

**Fig. 97.** The proportion of fused epiphyses in samples of camelid bone from two Chilean sites. Arranging the types of fragments in descending order of fused proportion reveals different patterns at Puripica (solid circles) and Tulán-52 (open circles). The explanation seems to be that one form of camelid (a smaller one) is represented in the Puripica sample mainly by toe bones.

formed a smooth curve, overall much younger than at Tulán-52, except that the proportions of phalanges were about 20 percent higher than expected (Fig. 97).

To explain this inconsistency, we examined the sources of the measurements. This revealed that the dimensions we were able to analyze came almost exclusively from bones of the feet. The mortality information, by contrast, was derived from all locations in the skeleton. The anomalous frequency for the fusion of toes resulted from two facts: (1) each size category of camelid was being harvested at different ages, and (2) the smaller form was represented largely by toe bones. When the Puripica harvest profile was segregated into two patterns, one for guanacos and the other for vicuñas, it became evident that vicuñas were dying at relatively mature ages, whereas guanacos were slaughtered young. Both kinds of camelid were dying at older ages in the sample from Tulán-52. This change in mode of exploitation can be attributed to the advent of domestication.

## CONCLUSION

The analysis of an animal bone category involves two basic steps. First, the taphonomic spaces (or groupings of excavation units) that define the population of bones must be examined to establish the comparability on archeological grounds of the units of analysis. Second, the similarities and differences in the proportions of bone elements or bone-element attributes within a grouping must be established. This procedure may yield important information that requires subdividing an animal bone category along lines of age, sex or carcass part. More critical is the contribution that this analysis makes to assessing the comparability of bone units from different contexts. Much research in animal bone studies is aimed at comparing faunas. Unless the composition of each category is clearly defined, much of the analysis of the assemblage at a higher level will produce results that are misleading and unreliable.

# 8    The Analysis of an Assemblage

## INTRODUCTION

The last step along the road from objectives to analysis in animal bone archeology is the characterization of the whole archeozoological collection recovered from a unit defined contextually or chronologically. The focus is on the "assemblage," or group of categories, and on the variability between rather than within the basic categories. There has been considerable sterile wrangling over the appropriate procedures to apply at this broad level of description. At the 1982 Internatonal Congress of Archaeozoology in London, no subject aroused more heated debate than whether Minimum Number of Individuals (MNI) or some other procedure is the best estimator of the frequency of a species in an archeological collection. Much of this confusion vanishes when a few general aspects of the process and description are considered.

Part of the problem is that the statistics used to describe assemblages estimate something about fairly large-scale phenomena. Archeological assemblages are expected to contain behavioral information about cultural groupings, which are the primary components of historical and anthropological reconstructions of past activities. Because assemblage descriptions represent the behavior of large numbers of people acting over large areas, however, they are subject to the widest possible range of biasing and distorting agents. Consequently, we should not expect them to be accurate analytic tools.

Further, we often move to the level of assemblage descriptions without sufficient preliminary attention to category analysis. Before whole collections can be compared profitably, we need to establish that the subcomponents of each sample reflect similar cultural or natural processes. Only then will differences in the statistics calculated for categories at the assemblage level represent what is actually desired: a measure of the relative intensity of some specific sphere of past animal-related behavior for a significant group of people.

It is not reasonable to assume that we will eventually find *the* correct statistic for measuring the abundance of an animal bone category. Each statistic has strengths and weaknesses, and therefore special applications. The fact that a statistic has been used frequently in the past does not automatically make it the right one to apply in the future.

In recent years, emphasis has been placed on making animal bone studies more consistent. One proposal is that certain assemblage-level values always be calculated. Unfortunately, animal bone statistics are not always computed in the same way nor could they be, given the variable nature of the collections. Moreover, few techniques do more than reduce a complex distribution of bone-fragment frequencies to a single value. Publishing a listing of TNF's, MNI's or RF's is analogous to reporting the means of a series of distributions but not their standard deviations. The utility of these statistics in comparative work is thus substantially reduced.

Assemblages may be described at various levels. Estimates of the abundances of categories can range from simple presence/absence information to quantitative values spread on ratio scales. Beyond the basic understanding that more refined scales (ordinal, interval, ratio) require larger samples, guidance is sparse as to when one level or another is appropriate. Grayson (1979) has argued that advancing beyond the ordinal scale of measurement is very risky. Computer simulations of various procedures indicate that very large samples are required to achieve high levels of reliability no matter what technique for estimating is employed.

For some time to come, therefore, it will be necessary to present the raw data from which summary descriptions are drawn. Because of this situation, we present several techniques for describing and summarizing the categories within assemblages. Where possible, we try to indicate the strengths and weaknesses of each method.

## MEASURING ASSEMBLAGE DIVERSITY

### Comparing Numbers of Categories

At the simplest level, assemblages can be presented as lists, with no attempt to assess the relative abundance of any of the categories. It has been suggested that the number of categories is a measure of culturally significant processes. For example, Bokonyi (1975) has argued that subsistence techniques are a conservative cultural feature. Animal husbandmen resist changing their basic approach even when their choice of animals and management methods is not proving successful. If this thesis is valid, increasing diversity is a measure of economic stress. Diversity may also be an index of the process of "settling in." Thus, the shift from a nomadic life-style focussing on the intense pursuit of a few species, perhaps in special places or at certain times of the year, to a sedentary existence with a more catholic exploitation of local resources should be reflected in increasing diversity in the faunal remains.

The difficulty with estimating diversity from a list of species is that the length of the list is often related to the size of the collection. The more bones that are recovered, the greater the likelihood that rare species will be represented. Thus, comparing the number of species at two sites or from two periods at the same site is only appropriate when the number of identifiable fragments is roughly the same. Further, the technique of recovery must be similar. If the minimum size of reliably recovered fragments is much different in two sites or contexts, the probability of identifying small taxa (which contribute the most to diversity) will be sufficiently biased that any contrast in diversity becomes meaningless.

Lists for different collections may also be examined for similarity following the procedure suggested by Simpson (discussed in Shipman (1981) for calculating the Faunal Resemblance Index (FRI):

$$FRI = 100 \times \frac{C \text{ (# of taxa common to both samples)}}{N \text{ (# of taxa in the smaller sample)}}$$

### Comparing Groups of Categories

The problem with all simple diversity and similarity measures is that they may obscure a "true" state of affairs. It is very common to discover that two collections are overwhelmingly dominated by the same few species, other taxa being represented by a scattering of fragments. If the scatterings derive from different species, the divergence of the two collections will seem large, whereas common sense indicates it is not. A solution is to assign the categories to groups, such as wild animals versus domestic stock, small rodents and birds versus larger animals, species whose presence in the deposit can be attributed to human activity versus commensals and other possibly natural accumulations. The diversities and similarities among these groups can be calculated and evaluated.

## ESTIMATING CATEGORY ABUNDANCE

A more frequent approach is to assess the abundance of each category in a sample. A wide variety of measures of abundance has been proposed and expectations about what these statistics represent also vary. At one extreme, the measures are seen as estimates of the absolute amount of some animal category deposited at the site. At the other, they are considered to be values that establish the locus of an animal category on an ordinal scale of abundance. The intermediate position is that category abundance can be estimated only in a relative way, using the ratios between frequencies. Deciding which of these expectations is reasonable for some analysis involves weighing such factors as the proportion of the site excavated, the intensity of the collecting effort, the complexity and duration of the occupation, and the existence of serious attritional processes. In terms of animal bone research, the most significant factors are the relationship between the sample and the hypothesized taphonomic space, and the intensity of destructive taphonomic processes. Most general considerations of this problem have led to the conclusion that ordinal-scale estimations are most frequently justified, relative scales less so, and absolute values rarely.

There is also the question of whether category abundance should be expressed in terms of frequency (relative or otherwise) or whether the relative significance of each category as a resource should be factored in. As has been noted, a recipe for elephant and rabbit stew that calls for one elephant and one rabbit will taste somewhat different from a dish prepared using one kilogram each of rabbit and elephant meat. The problem of converting category abundances to meat weights will be discussed in a subsequent section, but we recommend that this analysis be done in addition to rather than instead of providing the values of category abundance. Animals are resources in many realms of culture, from providing skins for clothing to conferring status for success in hunting (e.g. Gramley 1977, 1979; Turner and Santley 1979; Webster 1979). Reducing them to clusters of calories or piles of proteins cuts off numerous other interesting lines of research.

Methods for estimating category abundance should be applied to the comparison of categories of equivalent reliability of identification. In sites containing sheep, goats, cattle, and pigs, for example, it makes little sense to employ a single ratio of abundance:

*Ovis:Capra:Bos:Sus*

The reason is that cattle and pig bones are distinct from one another and from the bones of sheep and goats, whereas the latter are very difficult to separate. Thus, including only those fragments confidently assignable to either species would seriously understate their abundance. A preferable approach is to use two ratios based on equivalent reliability of information:

Ratio 1. *Ovis/Capra:Bos:Sus*
Ratio 2. *Ovis:Capra*

Five principal methods have been used to estimate abundance: (1) bone volume, (2) bone weight, (3) total number of fragments, (4) minimum number of individuals, and (5) relative frequency.

## Bone Volume

After the bone fragments have been washed, and while they are still wet, those from each excavation unit should be placed in a graduated container filled with water. Noting the level of the liquid before immersion and recording the amount displaced provides an estimate of the volume of the bone. This information can be grouped into taphonomic spaces and compared to similar information obtained for other categories of artifactual debris.

The relative proportions of bone to inorganic materials may reflect differential conditions of preservation within a site. On the assumption that the least resistant fragments will be destroyed first, a negative correlation between the relative amount of bone recovered and its relative density (i.e. the lower the volume per unit of weight, the higher the density of the bone) is evidence for bias in preservation.

Differences in the relative volume of bone may permit distinguishing secondary from primary refuse. The unpleasant nature of rotting organic matter leads many communities to segregate faunal debris from other categories of garbage. Thus, bone concentrations may represent refuse areas or locations some distance from habitations and work areas.

Bone volumes may be calculated for specific categories of remains as well as for total assemblages. They can be used to describe the proportion of each kind of bone that is preserved, a method that may be faster than preparing drawings for each category of fragment, as was suggested in an earlier chapter. The difficulty is establishing a standard for comparison, since the volume of bone in a skeletal element not only increases as the animal matures, but differs among the sex and age classes of polymorphic species. Thus, a series of standards must be developed and individual fragments matched with appropriate analogs, perhaps using measurements.

If the volume of each fragment recovered is established, the resulting data can be portrayed as a bar graph. If the X-axis is used to scale increasing size, the right side of the graph should form a smooth curve, assuming with Watson (1972) that the abundances of the fragment sizes are normally distributed. The point on the left side of the distribution at which the curve becomes erratic approximates the smallest fragments reliably recovered by the sampling method employed during excavation. This procedure is very time consuming and, unless volumes are needed for some other purpose, alternative approaches for detecting sampling bias should be tried first.

In archeological situations where the number of animals originally present in the deposit is known, it might be useful to calculate the volume of bone in a taxonomic category. The proportion recovered compared to the total amount of bone known to have been present at the inception of formation of the site (determined by multiplying the number of animals by the average skeletal volume per individual) would index preservational conditions, although not reveal much about the processes involved.

Estimating bone volume by immersion is stressful to archeological specimens because repeated soaking and drying increase the rate of post-excavation fracture and damage. The paucity of reference information about skeletal volume for even commonly encountered categories restricts the application of the data to the most general (all osseous material) and most specific (the individual skeletal element) levels of comparison.

## Bone Weight

A second method for estimating category abundance is weight, a datum that is convenient to record during initial processing of a collection. Like volume, weight can be used for comparing bones with other broad categories of artifactual debris. When suitably grouped into taphonomic units, differences in bone weights may reveal differential preservation and distinguish primary from secondary debris.

In order to assess differential preservation, the relative composition of the subsamples must be established by scoring each identifiable fragment by its density, as determined experimentally from modern material. This procedure insures that the archeological specimens are represented by their original density values rather than those obtaining after the experience of burial. Its realization is hampered, however, by the paucity of comparative data from fresh skeletons.

A cruder estimate can be produced by dividing weight by volume within each collection. Ideally, this would be done by weighing and taking the volume of each bone fragment, a very laborious procedure. An alternative approach is to estimate the density of the sample from each of the excavation units to be combined for analysis.

The weight of the fragments assigned to a category has been used to estimate the abundance of the category in an assemblage (Uerpmann 1973; Ziegler 1973). In practice, this value is converted to an estimate of the dietary resource it represents by multiplying the weights of the bones by the ratio of meat to bone (by weight) in a typical carcass of the category.

This procedure incorporates numerous methological problems. First, it obscures the fact that the amount of meat per carcass is highly variable. At a minimum, it is affected by the age, sex, and condition of the animal when it is slaughtered. Second, it assumes that whole carcasses are represented by the debris. In fact, dead animals tend to be subdivided into packets of meat, bone, and sinew that may be widely dispersed. Third, it reduces the economic importance of animals to a single category, protein, whereas they have a variety of non-dietary uses. Fourth, there are few reliable data on which to base conversions from bone weight to meat weight. Fifth, bone weight is not a constant through archeological time. Soil conditions alter both composition and weight through chemical action. These considerations significantly restrict the utility of the bone-weight method. In our opinion, it serves its greatest function as a basis for comparing samples of animal bone to other general categories of archeological debris.

## Total Number of Fragments (TNF)

Other techniques for estimating abundance involve either inspecting or manipulating arithmetically the number of bones assigned to a category. The simplest measure of frequency is the actual number of identified fragments. This value is often labeled TNF (Total Number of Fragments) or E, and is calculated as follows:

Let     F1, F2, . . . Fn = the types of fragments in a category and
Let     #Fn = the number of specimens of each type
Then    TNF = #F1 + #F2 + #F3 + . . . #Fn

Problems with using TNF to estimate abundance arise when the values are considered to reflect the sizes of the populations represented by the categories of animals. For instance, TNF values of 50% *Bos* and 50% *Equus* might easily be interpreted as evidence that a death assemblage (thanatocoenosis) contains half cattle and half horses. Unfortunately, this conclusion is not necessarily valid. The values actually indicate that the sample consists of 50% cattle parts and 50% horse parts. If the latter species is represented only by heads and the former by whole carcasses, many more horses than cows are included in the assemblage.

*Effect of Interdependence.* Another problem with TNF values is that they can be biased by interdependence; that is, the chance that two fragments from the same animal will not be recognized as such and will be counted twice. The bias may not be severe unless the degree of interdependence is different in the categories compared or TNF is expected to estimate the actual number of animals or animal parts rather than their relative frequencies. The degree of interdependence can be crudely estimated using the procedures suggested in the previous chapter. TNF should not be used when samples have widely divergent interdependence values, and never to estimate the actual size of the population composing the deposit.

Before TNF is computed, it should be shown that the taxa compared derive from equivalent areas of disarticulation and deposition (taphonomic spaces). This can be done using category analysis. At the same time that the similarities in the archeological animals are established, total bias in the pattern of skeletal preservation can be assessed by comparing the ratios of the frequencies of bone categories in living animals to those in the excavated sample.

**Unequal Potential Recovery.** Comparisons of abundances of different animals within assemblages using TNF results are affected by the number of types of fragments in each category. If one category is potentially represented by five types and another by ten, the second has a better chance of being recovered, identified, and counted. If one were comparing the relative abundance of *Equus* and *Bos,* the additional bones in the skeleton of the latter would give it an advantage in recoverability and produce an estimate of frequency exceeding the true contribution of cattle to the sample. Two methods can be used to deal with this problem.

One way to minimize the bias in TNF created by differing numbers of fragment types within categories is to consider the abundances as measures of trends across several temporal or spatial contexts. An example can be constructed using hypothetical TNF values (Table 8). In this case, all that is implied is that sheep and cows become relatively more frequent through time, whereas horses and pigs become less abundant. No conclusion may be drawn either about the total number of animals exploited in each period or the relative sizes of the populations of the species during any period.

**Adjustments to TNF.** Another possibility is to make adjustments in the way the TNF value is calculated. Correction factors might be developed from the relative number of fragment types in the animal categories compared, but this is likely to be very difficult since the relative probability of recovery of each type of fragment would have to be estimated. An easier approach is to make the lists for the animal categories to be compared as similar as possible by identifying the types of fragments the taxa have in common and using these to calculate TNF. It is advisable to identify this kind of count by giving it a different label, such as TNFcl (comparable lists). TNFcl can be calculated as follows:

> Let A1, A2, A3, . . . An = the fragment types in Category A matched in Category B
>
> Let B1, B2, B3, . . . Bn = the fragment types in Category B matched in Category A
>
> Plot the counts A1 . . . An and B1 . . . Bn as histograms and establish rough similarity.
>
> Then #A1 + #A2 + . . .#An = TNFcl for Category A, and #B1 + #B2 + . . . #Bn = TNFcl for Category B.

### Minimum Number of Individuals (MNI)

By far the most popular method of estimating category abundance is the statistic called Minimum Number of Individuals, usually abbreviated as MNI or MIND. First, it is widely applied and thus permits comparing the collection at hand to those from other sites. Second, it is easy to determine since its value is obtained by inspection. Third, depending on how it is applied, it can eliminate completely the bias of interdependence.

MNI is exactly what it says it is: the minimum number of animals (or animal parts) that would have to have existed to create a given sample. It contrasts conceptually with TNF, which estimates the maximum number of individuals required to explain a sample (the condition of complete sample independence). In its simplest form, it is determined by the most frequent type of fragment in a category. For example, the compilations in Table 9 indicate the MNI is 35 for cattle, 27 for pigs, and 15 for camels.

**Table 8.** The relative abundance of four species in three periods of occupation at a site. The values are expressed as percentages based on TNF. The only inference that can be drawn is that cow and sheep increased in abundance while horse and pig decreased.

|  | Species | | | |
|---|---|---|---|---|
| Period | Cow | Horse | Pig | Sheep |
| Late | 25 | 15 | 25 | 35 |
| Middle | 10 | 25 | 40 | 25 |
| Early | 5 | 30 | 50 | 15 |

**Table 9.** A hypothetical example of the determination of the statistic Minimum Number of Individuals (MNI), using an abbreviated archeological animal. The element with the most fragments establishes the MNI. Note that the estimate of abundance by MNI does not agree with that derived using TNF.

| Skeletal Element | Species | | |
| --- | --- | --- | --- |
| | Bos | Sus | Camelus |
| Atlas | 10 | 17 | 8 |
| Axis | 8 | 13 | 9 |
| Right mandible | 15 | 21 | 6 |
| Left mandible | 11 | 16 | 5 |
| Right distal humerus | 35 | 22 | 13 |
| Left distal humerus | 31 | 24 | 12 |
| Right proximal femur | 17 | 14 | 15 |
| Left proximal femur | 16 | 20 | 10 |
| Right distal tibia | 18 | 27 | 14 |
| Left distal tibia | 13 | 19 | 10 |
| Right astragalus | 10 | 20 | 14 |
| Left astragalus | 9 | 21 | 13 |
| Total (TNF) | 193 | 234 | 129 |
| MNI | 35 | 27 | 15 |

***Modifications to MNI.*** The calculation of MNI has been elaborated in several ways. Sometimes age is taken into consideration. As an example, consider a sample of sheep/goat bones containing 100 first phalanges and 90 second phalanges, bones that fuse at about the same point in the maturation of these animals. The simple MNI would be 100. However, if 90 of the first phalanges were mature and 10 immature, whereas 70 of the second phalanges were mature and 20 immature, it could be argued that a MNI of 100 underestimates the true value. The 100 first phalanges do not include enough immature examples to pair with all the immature second phalanges. To eliminate this discrepancy, the MNI should be increased to 110.

Size is another relevant variable in the example above. The proximal width of the mature second phalanges and the distal width of the mature first phalanges could be measured and, if the normal relationship between these two dimensions in sheep and goats were known, it might be possible to show that 10 of the mature second phalanges were either too large or too small to be paired with any of the mature first phalanges. These "extras" would have to be added to the MNI, raising the value to 120. As we learn more about the correlations within the osteometry of the species we study, we should enhance our ability to make such corrections.

Disease could also be factored in. Bone disease in joint areas usually affects all the articulated bones. Thus, if five of the proximal second phalanges showed exostoses, whereas none of the distal first phalanges did, then the MNI would have to be increased to 125.

To make these adjustments to MNI, each animal category was subdivided before the value for the sample was calculated. Sub-MNI's for large and small, old and young, healthy and diseased, were computed and then summed to provide a total MNI. In effect, reliable cases of non-interdependence were isolated on the basis of zoological considerations, adding bone fragments to each MNI count.

MNI estimates can also be modified using archeological information. As with TNF, MNI is determined for samples from groups of excavation units. In contrast to the TNF abundance estimator, however, whether one groups the excavation units before establishing the MNI or establishes the MNI independently for each excavation unit and then sums the results will have a dramatic effect on the final estimate of abundance (Grayson 1973). In fact, if the MNI is calculated from small enough excavation units before summing, it will begin to approach TNF. This is because selecting a subsample for calculating MNI amounts to specifying the size of the area over which interdependence is likely to be a problem.

Because of this behavior of the MNI statistic, attention must be paid to the character of the archeological excavation units. Both horizontal and vertical dimensions need to be considered. The two key questions are:

1. How far apart must two bones be to favor the probability that they do not come from the same animal?

2. How different in time do two deposits have to be to insure that parts of the same animal are not included in both?

Answering these questions establishes the taphonomic spaces appropriate for calculating MNI.

The result of all these adjustments is to increase the value of MNI in the direction of TNF (Lie 1980, Schram and Turnbull 1970). Coy (1977) suggests that these modified statistics could be labeled the Probable Number of Individuals (PNI). In our view, these corrections are important because MNI is intended to be used as an index for comparison. The "true" number of individuals that died to create a sample lies somewhere between MNI and TNF, but the spread between these two values is not a constant, making some MNI's more minimum than others (Fig. 98). Comparing MNI's is thus equivalent to taking the low end of a range rather than the mean or median. Calculating

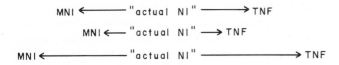

**Fig. 98.** Reducing error before comparing MNI's. MNI and TNF provide lower and upper limits to estimates for the "true" number of animals that contributed to a deposit. Since the range between these extremes is not a constant, comparing MNI's injects variation of the kind shown here into the estimates. Establishing the PNI (Probable Number of Individuals) diminishes this discrepancy, providing a more reliable basis for comparison.

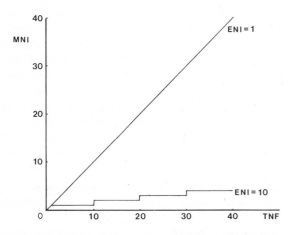

**Fig. 99.** The manner in which the relationship between MNI and TNF is controlled by ENI, the Effective Number of Individuals. If an animal category has 10 types of elements, then ENI can range from 1 to 10. When only one slot actually has any specimens, a plot of MNI and TNF will follow the diagonal line for all sample sizes. When all 10 types of elements are equally represented, the plot will follow the stepped line. The degree of divergence from the lower pattern is a measure of the distortion in the archeological animal from skeletal proportions in the living animal. Since smaller samples are likely to be more distorted, their ENI is likely to be lower than among large samples. This does not mean that the MNI's of small and large samples cannot be compared.

PNI tends to reduce the range and thus provides a more reliable basis for comparison.

***Comparing MNI and TNF.*** Considerable effort has been devoted to establishing the relationship between MNI and TNF (Bobrowsky 1982). When large numbers of pairs of these values derived from many collections are plotted, a curvilinear pattern emerges. Most of the deflection from a straight line occurs in the area of the graph near the origin. This result has been interpreted as evidence that MNI's from samples widely divergent in size cannot be compared.

The plot of TNF versus MNI is curved because the Effective Number of Individuals or ENI is likely to vary with sample size (Holtzman 1979). One can visualize the MNI counting procedure as placing fragments in boxes according to types. As sorting proceeds, every so often a fragment is placed in the box containing the most frequent type. The average number of bones intervening between these events is the ENI. This number can vary from one to the total number of types of fragments (Fig. 99). When MNI versus TNF is plotted for a series of samples of equivalent categories of animals from sites excavated in a similar manner, the curvilinear relationship tends to disappear because the archeological animals for these categories are similar (Hesse 1982a).

The curve in the plot of MNI and TNF measures the differences between archeological animals. Categories with few specimens are likely to be dominated by one or two types of fragments because the others are difficult to identify or seldom preserved. Thus, there is no reason to divide animal categories solely on the basis of sample size unless it can be shown that the most frequent element in each category was differentially preserved.

***MNI as an Estimator of Abundance.*** MNI can be recommended as an estimator of abundance where it is suspected that interdependence is radically different in the categories being compared. It is also useful when the archeological animals are sharply divergent. On the negative side, MNI effectively ignores the information provided by a large proportion of the sample by shifting the analysis from estimating the amount of animal resources to counting the number of animals represented by a sample of bones. In some computer simulations where differential bias was not severe, it did not perform as well as TNF or another abundance estimator, RF, discussed below (Gilbert and Singer 1982; Holtzman 1979).

### Relative Frequency (RF)

A third method of estimating abundance is Relative Frequency (RF) or the Weighted Abundance of Elements (WAE). It is the most complicated to apply since it involves a series of arithmetic operations. The two main goals of the procedure are to overcome the primary weaknesses of MNI (that the existence of a whole animal is inferred from one of its parts) and TNF (that the categories of animals are represented by variable numbers of types of fragments). RF is calculated by listing the types of bones representing a

**Table 10.** The calculation of Relative Frequency (RF) for the five main levels at Tepe Ganj Dareh. The corrected frequencies of the element types in each level have been added and divided by the number of types.

| Level | A | | B | | C | | D | | E | |
|-------|------|-----|-------|-----|-------|-----|-------|-----|-------|-----|
| | INNOM | 444 | INNOM | 500 | CALC | 116 | CALC | 588 | INNOM | 508 |
| | CALC | 380 | CALC | 420 | PRAD | 104 | DHUM | 568 | PRAD | 368 |
| | DHUM | 336 | ASTRA | 404 | DHUM | 96 | INNOM | 484 | DTIB | 360 |
| | DMTC | 328 | DHUM | 400 | PULN | 88 | ASTRA | 448 | DRAD | 344 |
| | PMTC | 316 | PMTC | 400 | PMTT | 80 | DFEM | 424 | PULN | 344 |
| | ASTRA | 312 | SCAP | 384 | SCAP | 76 | PHUM | 412 | CALC | 340 |
| | SCAP | 292 | PRAD | 348 | ASTRA | 76 | PMTC | 388 | PMTT | 336 |
| | PMTT | 284 | PULN | 344 | CALC | 72 | PFEM | 384 | DHUM | 328 |
| | PRAD | 276 | PMTT | 340 | N-C | 68 | PULN | 368 | PMTC | 280 |
| | PH-1 | 244 | DMTC | 336 | PMTC | 68 | PRAD | 348 | SCAP | 268 |
| | PULN | 244 | N-C | 312 | PTIB | 64 | SCAP | 332 | ASTRA | 252 |
| | N-C | 240 | DMTT | 280 | DRAD | 64 | PMTC | 324 | DMTC | 232 |
| | DMTT | 228 | PH-1 | 268 | INNOM | 64 | N-C | 320 | AXIS | 208 |
| | DTIB | 204 | PFEM | 258 | PH-1 | 62 | PH-1 | 316 | PFEM | 196 |
| | PFEM | 176 | C-T | 228 | DFEM | 56 | DMTT | 308 | DMTT | 188 |
| | PH-2 | 162 | PHUM | 228 | DTIB | 56 | DTIB | 284 | PH-1 | 186 |
| | DRAD | 156 | SCAPH | 216 | C-T | 56 | PMTT | 280 | N-C | 184 |
| | C-T | 156 | DTIB | 212 | PH-3 | 45 | PATE | 272 | PHUM | 168 |
| | SEML | 144 | SEML | 208 | PATE | 44 | C-T | 272 | DFEM | 160 |
| | PHUM | 140 | DRAD | 204 | DMTC | 44 | DRAD | 256 | PTIB | 116 |
| | PH-3 | 130 | PH-2 | 182 | PH-2 | 42 | SCAPH | 228 | PH-2 | 114 |
| | SCAPH | 128 | DFEM | 164 | PFEM | 40 | PH-2 | 215 | PATE | 108 |
| | DFEM | 128 | PH-3 | 160 | SEML | 40 | SEML | 200 | SCAPH | 104 |
| | AXIS | 112 | PTIB | 140 | DMTT | 40 | PTIB | 196 | SEML | 96 |
| | PTIB | 112 | PYRA | 120 | AXIS | 32 | PH-3 | 187 | ATLAS | 96 |
| | PYRA | 104 | AXIS | 112 | SCAPH | 32 | OSCRO | 156 | C-T | 92 |
| | PATE | 92 | PATE | 104 | OSCRO | 28 | AXIS | 120 | PH-3 | 88 |
| | OSCRO | 64 | OSCRO | 100 | PYRA | 24 | ATLAS | 112 | OSCRO | 64 |
| | ATLAS | 56 | ATLAS | 88 | ATLAS | 24 | PYRA | 108 | PYRA | 52 |
| TOTAL | | 5988 | | 7446 | | 1701 | | 8898 | | 6181 |
| RF | | 206 | | 257 | | 59 | | 307 | | 213 |

category and the number of fragments in each, obtaining the total number of fragments, and dividing it by the number of types (Table 10). This produces a sort of average MNI. RF works under the assumption that each type of element within a category constitutes an alternative estimator of the relative abundance of the category. Looked at this way, RF is analogous to a mean, whereas MNI represents the maximum of a distribution.

*Modifications to RF.* Several modifications have been made in calculating this statistic. One is to reduce the number of types of fragments used in the analysis. The types of a category are arranged in a ranked list and a proportion (perhaps half, two-thirds or three-quarters) is extracted from the middle of the distribution. RF is calculated from the counts in this sample. The goal of this procedure is to eliminate from the calculation those types of fragments that are over or

under preserved and thus likely to bias the result.

Elimination can also be done on a case-by-case basis. For example, in the samples excavated from the Bronze Age site of Karatas-Semayuk in southwest Turkey (Hesse and Perkins 1974), mandibles were outstandingly common compared to other parts of the skeleton among sheep/goat, but not among cattle remains. We suspected that this abundance reflected selection of mandibles for tools and/or sullegic bias. Thus, in comparing the relative frequency of *Ovis/Capra* and *Bos,* mandible fragments were eliminated. Extremely rare types of elements were also excluded because their recovery seemed likely to have been biased compared to other kinds of fragments.

The number of fragment types used as the divisor in the equation is also a matter for some consideration. In the cases presented so far, n was equal to the number of types represented by at least one specimen. Difficulty occurs when RF is being calculated for the same category in a series of contexts. Should n be the number of filled slots in each individual context or the number of filled slots in the collection as a whole? The first option incorporates the assumption that the animals were being deposited in different contexts in different ways. The second implies that all types in the category were being deposited and that differential preservation accounts for the empty slots.

*RF as an Estimator.* RF seems to perform better than MNI in simulations of category counting, but it is susceptible to distortion by widely different levels of interdependence. Further, it does not attempt to measure the "actual" number of individuals that contributed to the deposit. It has the distinct advantage of forcing consideration of how each category is represented. All the modifications to the standard calculation of RF restrict the lists of values used to estimate relative abundance in ways that make them similar and consequently comparable.

## THE ANALYSIS OF ABUNDANCE ESTIMATES

After category abundances have been estimated, they can be incorporated into the research design. Often, all that is required is the estimate itself, expressed either as a relative frequency or as a ranking. In other cases, it is necessary to transform the abundance estimates by considering how an example of each category would have been valued as a resource.

## Untransformed Estimates

The abundance of the house mouse, *Mus musculus,* in the samples from Tepe Ganj Dareh was used as an indicator of permanence of settlement (Hesse 1979). This interpretation was motivated by the observation that this animal is most successful in inhabiting dumps in seasonal environments when there is a continuous input of debris. Intermittent occupations would be unlikely to fit this condition and mice ought to be less common in such sites. The abundance of this tiny animal was measured by MNI and compared to the frequency of the other rodents in the collection *(Meriones* and *Ellobius)* and of the most common category, sheep/goat. MNI was selected as the estimator for the rodents because only one type of element, the mandible, was reliably recovered by the sampling technique and certainly identifiable to the species. Also, it was expected that interdependence would be high in the samples for these species. RF was used to measure the sheep/goat category. The increased abundance of *Mus* in the upper levels of the site reinforced the evidence for more permanent settlement implied by the concomitant appearance of mud-brick construction.

A second example also involves rodents. The Archaic sites of Tulán-52 and Puripica in the Salar de Atacama basin of northern Chile produced substantial quantities of chinchilla and viscacha. The former species is famous for its fur, though it is large enough to provide a significant amount of meat; the latter is a much larger animal with a somewhat less luxurient though still beautiful coat. Comparison to the most important animal resource at these sites, the camelids, showed rodents to be more abundant at Puripica than at Tulán, a record paralleled in the avian remains. When the frequencies of the two taxa were examined, using MNI and defining the taphonomic space as the whole site, they showed that the inhabitants of Puripica were more intensively pursuing viscachas than chinchillas. Viscachas are diurnal, whereas chinchillas are crepuscular. Increased pursuit of the former implies reallocation of time during the day previously devoted to other activities. The pursuit of chinchillas, an activity of early morning and evening, was apparently not affected. Since category analysis of the camelid remains suggested that the people of Puripica were at least part-time pastoralists, whereas the occupants of Tulán were hunters, two activity patterns were inferred. At Tulán, the hunters apparently pursued vicuñas and guanacos during the day, shifting to rodents in the morning and evening. At Puripica, pastoralists filled out their day of herding by hunting viscachas, probably as a buffer resource, while continuing to hunt chinchillas at dawn and dusk.

## Transforming Death Assemblages into Life Assemblages

The relative proportions of animals in the collection from a site cannot be assumed equivalent to those in the living community unless the sample is derived from a catastrophic event. Even then, the cause of mortality must be known so that the selective bias of the agent can be factored into the analysis. Further, the social behavior of the animal whose remains are being studied must be known well enough so that the slice of the biological environment from which the sample derives can be specified.

For attritional samples, living assemblages (biocoenoses) can only be inferred from death assemblages (thanatocoenoses) by transforming the mortality information. Two species whose estimated abundances are equal in the archeological samples would only have been equal in numbers in the ancient environment if they died at the same average age. A simplified example shows why this is so (Fig. 100). Reconstructions of this kind depend on the certainty that a sample incorporates all the mortality of some definable population of animals.

## Converting Category Abundance to Resource Abundance

In research designs, the concept of resource is frequently equated with food and the relative abundances of the animal categories are expected to reveal how much each contributed to the diet of the past society. Transforming quantities of bones into amounts of meat can be approached in two ways.

If the results of the category analysis indicate that an animal or portion of an animal is represented by only a few of its parts, it makes sense to proceed additively. Each type of element can be assigned an estimate of the quantity of meat that would have surrounded it when the animal was butchered. Then, the number of fragments can be multiplied by the meat weight in kilograms for each type and the total established for each category:

**CONDITIONS**

1. The animals of Herd A are being harvested between the ages of one and two; the animals of Herd B between the ages of four and five.

2. Animals of both species are only sexually mature after they reach five. One male is required for every five females and each female produces one young per year. Two in fifteen pregnancies end in abortion.

3. All animals of both species not harvested at the specified age survive to die a natural death on their eleventh birthday.

(The animals in brackets are dying or being harvested in each year. Each herd is losing 230 animals per year.)

| Age | For Slaughter | | For Reproduction | Young |
|-----|------|------|------|------|
| | Herd A | Herd B | Herd A or B | Herd A or B |
| 0–1 | 100 | 100 | 25 F + 5 M | |
| 1–2 | (100) | 100 | 25 F + 5 M | |
| 2–3 | | 100 | 25 F + 5 M | |
| 3–4 | | 100 | 25 F + 5 M | |
| 4–5 | | (100) | 25 F + 5 M | |
| 5–6 | | | 25 F + 5 M | 25 F & M |
| 6–7 | | | 25 F + 5 M | 25 F & M |
| 7–8 | | | 25 F + 5 M | 25 F & M |
| 8–9 | | | 25 F + 5 M | 25 F & M |
| 9–10 | | | 25 F + 5 M | 25 F & M |
| 10–11 | | | (25 F + 5 M) | 25 F & M |
| Totals | 200 | 500 | 275 | 55  (130 as 13% lost) |

Total Population of Herd A = 200 + 275 + 55 = 530

Herd B = 500 + 275 + 55 = 830

Thus two equal attritional death assemblages composed of:

Herd A — 13% fetal, 67% 1 yr. olds, 20% 11 yr. olds

Herd B — 13% fetal, 67% 4 yr. olds, 20% 11 yr. olds,

or a ratio of 1 : 1 actually implies a living ratio of 1 : 1.56.

**Fig. 100.** Attritional samples with equal proportions of fetal, immature, and mature individuals produced from living assemblages of distinct sizes and age compositions. This hypothetical example illustrates the pitfalls of attempts to infer details of animal husbandry from archeological information.

Species A

| Fragment type | Meat/ example | # of examples | Total |
|-----|-----|-----|-----|
| D Humerus | 2.3 | 35 | 80.5 |
| D Femur | 1.7 | 26 | 44.2 |
| . | . | . | . |
| . | . | . | . |
| | | Grand total | xxx.x |

Establishing acceptable estimates for amounts of meat requires considerable experimentation because of the variability among individuals. At a minimum, the ratio can be expected to change with the age, sex, and condition of the animal. Another problem is that important edible parts that do not encapsulate a bone, such as organs, are unrepresented. Further, if the meat was stripped from the bones before being transported to the site, the amount calculated will severely underestimate the true situation. What is measured by this approach is the minimum amount of meat available that is represented by a collection of bones. A somewhat more reliable result can be obtained by working with butchering units (Lyman 1979).

Alternatively, one can assume that most examples of each category were deposited in the space represented by the sample. Then, one of the abundance estimators that attempts to convert animal parts into whole animals (MNI or RF) can be transformed into meat by multiplying each value by an estimate of the meat contained in a single animal. It is important to remember that these multipliers are extremely variable in most species and to use modern analogs that replicate as closely as possible the ancient conditions. The MNI or RF should be broken down into components based on size, age, and sex for most barnyard stock because of the wide diversity in these characters. Among hunted animals, it must be remembered that their condition changes during the year and the season of slaughter may be a significant determinant of the amount of meat provided.

Meat weights can be converted into protein and calorie estimates for inclusion in research designs that emphasize the energetics of human adaptation. However, each step farther away from the bones introduces additional variability and uncertainty into the analysis and the results.

## Linking Category Abundance to Work Involved

Finally, category abundances can be used to estimate the amount of effort required to obtain the resource in question. The distributions, activity patterns, and defensive abilities of prey species can be converted into estimates of the time and energy required to catch an individual. When these are coupled with estimates of the relative frequencies of each species in a typical hunter's bag and the amount of food value each represents, an assessment of the relative efficiency of an ancient subsistence economy can be developed.

# 9     From Objectives to Analysis

The theme of this manual has been that animal bone archeology is a collaborative venture. Each step of the research requires cooperative decisions by the project director/archeologist and the animal bone specialist. The study of a large collection can be a daunting undertaking and the work must be partitioned to accomplish it efficiently. Analysis should be directed toward answering a series of cultural or historical questions rather than simply identifying and describing categories of material.

Below, in summary form, are the eight principal kinds of decisions that must be incorporated into the research design if the potential inherent in animal bone archeology is to be realized. The questions posed are sufficiently broad to allow fine-tuning for individual circumstances, yet they insure detailing the information necessary for successful collaboration. The time to define the significant questions is before going into the field.

## 1. Category Formation

What animal categories are important for historical or cultural interpretation? Two main spheres should be investigated. Zoology provides a template of categories that can be used to catalog the collection and to elucidate many aspects of environmental exploitation. Folk classification offers a number of general principles and observations that may be applied to group zoological categories into culturally relevant units. Animals interact in all spheres of human activity, from the technological to the ideological. All these areas must be accommodated in the research design.

## 2. Animal Bone Units

Which animal bone remnants are associated with each of the categories deemed important for analysis? The size and fragility of these fragments will establish the excavation strategy at the site. This includes preparation for field conservation and for description of finds in situ, as well as specifying recovery techniques.

## 3. Attribute Identification

What are the diagnostic features of the important animal bone remnants? How are they related to patterns of animal management or exploitation? Can they be recognized in archeological material? These questions determine what attributes of the bone fragments must be recorded (dimensions, modifications, morphology, etc.). The complexity of the anticipated data set will mandate the recording system and data-handling equipment necessary.

## 4. Site Formation Processes

What biasing agents are expected to have distorted the characteristics of the sample during and after its deposition? Can any of them be modeled and their effects estimated? Is the sample so badly transformed by non-cultural agents as to obscure the evidence of human activity? The collection may be segregated into parts on the basis of the expected bias. Some biasing agents leave traces on the bone fragments. These features must be added to the list of attributes recorded about the sample.

## 5.  Archeological Units

How can the site be subdivided into meaningful spaces for animal bone interpretation? The processing of carcasses can lead to the wide dispersal of the remains of a single animal. Is it possible to identify the limits of the typical dispersal area and use this as the spatial unit of excavation and subsequent analysis? If not, can it at least be said that the archeological areas to be compared and contrasted in terms of the bone fragments they contain are similar in architecture, artifacts or other cultural remains?

## 6.  Level of Description

How precise do the category summaries have to be to answer cultural and historical questions? Can information be presented as nominal data or must a higher level of description (ordinal, interval or ratio) be used?

## 7.  Animal Category Comparison

Are the measures used to estimate the frequency of animal categories really analogous? Each animal category is made up of a number of types of fragments. If the relative frequencies of these types are not similar across the archeological areas being compared, they are unlikely to measure the same behavior.

## 8.  Sample Interdependence

How likely is it that interdependence affects each of the animal categories differently? The answer to this question (a probability statement about the chance of finding a second fragment from the same individual) will profoundly influence the choice of an estimator for the frequency of any category more general than a single type of bone.

# Literature Cited

Armitage, Philip
  1982  A System for Ageing and Sexing the Horn Cores of Cattle from British Post-medieval Sites (with Special Reference to Unimproved British Longhorn Cattle). In Ageing and Sexing Animal Bones from Archaeological Sites, edited by B. Wilson, C. Grigson, and S. Payne, pp. 37–54. BAR British Series 109.

Armitage, Philip and Juliet Clutton-Brock
  1976  A System for Classification and Description of Horn Cores of Cattle from Archaeological Sites. Journal of Archaeological Science, Volume 3, pp. 329–348.

Bacher, A.
  1967  Vergleichend morphologische Untersuchungen an Einzelknochen des postkranialen Skelettes in Mitteleuropa vorkommender Schwäne und Gänse. München.

Baker, John R. and Don R. Brothwell
  1980  Animal Diseases in Archaeology. Academic Press, London.

Ballinger, Diane
  n.d.  Butchering Marks on the Cattle Bones from Tell Jemmeh. Manuscript on file, Department of Anthropology, University of Alabama, Birmingham.

Bates, Daniel G.
  1973  Nomads and Farmers: A Study of the Yörük of Southeastern Turkey. Occasional Contribution No. 52. Museum of Anthropology, University of Michigan, Ann Arbor.

Baumgartner, H. and R. Lanooy
  1982  Eine Methode zur Wassersättigung Trockener, Fossiler, Knochen, Zähne und Hölzer, für die Konservierung mit PEG 6000 - 12000. Der Präparator, Volume 28, pp. 269–274.

Beckerman, Steven and Tom Sussenbach
  1983  A Quantitative Assessment of the Dietary Contribution of Game Species to the Subsistence of South American Tropical Forest Tribal Peoples. In Animals and Archaeology 1. Hunters and their Prey. edited by J. Clutton-Brock and C. Grigson, pp. 337–350. BAR International Series 163.

Behrensmeyer, Anna K.
  1975  Taphonomy and Paleoecology of the Plio-Pleistocene Vertebrate Assemblages East of Lake Rudolf, Kenya. Museum of Comparative Zoology Bulletin 146, pp. 473–578. Harvard University, Cambridge.
  1978  Taphonomic and Ecologic Information from Bone Weathering. Paleobiology, Volume 4 (2), pp. 150–162.

Bennett, John W.
  1964  Attitudes Towards Animals and Nature in a Great Plains Community. Plains Anthropologist, Volume 9, pp. 3–47.

Berlin, Brent
  1976  The Concept of Rank in Ethnobiological Classification: Some Evidence from Aguaruna Folk Botany. American Ethnologist, Volume 3, pp. 381–399.

Berlin, Brent, Dennis E. Breedlove, and Peter H. Raven
  1973  General Principles of Classification and Nomenclature in Folk Biology. American Anthropologist, Volume 75, pp. 214–242.

Binford, Lewis R.
  1978  Nunamuit Ethnoarchaeology. Academic Press, New York.
  1981  Bones: Ancient Men and Modern Myths. Academic Press, New York.
  1983  Reply. Current Anthropology, Volume 24, pp. 372–376.

Binford, Lewis R. and Jack B. Bertram
1977 Bone Frequencies and Attritional Processes. In For Theory Building in Archaeology, edited by L.R. Binford, pp. 77–153. Academic Press, New York.

Bobrowsky, Peter T.
1982 An Examination of Casteel's MNI Behavior Analysis: A Reductionist Approach. Midcontinental Journal of Archaeology, Volume 7, pp. 171–184.

Boessneck, Joachim
1970 Osteological Differences between Sheep (*Ovis aires* Linne) and goats (*Capra hircus* Linne). In Science in Archaeology, edited by D.R. Brothwell and E.S. Higgs, pp. 331–358. Praeger, New York.

Boessneck, Joachim, J.-P. Jéquier and Hans R. Stampfli
1963 Seeberg Burgäschisee-Süd, Teil 3: Die Tierreste. Acta Bernensia II. Bern.

Boessneck, Joachim, H.H. Müller and M. Teichert
1963 Osteologische Unterscheidungsmerkmale zwischen Schaf (*Ovis aires* Linne) and Ziege (*Capra hircus* Linne). Kühn Archiv, Volume 78, pp. 1–129.

Boessneck, Joachim and Angela Von den Dreisch
1975 Tierknochenfunde vom Korucutepe bei Elazig in Ostanatolien. In Korucutepe, edited by M.N. van Loon. Elsevier Publishing Company, New York.

Bogan, Arthur E. and Neil D. Robison
1978 A History and Selected Bibliography of Zooarchaeology in Eastern North America. Tennessee Anthropological Association Miscellaneous Paper No. 2.

Bökönyi, Sandor
1975 Effects of Environmental and Cultural Changes on Prehistoric Fauna Assemblages. In Gastronomy: The Anthropology of Food and Food Habits, edited by M.C. Arnott, pp. 3–12. Mouton, The Hague.

Bowen, Joanne
1975 Probate Inventories: An Evaluation from the Perspective of Zooarchaeology and Agricultural History at Mott Farm. Historical Archaeology, Volume 9, pp. 11–25.

Brain, C.K.
1967 Hottentot Food Remains and Their Bearing on the Interpretation of Fossil Bone Assemblages. Scientific Papers of the Namib Desert Research Station, Volume 32, pp. 1–11.
1980 Some Criteria for the Recognition of Bone-Collecting Agencies in African Caves. In Fossils in the Making: Vertebrate Taphonomy and Paleoecology, edited by A.K. Behrensmeyer and A.P. Hill, pp. 108–130. University of Chicago Press, Chicago.

1981 The Hunters or the Hunted? University of Chicago Press, Chicago.

Brothwell, Don
1976 Further Evidence of Bone Chewing by Ungulates: The Sheep of North Ronaldsay, Orkney. Journal of Archaeological Science, Volume 3, pp. 179–182.

Brown, Cecil H.
1979 Folk Zoological Life-forms: Their Universality and Growth. American Anthropologist, Volume 81, pp. 791–817.
1981 More on Folk Zoological Life-forms. American Anthropologist, Volume 83, pp. 398–401.

Brown, J. Clevedon
1976 Mammals of the Past - Field Methods. Mammal Review, Volume 6, pp. 161–166.

Bulmer, Ralph
1979 Mystical and Mundane Kalam Classification of Birds. In Classifications in Their Social Contexts, edited by Roy F. Ellen and David Reason, pp. 57–79. Academic Press, London.

Burleigh, Richard and Don Brothwell
1978 Studies on Amerindian Dogs, 1: Carbon Isotopes in Relation to Maize in the Diet of Domestic Dogs from Early Peru and Ecuador. Journal of Archaeological Science, Volume 5, pp. 355–362.

Casteel, Richard W.
1977 Characterization of Faunal Assemblages and the Minimum Number of Individuals Determined from Paired Elements: Continuing Problems in Archaeology. Journal of Archaeological Science, Volume 4, pp. 125–134.

Caughley, Graeme
1977 Analysis of Vertebrate Populations. John Wiley and Sons, New York.

Chaplin, Raymond E.
1971 The Study of Animal Bones from Archaeological Sites. Seminar Press, New York.

Clark, John and Kenneth K. Kietzke
1967 Paleoecology of the Lower Nodule Zone, Brule Formation, in the Big Badlands of South Dakota. Fieldiana: Geology Memoir 5, pp. 111–129.

Clutton-Brock, Juliet
1974 The Buhen Horse. Journal of Archaeological Science, Volume 1, pp. 89–100.
1975 A System for the Retrieval of Data Relating to Animal Remains from Archaeological Sites. In Archaeozoological Studies, edited by A.T. Clason, pp. 21–34. North Holland, Amsterdam.
1981 Domesticated Animals from Early Times. University of Texas Press, Austin.

Clutton-Brock, Juliet and Caroline Grigson
1983 Animals and Archaeology, Volumes 1–4. BAR International Series 163, 183, and forthcoming.

Cole, D.P.
1975   Nomads of the Nomads; The Al Murrah Be-
       douin of the Empty Quarter. Aldine, Chicago.
Cole, L.C.
1957   Sketches of General and Comparative Demo-
       graphy. Cold Springs Harbor Symposium on
       Quantitative Biology, Volume 22, pp. 1–15.
Coon, Carleton
1951   Cave Explorations in Iran, 1949. Museum
       Monographs. The University Museum, Phila-
       delphia.
Cornwall, I.W.
1956   Bones for the Archaeologist. Phoenix House,
       London.
Cowgill, George L.
1970   Some Sampling and Reliability Problems in Ar-
       chaeology. In Archeologie et Calculateurs,
       edited by J.C. Gardin, pp. 161–175. CNRS,
       Paris.
Coy, Jennie
1975   Iron Age Cookery. In Archaeozoological Stud-
       ies, edited by A.T. Clason, pp. 426–430. North
       Holland, Amsterdam.
1977   Appendix 4: Animal Remains. In Kephala: A
       Late Neolithic Settlement and Cemetery, edited
       by J.E. Colman. Keos, Volume 1, pp. 129–133.
Crabtree, Pam Jean
1982   Patterns of Anglo-Saxon Animal Economy: An
       Analysis of the Animal Bone Remains from the
       Early Saxon Site of West Stow, Suffock. Ph.D.
       Dissertation, University of Pennsylvania.
Crader, Diana C.
1983   Recent Single Carcass Bone Scatters and the
       Problem of "Butchery" Sites in the Archaeo-
       logical Record. In Animals and Archaeology 1.
       Hunters and their Prey, edited by Juliet Clut-
       ton-Brock and Caroline Grigson, pp. 107–142.
       BAR International Series 163.
Dahl, Gudrun and Anders Hjort
1976   Having Herds; Pastoral Herd Growth and
       Household Economy. Stockholm Studies in
       Social Anthropology 2.
Davis, Leslie B.
1978   Twentieth Century Commercial Mining of
       Northern Plains Bison Kills. Plains Anthropo-
       logist, Volume 82, No. 2.
DeBlase, Anthony and Robert E. Martin
1974   A Manual of Mammalogy. William C. Brown
       Co., Dubuque.
Deniz, Esref and Sebastian Payne
1982   Eruption and Wear in the Mandibular Dentition
       as a Guide to Ageing Turkish Angora Goats. In
       Ageing and Sexing Animal Bones from Archae-
       ological Sites, edited by B. Wilson, C. Grigson,
       and S. Payne. BAR British Series 109, pp. 155–
       205.

Douglas, Mary
1966   Purity and Danger. Routledge and Kegan Paul,
       London.
Drew, Isabella M., Dexter Perkins Jr. and Patricia Daly
1971   Prehistoric Domestication of Animals: Effects
       on Bone Structure. Science, Volume 171, pp.
       280–282.
Driver, Jonathan C.
1981   Minimum Standards for Reporting of Animal
       Bones in Salvage Archaeology: Southern Al-
       berta as a Case Study. 14th Annual Conference
       of the University of Calgary Archaeology As-
       sociation.
1982   Medullary Bone as an Indicator of Sex in Bird
       Remains from Archaeological Sites. In Ageing
       and Sexing Animal Bones from Archaeological
       Sites, edited by B. Wilson, C. Grigson, and S.
       Payne, pp. 251–254. BAR British Series 109.
Ducos, Pierre
1968   L'Origine des Animaux Domestiques en Pales-
       tine. Travaux de l'Université de Bordeaux 6.
Duerst, J. Ulrich
1930   Methoden der Vergleichenden Morphologis-
       chen Forschung 1. Teil Untersuchungmethoden
       am Skelett bei Saugern. Urban und Schwarzen-
       berg, Berlin.
Dwyer, Peter D.
1977   An Analysis of Rofaifo Mammal Taxonomy.
       American Ethnologist, Volume 3, pp. 425–445.
Ebersdobler, K.
1968   Vergleichend Morphologische Untersuchungen
       an Einzelknochen des Postkranialen Skelettes
       in Mitteleuropa Vorkommender Mittelgrosse
       Hühnervögel. München.
Efremov, J.A.
1940   Taphonomy: New Branch of Paleontology.
       Pan-American Geologist, Volume 74, pp. 81–93.
Eisenmann, Vera
1980   Les Chevaux (Equus sensu lato) Fossiles et
       Actuels: Cranes et Dents Jugales Supérieures.
       Cahiers de Paléontologie. CNRS, Paris.
Epstein, H.
1971   The Origin of the Domestic Animals of Africa.
       Vols. 1 and 2. Africana Press, New York.
Ewbank, J.M., D.W. Phillipson, R.D. Whitehouse, with
       E.S. Higgs
1964   Sheep in the Iron Age: A Method of Study.
       Publications of the Prehistoric Society, Volume
       30, pp. 423-436.
Feduccia, J. Alan
1971   A Rapid Method for the Preparation of Avian
       Skeletal Material. Texas Journal of Science,
       Volume 23, pp. 147–148.
Fick, O.K.W.
1974   Vergleichend Morphologische Untersuchungen

an Einzelknochen Europäischer Taubarten. München.

Freeman, L.G.

1983   More on the Mousterian: Flaked Bone from Cueva Morin. Current Anthropology, Volume 24, pp. 366–377.

Ghetie, Basile and Cornelius N. Mateesco.

1977   L'Elévage et Utilisation Bovina au Néolithique Moyen et Tardif du Bas-Danube et du Sud des Balkans. L'Anthropologie, Volume 81, pp. 115–128.

Gifford, Diane P. and Diana C. Crader

1977   A Computer System for Archaeological Faunal Remains. American Antiquity, Volume 42, pp. 225–238.

Gilbert, Allan S.

1979   Urban Taphonomy of Mammalian Remains from the Bronze Age of Godin Tepe, Western Iran. Ph.D. Dissertation, Columbia University.

Gilbert, Allan S. and Burton H. Singer

1982   Reassessing Zooarchaeological Quantification. World Archaeology, Volume 14, pp. 21–40.

Gilbert, Allan S. and Paul Steinfield

1977   Faunal Remains from Dinkha Tepe, Northwestern Iran. Journal of Field Archaeology, Volume 4, pp. 329–351.

Gilbert, B. Miles

1980   Mammalian Osteology. Laramie.

Gilbert, B. Miles, Larry D. Martin and Howard G. Savage

1981   Avian Osteology. Laramie.

Goffer, Zvi

1980   Archaeological Chemistry. John Wiley and Sons, New York.

Gould, Richard A. and Patty Jo Watson

1982   A Dialogue on the Meaning and Use of Analogy in Ethnoarchaeological Reasoning. Journal of Anthropological Archaeology, Volume 1, pp. 355–381.

Graham, Russell W.

1976   Late Wisconsin Mammalian Faunas and Environmental Gradients of the Eastern United States. Paleobiology, Volume 2, pp. 243–350.

Graham, Russell W. and Holmes A. Semken

1976   Paleoecological Significance of the Short-tailed Shrew *(Blarina)* with a Systematic Discussion of *Blarina brevicauda.* Journal of Mammalogy, Volume 57, pp. 433–439.

Gramley, Richard M.

1977   Deerskins and Hunting Territories: Competition for a Scarce Resource of the Northeastern Woodlands. American Antiquity, Volume 42, pp. 601–605.

1979   Reply to Webster and Turner and Santley. American Antiquity, Volume 44, pp. 820–821.

Grant, Annie

1975   Appendix B. The Use of Tooth Wear as a Guide to the Age of Domestic Animals. In Excavations at Portchester Castle. 1. Roman, edited by B.W. Cunliffe. Reports of the Research Committee of the Society of Antiquaries of London, No. 32, pp. 437–450.

1978   Variation in Dental Attrition in Mammals and its Relevance to Age Estimation. In Research Problems in Zooarchaeology, edited by D.R. Brothwell, K.D. Thomas, and J. Clutton-Brock, pp. 103–106. Occasional Publication 3, Institute of Archaeology, University of London.

1982   The Use of Tooth Wear as a Guide to the Age of Domestic Ungulates. In Ageing and Sexing Animal Bones from Archaeological Sites, edited by B. Wilson, C. Grigson, and S. Payne, pp. 91–108. BAR British Series 109.

Grayson, Donald K.

1973   On the Methodology of Faunal Analysis. American Antiquity, Volume 38, pp. 432–439.

1979   A Critical View of the Use of Archaeological Vertebrates in Paleoenvironmental Reconstruction. Journal of Ethnobiology, Volume 1, pp. 28–38.

Grigson, Caroline

1974   The Craniology and Relationships of Four Species of *Bos.* 1. Basic Craniology: *Bos taurus* L. and its Absolute Size. Journal of Archaeological Science, Volume 1, pp. 353–379.

1975   The Craniology and Relationships of Four Species of *Bos.* 2. Basic Craniology: *Bos taurus* L. Proportions and Angles. Journal of Archaeological Science, Volume 2, pp. 109–128.

1976   The Craniology and Relationships of Four Species of *Bos.* 3. Basic Craniology: *Bos taurus* L. Sagittal Profiles and Other Non-measureable Characters. Journal of Archaeological Science, Volume 3, pp. 115–136.

1978a  The Craniology and Relationships of Four Species of *Bos.* 4. The Relationship between *Bos primigenius* Boj. and *Bos taurus* L. and its Implications for the Phylogeny of the Domestic Breeds. Journal of Archaeological Science, Volume 5, pp. 123–152.

1978b  Towards a Blueprint for Animal Bone Reports in Archaeology. In Research Problems in Zooarchaeology, edited by D.R. Brothwell, K.D. Thomas, and J. Clutton-Brock, pp. 121–127. Occasional Publication 3, Institute of Archaeology, University of London.

Gromova, Vera

1950   Key to the Mammals of the U.S.S.R. Based on Bones of the Skeleton. The Works of the Committee for the Study of the Quaternary Period. Publications of the Soviet Academy of Science, Moscow.

Gross, Jack E. and Betty L. Gross
1966    Jackrabbit Humerii Cleaned with Clorox. Journal of Wildlife Management, Volume 30, p. 212.

Groves, Colin P. and David P. Willoughby
1981    Studies on the Taxonomy and Phylogeny of the Genus *Equus*. 1. Subgeneric Classification of the Recent Species. Mammalia, Volume 45, pp. 321–354.

Guilday, John E., Paul W. Parmalee and Donald P. Tanner
1962    Aboriginal Butchering Techniques at the Eschelman Site (36La12), Lancaster County, Pennsylvania. Pennsylvania Archaeologist, Volume 32, pp. 59–83.

Habermehl, K-H.
1961    Die Altersbestimmung bei Haustieren, Pelztieren und beim Jagdbaren Wild. Verlag Paul Parey, Hamburg.

Hare, P.E.
1980    Organic Geochemistry of Bone and its Relation to the Survival of Bone in the Natural Environment. In Fossils in the Making, edited by A.K. Behrensmeyer and A.P. Hill, pp. 208–219. University of Chicago Press, Chicago.

Harris, Marvin
1966    The Cultural Ecology of India's Sacred Cattle. Current Anthropology, Volume 7, pp. 51–66.

Harshbarger, Thad R.
1971    Introductory Statistics; A Decision Map. Macmillan, New York.

Hatting, T.
1975    The Influence of Castration on Sheep Horns. In Archaeozoological Studies, edited by A.T. Clason, pp. 345–351. North Holland, Amsterdam.

Hayden, Brian and Aubrey Cannon
1983    Where the Garbage Goes: Refuse Disposal in the Maya Highlands. Journal of Anthropological Archaeology, Volume 2, pp. 117–163.

Haynes, Gary
1980    Evidence of Carnivore Gnawing on Pleistocene and Recent Mammalian Bones. Paleobiology, Volume 6, pp. 341–351.

Hecker, Howard
1975    The Faunal Analysis of the Primary Food Animals from Pre-pottery Neolithic Beidha, Jordan. Ph.D. Dissertation, Columbia University.

Hesse, Brian C.
1978    Evidence for Husbandry from the Early Neolithic Site of Ganj Dareh in Western Iran. Ph.D. Dissertation, Columbia University.
1979    Rodent Remains and Sedentism in the Neolithic: Evidence from Tepe Ganj Dareh, Western Iran. Journal of Mammalogy, Volume 60, pp. 856–857.
1982a    Bias in the Zooarcheological Record: Suggestions for Interpretations of Bone Counts in Faunal Samples from the Plains. Smithsonian Contributions to Anthropology, Volume 30, pp. 157–172.
1982b    Archaeological Evidence for Camelid Exploitation in the Chilean Andes. Saugtierkundliche Mitteilungen, Volume 30, pp. 201–211.
1982c    Slaughter Patterns and Domestication: The Beginnings of Pastoralism in Western Iran. Man, Volume 17, pp. 403–417.
1983    Flamingo Bonnets and Chinchilla Wraps: Buffer Resources in Preceramic Northern Chile. Paper delivered at 6th Ethnobiology Conference, Norman, Oklahoma.

Hesse, Brian C. and Susan Henson
1983    Faunal Remains from the Rogers-CETA Site. Paper delivered at Southeastern Archaeological Conference, Columbia, S.C.

Hesse, Brian C. and Dexter Perkins Jr.
1974    Faunal Remains from Karatas-Semayuk in Southwest Anatolia: An Interim Report. Journal of Field Archaeology, Volume 1, pp. 149–160.

Hesse, Brian C. and Paul Wapnish
1981    Animal Remains from the Bab edh-Dhra Cemetry. Annual of the American Schools of Oriental Research, Volume 46, pp. 133–136.

Higgs, Eric S.
1975    Palaeoeconomy. Cambridge University Press, Cambridge.

Higham, C.W.F.
1968    Trends in Prehistoric European Caprovine Husbandry. Man, Volume 3, pp. 64–75.
1969    An Assessment of a Prehistoric Technique of Bovine Husbandry. In Science in Archaeology, Second Edition, edited by D.R. Brothwell and E.S. Higgs, pp. 315–330. Praeger, New York.

Hill, Andrew P.
1975    Taphonomy of Contemporary and Late Cenozoic East African Vertebrates. Ph.D. Dissertation, University of London.
1979    Butchery and Natural Disarticulation: An Investigatory Technique. American Antiquity, Volume 44, pp. 739–744.

Hill, F.C.
1975    Techniques for Skeletonizing Vertebrates. American Antiquity, Volume 40, pp. 216–219.

Hoffman, Michael A.
1974    The Social Context of Trash Disposal in an Early Dynastic Egyptian Town. American Antiquity, Volume 39, pp. 35–50.

Hole, Frank, Kent V. Flannery and James A. Neely
1969    Prehistory and Human Ecology of the Deh Luran Plain. Memoirs of the Museum of Anthropology, No. 1. University of Michigan, Ann Arbor.

Holtzman, Richard C.
1979    Maximum Likelihood Estimation of Fossil As-

semblage Composition. Paleobiology, Volume 5, pp. 77–89.

Howard, Hildegarde
1929    The Avifauna of Emeryville Shellmound. University of California Publications in Zoology, Volume 32, pp. 301–394.

Huelsbeck, David R. and Gary Wesson
1982    Thoughts on the Collection, Conservation and Curation of Faunal Remains. Northwest Anthropology Research Notes, Volume 16, pp. 221–230.

Hunn, Eugene S.
1975    A Measure of the Degree of Correspondence of Folk to Scientific Biological Classifications. American Ethnologist, Volume 21, pp. 309–327.

1977    Tzeltal Folk Zoology; The Classification of Discontinuities in Nature. Academic Press, New York.

1978    Fuzzy Sets and Folk Biology. Folk Classification Bulletin, Volume 2, pp. 1–3.

1982    The Utilitarian Factor in Folk Biological Classification. American Anthropologist, Volume 84, pp. 830–847.

Johnson, Ralph Gordon
1960    Models and Methods for Analysis of the Mode of Formation of Fossil Assemblages. Bulletin of the Geological Society of America, Volume 71, pp. 1075–1086.

Jourdan, Lucien
1976    La Faune du Site Gallo-Romain et Paléochrétien de la Bourse (Marseille). CNRS, Paris.

Kensinger, Kenneth M. and Waud H. Kracke, Editors
1981    Food Taboos in Lowland South America. Working Papers on South American Indians, No. 3. Bennington College.

Kent, Jonathan D.
1982    The Domestication and Exploitation of the South American Camelids; Methods of Analysis and their Application to Circum-lacustrine Archaeological Sites in Bolivia and Peru. Ph.D. Dissertation, Washington University.

Kent, Susan
1982    Analyzing Activity Areas; An Ethnoarchaeological Study of the Use of Space. University of New Mexico Press, Albuquerque.

Klein, Richard G.
1978    Stone Age Predation on Large African Bovids. Journal of Archaeological Science, Volume 5, pp. 195–217.

Klevezal, G.A. and S.E. Kleinberg
1969    Age Determination of Mammals from Annual Layers in Teeth and Bone. Israel Program for Scientific Translations, Kiryat Moshe, Jerusalem.

Kraft, E.
1972    Vergleichend Morphologische Untersuchungen an Einzelknochen Nord- und Mitteleuropäischer Kleineren Hühnvogel. München.

Krantz, Grover S.
1968    A New Method of Counting Mammal Bones. American Journal of Archaeology, Volume 72, pp. 286–288.

Krauss, R.
1975    Tierknochenfunde aus Bastam in Nordwest-Azerbaidjan/Iran. Inaugural Dissertation. Fachbereichs der Universität München, München.

Larson, Lewis H.
1980    Aboriginal Subsistence Technology on the Southeastern Coastal Plain During the Late Prehistoric Period. Ripley P. Bullen Monographs in Anthropology and History 2. Florida State Museum, Gainesville.

Lavocot, R.
1966    Faunes et Flores Préhistoriques de l'Europe Occidentale. Ed. N. Boubée et Cie., Paris.

Lawler, Timothy E.
1976    Handbook to the Orders and Families of Living Mammals. Mad River Press, Eureka.

Lawrence, Barbara
1951    Post-cranial Skeletal Characters of Deer, Pronghorn, and Sheep-Goat with Notes on *Bos* and *Bison*. Part II. Papers of the Peabody Museum of Archaeology and Ethnology, Volume 35, No. 3. Harvard University.

Levine, Marsha A.
1982    The Use of Crown Height Measurements and Eruption-Wear Sequences to Age Horse Teeth. In Ageing and Sexing Animal Bones from Archaeological Sites, edited by B. Wilson, C. Grigson, and S. Payne. BAR British Series 109, pp. 243–250.

Lie, Rolf W.
1980    Minimum Number of Individuals from Osteological Samples. Norwegian Archaeological Review, Volume 13, pp. 24–30.

Lipton, James
1968    An Exaltation of Larks. Grossman, New York.

Losey, Timothy C.
1973    The Relationship of Faunal Remains to Social Dynamics at Fort Enterprise, NWT. In Historical Archaeology in Northwestern North America, edited by R.M. Getty and K.R. Fladmark, pp 133–143. University of Calgary Archaeological Association.

Lyman, R. Lee
1977    Analysis of Historic Faunal Remains. Historical Archaeology, Volume 11, pp. 67–73.

1979    Available Meat from Faunal Remains: A Consideration of Techniques. American Antiquity, Volume 44, pp. 536–546.

Lyon, P.J.
1970    Differential Bone Destruction: An Ethnographic Study. American Antiquity, Volume 35, pp. 213–215.

Mason, I.L.
1980    Prolific Tropical Sheep. FAO Animal Production and Health Paper 17. FAO, Rome.

Mayr, Ernst
1969    Principles of Systematic Zoology. McGraw-Hill, New York.
1982    The Growth of Biological Thought. The Belknap Press, Cambridge, Mass.

McArdle, John
1975-    A Numerical (Computerized) Method for
1977    Quantifying Zooarchaeological Comparison. Paléorient, Volume 3, pp. 181–190.

Meadow, Richard H.
1975    Mammal Remains from Hajji Firuz: A Study in Methodology. In Archaeozoological Studies, edited by A.T. Clason, pp. 265–283. North Holland, Amsterdam.
1978a   Effects of Context on the Interpretation of Faunal Remains: A Case Study. Peabody Museum Bulletin, Volume 2, pp. 15–21.
1978b   "Bonecode" - A System of Numerical Coding for Faunal Data from Middle Eastern Sites. Peabody Museum Bulletin, Volume 2, pp. 169–186.
1980    Animal Bones: Problems for the Archaeologist Together with some Possible Solutions. Paléorient, Volume 6, pp. 65–77.

Mech, L.D.
1970    The Wolf. Natural History Press, Garden City.

Meek, Theophile J.
1969    Translation, The Code of Hammurabi. In Ancient Near Eastern Texts Relating to the Old Testament, edited by James B. Pritchard. Princeton University Press, Princeton.

Metzger, Mary
1984    Archaeozoological Perspectives on the Bronze Age Village of Tell el-Hayyat, Jordan. M.A. Thesis, University of Alabama, Birmingham.

Miller, George R.
1979    An Introduction to the Ethnoarchaeology of the Andean Camelids. Ph.D. Dissertation, University of California, Berkeley.

Müller, Hans-Hermann
1982    Bibliographie zur Archäo-Zoologie und Geschichte der Haustiere (1980–1981). Akademie der Wissenschaften der DDR, Berlin.

Munk, Michael L, Eli Munk and I.M. Levinger
1976    Shechita. Part II of Edut Ne'emana. Religious and Historical Research on the Jewish Method of Slaughter and Medical Aspects of Shechita. Gur Aryeh, Brooklyn.

Murie, A.
1944    The Wolves of Mount McKinley. Fauna of the National Parks of the United States, Fauna Series No. 5. Washington, D.C.

Murra, John V.
1965    Herds and Herders in the Inca State. In Man, Culture and Animals, edited by Anthony Leeds and A.P. Vayda, pp. 185–215. American Association for the Advancement of Science Publication 78.

Nance, C. Roger
1983    Archaeology of the Rogers-CETA Site, a Lamar Village in Northeastern Alabama. Southeastern Archaeological Conference, Columbia, South Carolina.

Newesely, H. and B. Herrmann
1980    Ab- und Umbauvorgänge der Biologischen Hartgewebe (Knochen, Zähne) unter Langer Liegezeit. Berliner Beiträge zur Archaeometrie, Volume 5, pp. 175–186.

Olsen, Stanley J.
1964    Mammal Remains from Archaeological Sites. Part 1. Southwestern and Southeastern United States. Papers of the Peabody Museum of Archaeology and Ethnology, Volume 56, No. 1. Harvard University.
1968    Fish, Amphibian, and Reptile Remains from Archaeological Sites. Part 1. Southeastern and Southwestern United States. Papers of the Peabody Museum of Archaeology and Ethnology, Volume 56, No. 2. Harvard University.
1979    Osteology for the Archaeologist. Papers of the Peabody Museum of Archaeology and Ethnology, Volume 56, Nos. 3–5. Harvard University.
1982    An Osteology of Some Maya Mammals. Papers of the Peabody Museum of Archaeology and Ethnology, Volume 83. Harvard University.

Oppenheim, A. Leo, Editor
1962    The Assyrian Dictionary of the University of Chicago, Volume 16. University of Chicago Press, Chicago.

Ortner, Donald J. and Walter G.J. Putschar
1981    Identification of Pathological Conditions in Human Skeletal Remains. Smithsonian Contributions to Anthropology, Volume 28.

Ossian, C.R.
1970    Preparation of Disarticulated Skeletons Using Enzyme-Based Laundry "Pre-Soaks." Copeia, Volume 1, pp. 199–200.

Pales, Leon and Charles Lambert
1971    Atlas Ostéologique. Volumes 1 and 2. CNRS. Paris.

Parker, Ronald B. and Heinrich Toots
1980    Trace Elements in Bones as Paleobiological Indicators. In Fossils in the Making: Vertebrate

Taphonomy and Paleoecology, edited by A.K. Behrensmeyer and Andrew P. Hill, pp. 197–207. University of Chicago Press, Chicago.

Payne, Sebastian
1973    Kill-Off Pattern in Sheep and Goats; The Mandibles from Asvan Kale. Anatolian Studies, Volume 23, pp. 281–304.

Perkins Jr., Dexter and Patricia Daly
1968    A Hunters' Village in Neolithic Turkey. Scientific American, Volume 219, No. 5, pp. 96–106.

Petrie, William Matthew Flinders
1931    Ancient Gaza I. Tell El Ajjūl. British School of Archaeology, London.
1932    Ancient Gaza II. Tell El Ajjūl. British School of Archaeology. London.

Pollard, Gordon and Isabella M. Drew
1975    Llama Herding and Settlement in Prehispanic Northern Chile; Application of an analysis for Determining Domestication. American Antiquity, Volume 40, pp. 296–305.

Poplin, François
1975    La Faune Danubienne d'Armeau (Yonne, France); Ses Données sur l'Activité Humaine. In Archaeozoological Studies, edited by A.T. Clason, pp. 179–192. North Holland, Amsterdam.
1981    Un Problème d'Ostéologie Quantitative, Calcul d'Effectif Initial d'Après Appariements. Généralisation aux Autres Types de Remontages et à d'Autres Matériels Archéologiques. Revue d'Archéométrie, Volume 5, pp. 159–165.

Rabagliati, D.S.
1924    The Dentition of the Camel. Cairo.

Redding, Richard W.
1981    Decision Making in Subsistence Herding of Sheep and Goats in the Middle East. Ph.D. Dissertation, University of Michigan, Ann Arbor.

Reed, Charles A, and Dale J. Osborn
1978    Taxonomic Transgressions in Tutankhamun's Treasures. American Journal of Archaeology, Volume 82, pp. 273–283.

Reise, Detlef
1973    Clave para la Determinación de los Cráneos de Marsupiales y Roedores Chilenos. Gayana (Zoología), Volume 27, pp. 1–20.

Reitz, Elizabeth and Dan Cordier
1982    Use of Allometry in Zooarchaeological Analysis. Paper presented to the IVth International Congress of Archaeozoology, London.

Reitz, Elizabeth and Nicholas Honerkamp
1983    British Colonial Subsistence Strategy on the Southeastern Coastal Plain. Historical Archaeology, Volume 17, pp. 4–26.

Robinson, W.S.
1981    First Aid for Marine Finds. Handbooks in Maritime Archaeology 2. Trustees of the National Maritime Museum, Greenwich, London.

Rosch, Eleanor
1978    Principles of Categorization. In Cognition and Categorization, edited by E. Rosch and B.B. Lloyd, pp. 27–48. Lawrence Erlbaum Associates, Hillsdale, New Jersey.

Rosch, Eleanor, C.B. Mervis, W. Gray, D. Johnson, and Braem P. Boyes
1976    Basic Objects in Natural Categories. Cognitive Psychology, Volume 8, pp. 382–439.

Schaller, George B.
1977    Mountain Monarchs, Wild Sheep and Goats of the Himalayas. University of Chicago Press, Chicago.

Schiffer, Michael B.
1976    Behavioral Archaeology. Academic Press, New York.
1983    Toward the Identification of Formation Processes. American Antiquity, Volume 48, pp. 675–706.

Schmid, Elizabeth
1972    Atlas of Animal Bones. Elsevier Publishing Co., Amsterdam.

Schram, Frederick R. and William D. Turnbull
1970    Structural Composition and Dental Variations in the Murids of the Brown Cave Fauna, Late Pleistocene, Wombeyan Caves Area, N.S.W., Australia. Records of the Australian Museum, Volume 28, pp. 1–24.

Schulz, Peter D. and Sherri M. Gust
1983    Faunal Remains and Social Status in 19th Century Sacramento. Historical Archaeology, Volume 17, pp. 44–53.

Shipman, Pat
1981    Life History of a Fossil; An Introduction to Taphonomy and Paleoecology. Harvard University Press, Cambridge, Mass.
1984    Scavenger Hunt. Natural History, Volume 93, No. 4, pp. 20–27.

Shipman, Pat and Jennie Rose
1983    Early Hominid Hunting, Butchering, and Carcass-Processing Behavior; Approaches to the Fossil Record. Journal of Anthropological Archaeology, Volume 2, pp. 57–98.

Sillen, Andrew
1981    Post-Depositional Changes in Natufian and Aurignacian Faunal Bones from Hayonim Cave. Paléorient, Volume 7, pp. 81–86.

Silver, I.A.
1969    The Ageing of Domestic Animals, In Science and Archaeology, 2nd Edition, edited by Don Brothwell and Eric S. Higgs, pp. 283–302. Thames and Hudson, London.

Simpson, George G.
1961    Principles of Animal Taxonomy. Columbia University Press, New York.

Simpson, George G., A. Roe and R.C. Lewontin
1960    Quantitative Zoology. Harcourt Brace and World, New York.

Sisson, S. and J.D. Grossman
1953    The Anatomy of Domestic Animals. 4th Edition. W.B. Saunders, Philadelphia.

Smith, Eric A.
1983    Anthropological Applications of Optimal Foraging Theory: A Critical Review. Current Anthropology, Volume 24, pp. 625–651.

Smith, Philip E.L.
1975    Ganj Dareh Tepe. Iran, Volume 13, pp. 179–182.

Somer, H.G. and S. Anderson
1974    Cleaning Skeletons with Dermestid Beetles - Two Refinements in the Method. Curator, Volume 17, pp. 190–198.

South, Stanley
1977    Method and Theory in Historical Archeology. Academic Press, New York.

Stallibrass, Sue
1982    The Use of Cement Layers for Absolute Ageing of Mammalian Teeth; A Selective Review of the Literature with Suggestions for Further Studies and Alternative Applications. In Ageing and Sexing Animal Bones from Archaeological Sites, edited by B. Wilson, C. Grigson, and S. Payne, pp. 109–126. BAR British Series 109.

Stanford, Dennis J.
1984    The Jones-Miller Site: A Study of Hell Gap Bison Procurement and Processing. Research Reports, Volume 16, pp. 615–635. National Geographic Society, Washington D.C.

Steele, D. Gentry
1981    The Analysis of Animal Remains from Two Late Roman Middens at San Giovanni de Rutoi. In Lo Scavo di S. Giovanni di Ruoti ed il Periodo Tardoantico in Basilicata. Centro Academico Canadese in Italia, Rome.

Sullivan, Alan P.
1978    Inference and Evidence in Archaeology: A Discussion of the Conceptual Problems. Advances in Archaeological Method and Theory, Volume 1, pp. 183–222.

Sutcliffe, A.J.
1973    Similarity of Bones and Antlers Gnawed by Deer to Human Artifacts. Nature, Volume 246, pp. 428–430.

Szilvassy, J.
1979    A Method for the Hardening of Skeletons. Beiträge Gerichtlichen Medizin, Volume 37, pp. 73–74.

Tambiah, S.J.
1969    Animals are Good to Think and Good to Prohibit. Ethnology, Volume 8, pp. 428–459.

Tchernov, Eitan
1968    Succession of Rodent Faunas During the Upper Pleistocene of Israel. Verlag Paul Parey, Berlin.

Thomas, David H.
1976    Figuring Anthropology. Holt, Rinehart and Winston, New York.

Todd, T.W. and A.W. Todd
1938    The Epiphyseal Union Pattern of the Ungulates with a Note on Sirenia. American Journal of Anatomy, Volume 63, pp. 31–36.

Turner, E. Randolph and Robert S. Santley
1979    Deerskins and Hunting Theories Reconsidered. American Antiquity, Volume 44, pp. 810–816.

Tuzin, Donald F.
1981    Food Taboos in Lowland South America; A Discussion. In Food Taboos in Lowland South America, edited by K. M. Kensinger and W.H. Kracke, pp. 186–191. Working Papers on South American Indians, No. 3. Bennington College, Bennington.

Uerpmann, Hans-Peter
1973    Animal Bone Finds and Economic Archaeology: A Critical Study of "Osteo-Archaeological" Method. World Archaeology, Volume 4, pp. 307–332.
1978    The "Knocod" System for Processing Data on Animal Bones from Archaeological Sites. Peabody Museum Bulletin, Volume 2, pp. 149–168.
1979    Probleme der Neolithisierung des Mittelmeerraums. Dr. Ludwig Reichert Verlag, Wiesbaden.

Valdez, Raul
1982    The Wild Sheep of the World. Wild Sheep and Goat International, Mesilla, New Mexico.

Von den Driesch, Angela
1976    The Measurement of Animal Bones from Archaeological Sites. Peabody Museum Bulletin, Volume 1.

Voorhies, M.R.
1969    Taphonomy and Population Dynamics of an Early Pliocene Vertebrate Fauna, Knox County, Nebraska. Contributions to Geology, Special Paper No. 1. University of Wyoming, Laramie.

Wapnish, Paula
1981    Camel Caravans and Camel Pastoralists at Tell Jemmeh. Journal of the Ancient Near Eastern Society of Columbia University, Volume 13, pp. 101–121.
1984    The Dromedary and Bactrian Camel in Levantine Historical Settings: The Evidence from Tell Jemmeh. In Animals and Archaeology, 3. Early Herders and their Flocks, edited by J. Clutton-

Brock and C. Grigson, pp. 171–200. BAR International Series 202.

Watson, J.P.N.
1972    Fragmentation Analysis of Animal Bone Samples from Archaeological Sites. Archaeometry, Volume 14, pp. 221–227.
1975    Domestication and Bone Structure in Sheep and Goats. Journal of Archaeological Science, Volume 2, pp. 375–383.
1978    The Interpretation of Epiphyseal Fusion Data. Occasional Publication No. 3, pp. 97–101. Institute of Archaeology, University of London.
1979    The Estimation of Relative Frequencies of Mammalian Species: Khirokitia 1972. Journal of Archaeological Science, Volume 6, pp. 127–137.

Webb, Marianne
1982    Care and Treatment of Bone and Ivory. Ontario Museum Quarterly, Volume 2, Number 3, pp. 27–28.

Webster, Gary S.
1979    Deer Hides and Tribal Confederacies; An Appraisal of Gramly's Hypothesis. American Antiquity, Volume 44, pp. 816–820.

Wheat, Joe Ben
1972    The Olsen-Chubbuck Site; A Paleo-Indian Bison Kill. Society for American Archaeology, Memoir 26.

Wheeler, Jane C.
1982    Ageing Llamas and Alpacas by their Teeth. Llama World, Volume 1, No. 2, pp. 12–17.
1984    On the Origin and Early Development of Camelid Pastoralism in the Andes. In Animals and Archaeology, 3. Early Herders and their Flocks, edited by J. Clutton-Brock and C. Grigson, pp. 395–410. BAR International Series 202.

Wilkinson, P.F.
1975    The Relevance of Musk-Ox Exploitation to the Study of Prehistoric Animal Economies. In Palaeoeconomy, edited by E.S. Higgs, pp. 9–53. Cambridge University Press, Cambridge.
1976    'Random' Hunting and the Composition of Faunal Samples from Archaeological Excavations; A Modern Example from New Zealand. Journal of Archaeological Science, Volume 3, pp. 321–328.

Wilson, Bob, Caroline Grigson and Sebastian Payne
1982    Ageing and Sexing Animal Bones from Archaeological Sites. BAR British Series 109.

Wilson, Edmund
1975    Sociobiology. The Belknap Press, Cambridge, Mass.

Wing, Elizabeth S.
1972    Appendix IV. Utilization of Animal Resources in the Peruvian Andes. In Excavations at Kotosh, Peru, edited by S. Izumi and K. Terada, pp. 327–351. University of Tokyo Press, Tokyo.

Wing, Elizabeth and Antoinette B. Brown
1979    Paleonutrition: Method and Theory in Prehistoric Foodways. Academic Press, New York.

Woelfle, E.
1967    Vergleichend Morphologische Untersuchungen an Einzelknochen des Postkranialen Skelettes in Mitteleuropa Vorkommender Enten, Halbgänse und Säger. München.

Wolff, R.G.
1973    Hydrodynamic Sorting and Ecology of a Pleistocene Mammalian Assemblage from California (USA). Palaeogeography, Palaeoclimatology, and Palaeoecology, Volume 13, pp. 91–101.

Wylie, Alison
1982    An Analogy by any Other Name is Just as Analogical. A Commentary on the Gould-Watson Dialogue. Journal of Anthropological Archaeology, Volume 1, pp. 382–401.

Yellen, John E.
1977    Cultural Patterning in Faunal Remains; Evidence from the !Kung Bushmen. In Experimental Archaeology, edited by D. Ingersoll, J.E. Yellen, and W. MacDonald, pp. 217–331. Columbia University Press, New York.

Zeder, Melinda
1978    Differentiation Between the Bones of Caprines from Different Ecosystems in Iran by the Analysis of Osteological Microstructure and Chemical Composition. Peabody Museum Bulletin, Volume 2, pp. 69–84.

Zeuner, Frederick F.
1955    The Goats of Early Jericho. Palestine Exploration Quarterly, Volume 87, pp. 70–86.
1963    A History of Domesticated Animals. Hutchinson, London.

Ziegler, A.C.
1973    Inference from Prehistoric Faunal Remains. Addison Wesley Module in Anthropology 43.

# Analytical Table of Contents